Marcia and Jon Pankake

Joe's Got a Head
Like a Ping-Pong Ball:
A Prairie Home Companion
Folk Song Book

Foreword by

Garrison Keillor

Illustrations by John Palmer Low

Penguin Books

PENGUIN BOOKS
Published by the Penguin Group
Viking Penguin, a division of Penguin Books USA Inc.,
375 Hudson Street, New York, New York 10014, U.S.A.
Penguin Books Ltd, 27 Wrights Lane, London W8 5TZ, England
Penguin Books Australia Ltd, Ringwood, Victoria, Australia
Penguin Books Canada Ltd, 2801 John Street, Markham, Ontario, Canada L3R 1B4
Penguin Books (N.Z.) Ltd, 182–190 Wairau Road, Auckland 10, New Zealand

Penguin Books Ltd, Registered Offices: Harmondsworth, Middlesex, England

First published in the United States of America as
A Prairie Home Companion Folk Song Book by Viking Penguin Inc. 1988
Published in Penguin Books 1990

1   3   5   7   9   10   8   6   4   2

Copyright © Marcia Pankake and Jon Pankake, 1988
Foreword copyright © Garrison Keillor, 1988
All rights reserved

Ping-Pong® is a registered trademark of Indian Industries Inc.

"A Prairie Home Companion" is a production of Minnesota Public Radio and
is broadcast nationally on American Public Radio stations.

Grateful acknowledgment is made for permission to reprint
the following copyrighted works:

"Lutefisk, O Lutefisk" adapted from "O Lutefisk" by E. C. "Red" Stangland.
© 1978 E. C. "Red" Stangland, Norse Press, Sioux Falls, SD. Used by permission.

"Because I Could Not Stop for Death," from *The Poems of Emily Dickinson*,
edited by Thomas H. Johnson, Cambridge, Massachusetts, The Belknap Press
of Harvard University Press. Copyright 1951, © 1955, 1979, 1983 by The
President and Fellows of Harvard College. Reprinted by permission
of the publishers and the Trustees of Amherst College.

"Stopping by Woods on a Snowy Evening," from *The Poetry of Robert Frost*,
edited by Edward Connery Lathem. Copyright 1923 by Holt, Rinehart and
Winston, Inc., and renewed 1951 by Robert Frost. Reprinted by
permission of Henry Holt and Company, Inc.

Excerpt from "Fair Nottamun Town" from *Celebration of Life*, Geordie
Music Publishing Co. Copyright 1971, Jean Ritchie. Used by permission.

"The Dreidel Song," reprinted by permission of the Board of Jewish
Education of Greater New York, Inc.

"Wait 'Til We Get 'Em Up in the Air, Boys," by Lew Brown and Albert Von Tilzer.
Copyright 1919 Broadway Music Corp., copyright renewed. Used by permission.

Special thanks for unique material from: Malayna Joy Halvorson, Franklin Grapel,
Warren Fay, Tom and Deborah Gilboy, Kathryn J. Lord, Wes Ward,
Cindy Stocker, Floyd S. Nixon, and Nancy Koppin.

Portions of the royalties from this book are donated to the Archives of
Folk Culture of the Library of Congress.

LIBRARY OF CONGRESS CATALOGING IN PUBLICATION DATA
Prairie home companion folk song book.
Joe's got a head like a ping-pong ball.

Words printed as text; each song followed by tune
indication or melody with chord symbols.
Previously published as: A Prairie home companion
folk song book.
Includes indexes.
1. Humorous songs.   2. Folk music—United States.
3. Folk–songs, English—United States.   I. Pankake,
Marcia.   II. Pankake, Jon.   III. Prairie home
companion.   IV. Title.
M1977.H7P7   1990
ISBN 0 14 01.0905 6   90–751743

Printed in the United States of America
Set in ITC Garamond Light
Designed by Amy Hill
Illustrations by John Palmer Low

To Mary C. Turpie, friend and teacher

Contents

Chapter 11: The Grab Bag

Alaska: Home on the Snow; When It's Springtime in Alaska; Cape Cod Girls; Birmingham's My Home; Minnesota!; Oh, Ay Liff in Minneapolis; My Home's in Montana; The Nose of Oklahoma Smells You; Sweet Dakotaland; South Dakota Is the Sunshine State; I Don't Give a Darn for the Whole State of Iowa; New Mexico, We Love You; We're from Kansas; Smiles That Are Best of All; There Are Ships; The Rummy Dummy Line; Never Go Camping on Labor Day; Johnny Macree; She Sat on Her Hammock; Wait 'Til We Get 'Em Up in the Air, Boys; When We Went to Sunday School; I Ain't Got No Money; My Pappy's Whiskers.

Billy Boy; Brother John; White Coral Bells; Old Folks at Home; Little Brown Jug; Camptown Races; Crawdad; Clementine; Jesse James; Polly-Wolly-Doodle; Goodbye, Old Paint; Go Tell Aunt Rhody; She'll Be Comin' 'Round the Mountain; I Wish I Was Single Again; Over the River and Through the Woods; Long, Long Ago; The Titanic; When the Work's All Done This Fall; The Soldier's Poor Little Boy; Babes in the Woods; Sweet and Low; Skip to My Lou; Vive la Compagnie; Farther Along; Down in the Valley; Tell Me Why.

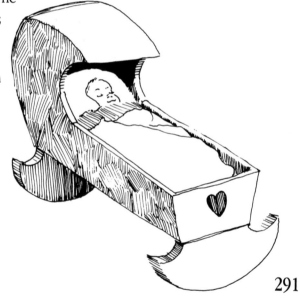

Foreword

Sometimes when a person starts up a radio show, he doesn't have a clear idea of what it ought to sound like or why, only a high-minded notion of bringing music and laughter into the lives of hundreds. I'd been to Nashville and seen the Opry and thought I'd start one like it. That was in 1974. In 1983, nine years after our debut—the year that "Prairie Home" invited listeners to send us these folk songs so we could sing them on the air—I was still looking around for the handle. According to everyone I talked to at the time, the show was a big success, which, in public broadcasting, means that your show gets attention in the press, it pulls in money during the fund-raising drives, and it wins a Peabody, but those things are pale comfort when you arrive at Thursday night every week, six o'clock, and still don't have a show in mind for Saturday. I'd sit in the office in downtown Saint Paul and look west up Seventh toward Mickey's Diner and the Greyhound depot and try to imagine my friends calling me the next Tuesday and saying, "That was a really terrific show last week, _____ was absolutely wonderful," and if I could just fill in the blank I felt we had a show, but half the time I couldn't, and when you've got musicians, a good sharp crew, a big satellite dish, a gloomy old theater, a pockmarked stage and ratty black curtain, six emergency exits, a candy counter and a couple dozen fifty-pound bags of popcorn and two big drums of butter, but you don't have a *show,* it's miserable. It's like you've got a dance to go to and nobody to dance with; you go to the ballgame and nobody remembered to bring a ball; you go to church but it's only for good people. Without a show, you've got no reason to be on the air, and in the face of that big blank hole on stage, cleverness does not suffice, not the Songwriters Named Bob Hall of Fame Special or An Evening with the Key of C Major or the Salute to Flat Spaces, it's time to get back to the basics.

Folk music was the ground that "A Prairie Home Companion" sprang from, the music that was in the air around the University of Minnesota in the fall of 1960 when I arrived for my freshman year, anxious to put the miseries of adolescence behind. At least it was in the air around me, thanks to a series of lucky accidents. I'd been crazy about a Danish exchange student at Anoka High School and went to see the Danish Royal Ballet that September when it came on tour to Northrop Auditorium and got the dreamy idea of interviewing lovely pale long-legged Danish girls for the student radio station, WMMR. I went up to the studio on the third floor of Coffman Union, walked back and forth past the door a few times, screwed up my courage and slipped in and proposed my radio idea, "The Danish Royal Ballet: A Portrait in Sound," not knowing how short-handed they were. They made me a staff member on the spot and gave me a daily fifteen-minute noontime newscast a few minutes after I arrived. Joining the station put me in the vicinity of Maury Bernstein, a WMMR

producer with a big collection of folk records. My friend Jim Milton owned a few Kingston Trio and Tarriers records that I liked to hear over and over again, but Bernstein's collection, played on his radio shows, ranged out to all the corners of folk music, to great folks such as Almeda Riddle, Dock Boggs, Mahalia Jackson, Pete Seeger, Mississippi John Hurt, The New Lost City Ramblers, Lester Flatt & Earl Scruggs, the Carter Family, and Jean Redpath. Folk music was the real thing. It was the true spirit of America, an invisible circle that united everyone in the country. It was generous, democratic, contemplative, moral, mysterious, not exploitive, and ambitious. A concert by Pete Seeger or Jean Redpath was the next thing to going to church. It was peaceful. You knew that ninety-eight percent of the audience around you in the dark was against the war, too, and doing what they could to stop it. The U.S. government was crazed, corrupt, dishonest, but the culture of the American people was honest, decent, and profoundly sane, and the germs of this sanity were carried by folk songs. In the fall of 1968, about the time when sanity seemed at a low ebb, I got to meet Jon and Marcia Pankake.

Jon had been a founding editor of *The Little Sandy Review,* a folk music journal full of passionate writing, in which words such as "authentic," "indigenous," and "native" were among the more passionate. He and Marcia played in a distinguished old string band called Uncle Willy and The Brandy Snifters who had four songs on an Elektra record, "The String Band Project," which was in my collection between the Brandenburg Concerti and Dave Brubeck. The Brandy Snifters played at The Ten O'Clock Scholar in Dinkytown near campus and at Mattie's Bar-B-Q on Lake Street, and other folk dives, and at benefits for Democratic insurgent candidates and good left-wing causes, but even in those uproarious times, playing to flaming self-conscious radicals with poofy hair and tie-dyed bib overalls in some wealthy radical's backyard to raise money for Hearing-Impaired Lutheran Lesbian Farmers United Against War & Racism, the Snifters remained exactly themselves, their repertoire as firmly fixed as the boundaries of South Dakota. They sang no songs of their own composition about being lonely and misunderstood, but stuck absolutely to the authentic banjo-frailing, fiddle-sawing hillbilly sound of old-time gospel songs and dance tunes and ballads, and consequently were lonely and misunderstood, and that is how I found them. I was lonely, too. I went to see them play at the Coffeehouse Extempore and afterward, feeling like a real idiot the way true fans always do and apologizing for it ("I've never done this before," I told them), I went up and said hello.

Jon and Marcia were graduate students, he in American Studies and she in library science, and lived in a green bungalow overlooking the Soo Line tracks near the underpass at Como and 23rd

Avenue Southeast. He was from Dassel, she was from Osseo, two farming towns not far from Minneapolis. The decor at their place was Early Comfortable with a Salvation Army accent; they spent their money on good groceries, books, tickets to movies, and records. They had shelves and shelves of records and tapes, mostly folk music, which reflected a special fondness for arcane folks, eephers and yodelers, maudlin singers and weepy duets dipping into the swamp of tears for a few verses about mother and dying soldiers and the old home place, dad-and-boy duets like Asher Sizemore and Little Jimmy, one-of-a-kind items such as the Cackle Sisters, a duo of Minnesota girls who yodeled and chirped and cackled in perfect harmony, and novelty artists of all kinds including washboard bands and cowgirl trios and singers of sly double-entendre numbers called "party songs." They possessed a gorgeous treasury of folk music of many genres, none of which were taught to us in grade school when we learned "Red River Valley." Most of their favorite artists were from the twenties and thirties, old radio artists, and gradually they got me interested in the old shows, such as "The Grand Ole Opry," where Uncle Dave Macon and Sam and Kirk McGee and the Fruit Jar Drinkers and Roy Acuff and His Smoky Mountain Boys had played string-band music on Saturday nights. I remembered hearing the network portion of the "Opry" when I was a kid and how much I'd liked that music.

I was public affairs director at station KUOM at the University when I started listening to Jon and Marcia, and one night I lugged the old Ampex tape recorder to a coffeehouse (same Ampex I'd recorded Eugene McCarthy, Betty Friedan, William Sloane Coffin, and Stokely Carmichael on) and made an authentic field recording of the Uncle Willie band just as John Lomax had done for Huddie Ledbetter, and then brought them into Studio A in the basement of Eddy Hall to record some more, and pieced it together into a Saturday afternoon music show and broadcast it. A man heard it as he drove across southern Minnesota and pulled over at a phone booth and called up to say it was the most wonderful thing he'd ever heard. One enthusiastic listener response was a lot for me in those days, so we did more. In 1971 the Snifters rode in "Uncle" Willard Johnson's taxi over to Saint Paul to another basement studio, where I was doing a 6:00 A.M. show on KSJN-FM and, while the meter was running, did a few songs live, and a few years later, Marcia and Jon and I did "The Pankake Breakfast Hour," a fifteen-minute show with a great theme song that began "I want to wake up in the morning where the morning glories grow." They were two intellectuals who loved to sing and play instruments, who found their work amusing, and whose music was the expression of their souls. They each had a few songs they held especially close to their hearts. Neither of them could imagine their earning a living as performers, working so desperately hard

for as long as it takes to be recognized, offering these cherished songs for public approval. Why would you ask strangers to applaud your music any more than you'd invite them to troop through your house?

Folk songs are far beyond our approval, they occupy a realm of art that borders on religion, where applause and personal attention are not wanted. So in 1983 when "Prairie Home" was heard all over and applauded and written about and still didn't know what to do with itself, it seemed exactly right to put out the call for folk songs and carve out a ten-minute segment after the Lake Wobegon story called "The Department of Folk Song." My friend Margaret Moos, who produced the show, may have been the one who thought it up first. So much of the show developed conversationally between her and me at the office or in the car driving home or around the house, it's hard to recall who thought what, but whoever's idea it was, we both jumped at the thought and were tickled to see the first batch of mail drift in. "On Top of Old Smoky" was in it, both the "all-covered-with-sand/old-rubber-band" version and, just in case we weren't familiar with it, the Original. Most of the submissions were handwritten, many in a shaky hand by old people: "Learned from my Mother," said some, but even more were attributed to fathers and uncles, as I recall. Some songs had words missing or whole lines, for which the writer apologized—"Sorry, it's been fifty years since I thought about this." Every week, opening the envelopes and looking through the songs, Ilene Zatal or Rosalie Miller or Jennifer Howe or Helen Edinger or Marge Ostroushko or Karen Tofte would smile and look up and say, "I remember this! *We* sang this!" and indeed, who could forget classics like "Greasy Grimy Gopher Guts," "Do Your Ears Hang Low?" or "Did You Ever Think"?

Greg Brown chaired the Department when he was on hand, or else I did it, and all the guests on the broadcast were welcome to take part, to sing a song or add a little harmony. The Department received thirty or forty letters a week, some containing a sheaf of songs, which we reduced to half by Friday afternoon rehearsal. The eight or ten we wound up singing on the air were largely determined by the performers who happened to be on hand that week, whichever songs they knew or cared for. Some of them enjoyed it, others seemed to look on it as a chore. I thought that, along with the birthday and anniversary greetings, the Folk Song Department threatened to be the best part of the show. At first, I was a little shy about singing, I wandered around the rehearsal humming, wishing someone would invite me to join the Department, but later it dawned on me that it was my show and I'd have to invite myself, so I just hauled off and sang when I wanted to. The segment came to an end in October 1984, when Greg Brown went east on an extended tour, and was briefly revived in a slightly different form two years later, when Jon Pankake appeared as

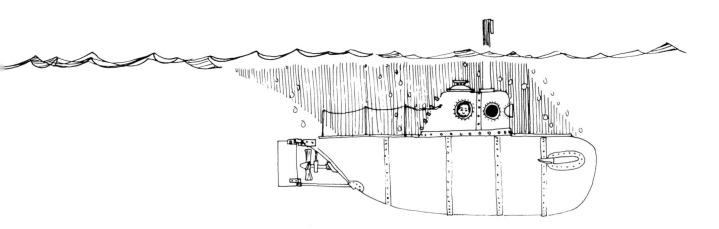

The Masked Folksinger, "A Performer as Anonymous as the Folk Song Itself," and sang unaccompanied ballads wearing a bright red harlequin mask.

It was sad to see the Department end, and then the old radio show itself came tumbling down, toppled by weariness and the natural stress that comes from playing one town for so long. After twelve years, Saint Paul had read and heard enough about me and Lake Wobegon to gag a goat. But these old songs never wear out, and there is no doubt they will live forever, in Saint Paul and wherever fine songs are sung. They're so good to sing, nobody can resist them for long. You sing one of them out of this book and get to like it, you want to sing it some more, eventually you get tired of hauling the book around, you learn the words, and then it becomes a folk song. A portable treasure you carry around in your head to know you'll never be so poor as to be without something of beauty.

A sweet old sad song I have in my head is one that was sung by my cousins Rachel and Susy and Janice and my sister Judy and me when we were little kids up at Uncle Jim's farm north of Anoka, sitting in a green Model A Ford parked under a tree in the middle of the yard. We all sat and sang, "Go tell Grandma. Go tell Grandma. Go tell Grandma the old gray goose is dead." We sang it slowly, as if riding in the poor goose's funeral cortege, and rocked back and forth, but we were embarrassed if a grownup came around, and we stopped immediately. The song was private to us. The words were about a goose Grandma had been saving to make a feather bed, who died in the millpond standing on her head, now the goslings were crying because their mother's dead, and we sang with deep feeling, though we knew geese and were scared of them, they ran at us flapping their wings and hissing, long evil necks stretched out to bite us. The emotional meaning of the song had nothing to do with geese; when we came to the goslings crying because their mother's dead, tears came to our eyes, as we felt the truth of it: we were little goslings huddled in the nest, all alone in the cold world, death was nearby. Death could strike our mother too and then there would be no more love for us. Even when I grew up and become a gander, my upper lip always trembled a little, singing that verse. I sang the song to my son years later, rocking him to sleep every night, part of a lullaby medley that included "Blessed Quietness" and "How Tasteless and Tedious the Hours" and "In My Life" and anything else that came to mind, and when it came to the goslings crying and the old gander weeping, I held the poor child close and I cried him to sleep.

—Garrison Keillor

New York

June 1988

Preface

On the August 20, 1983, broadcast of "A Prairie Home Companion," Garrison Keillor introduced a new feature called "The Department of Folk Song." Greg Brown, designated the "Chairman" of the Department, sang the old nonsense song "Ain't We Crazy," assisted by Garrison and PHC regulars Peter Ostroushko and Butch Thompson. At the end of the segment, Garrison invited listeners to send in their own favorite folk songs to be sung on the Department, the ground rules being two: songs must be "ones you have heard from someone else," and ones "to which you remember the words mostly."

Listeners responded with a will. Over the next three years until the last broadcast of the Department on January 3, 1987, during which forty-five editions of the Department were aired, nearly 1,800 PHC listeners submitted songs in letters, on sheet music (often in painstaking notation of their own devising), and on tape cassettes sung by themselves. Some listeners sent single songs; others sent sheaves of songs.

Garrison's ground rules provided listeners with a fairly good working definition of the principal characteristics of "folk song." Songs "you have heard from someone else" implies that the song has not been learned from some definitive written or recorded source, which differentiates the folk song from the popular or classical song which has a "correct" version from which a performance ought not to deviate. Thus, a song is a "folk song" less in how it originates than in how it is preserved over time and transmitted between performers. Songs "to which you remember the words mostly" implies that a dynamic of change exists in folk songs: a singer may forget some original lyrics, may make up some new ones, may be unable to hit the high note of a song and substitute a lower one which he or she can sing comfortably. The changes may then be perpetuated by the next singer to learn the song from that performer, and thus the song changes over time.

The Department received folk songs of nearly every description, from sea chanteys to lullabies, from native American ballads to parodies of old popular tunes, from generations-old nonsense songs to songs which defy description (some of which, we suspect, contrary to the ground rules, were composed by the senders).

When Garrison proposed that we publish the best of this mass of material in a song collection, our enthusiasm lay in what we felt was the uniqueness of the enterprise. Had anyone ever collected folk songs in such a way before, using a mass medium to reach contributors in a national folk "community," rather than in the local communities usually visited by folklorists who collect songs?

We found that in fact we had a very distinguished predecessor. From 1923 to 1927 the folklorist Robert Winslow Gordon edited a column called "Old Songs That Men Have Sung" in a national pulp magazine titled *Adventure*. In his column, Gordon discussed and reprinted

texts of interesting folk songs, and invited his (presumably blue-collar male) readers to send in "all the old songs of every variety." In his four years as editor, Gordon collected hundreds of lyric songs, work songs, and ballads (including fifty-three texts of "Casey Jones"), which collection now resides in the Archive of Folk Culture in the Library of Congress. The pages of *Adventure* provided Gordon with a national audience from whom to collect material, which sets his work apart from the more conventional local or regional focus of other extensive song collections such as Vance Randolph's *Ozark Folksongs* or Frank C. Brown's *North Carolina Folklore.*

Although the Department of Folk Song enjoyed a national forum in a popular medium, as did Gordon's magazine column, our collection as a whole differs greatly from Gordon's or from others we have seen. Any folk song collection is a mirror in which one sees reflected the tastes, needs, interests, and experiences of the people who contributed the songs, and to compare collections is inevitably to compare the groups of people who contributed the songs. The "A Prairie Home Companion" listening audience is a unique social group for whom strict comparisons with other demographically different groups of informants (such as rural North Carolinians) would be invalid. But we can make two general observations on how this collection differs from other collections with which the reader may be familiar.

First, the reader will find here very few songs which represent the "Anglo-American common stock" of material which usually makes up the core of a folk song collection. PHC listeners sent no texts of "The House Carpenter" or "Barbara Allen" or "The Merry Golden Tree," no versions of "Casey Jones" other than a parody, no "Wreck of the Old 97" and no "John Henry," and evidently these songs no longer circulate among PHC listeners. Very little narrative song appears at all, while most older collections contain a core of ballads which reflects a very strong story-telling urge among singers of folk songs, the seemingly innate human desire to weave cause and effect and to see "how it comes out" in spinning a yarn. Perhaps our need to enjoy narrative is satisfied in our time by books and television (or radio monologues), and we no longer look to or need folk songs as a means of telling a story. Then, too, our attention spans are shorter, attuned to the length of a 45-rpm single (and, increasingly, the thirty-second TV commercial), and most of us would become restless at hearing a twenty- or thirty-stanza story in song.

Second, the reader will find the emotional range of the songs in this collection considerably narrower than that of older folk song collections. The tiresome cliché that folk songs concern murders, feuds, train wrecks, and broken-hearted lovers is true to the extent that folk songs can and do dramatize the full range of human feelings, and do not hesitate to strive at times to portray high tragedy or the workings of desire. Our collection, in contrast, is almost entirely

jocular, and those who may seek Barbara Allen's passion or John Henry's tragedy need not enter here. Perhaps we no longer need the stilted tragedies of murder ballads so much as we need the balm of laughter. Certainly, as our ballad-singing traditions wear away, jokes and funny songs traded around the water cooler or the campfire will be the last to go, and the Department's laughter-rich folk songs may in some way be the model of those of the next century: short, snappy, and funny.

Our guiding philosophy in compiling this book was simply to include as many and as representative a selection as possible of the songs sent to the Department. We excluded songs which have been recently published and which were submitted in versions unchanged from the published ones, for example, "Lazy Bones" and "Mairzy Doats" (both of which, however, may eventually become folk songs). Also, we departed from scholarly folkloristic considerations in editing the song texts for the book. Since so many of the songs were sent in differing versions by several listeners, we have in some cases compiled composite texts which preserve the best lines and stanzas offered to the Department, without cluttering the book with variants. Only where versions substantially differ do we include numbered variants. Consequently, we do not identify contributors with songs, although this information is preserved in the files of the Department.

The musical notations have been transcribed from the tapes submitted by listeners, or have been newly arranged for this book from listeners' materials. We have used no musical notation from previously published sources. Many songs were submitted as texts only, with no indication as to how they are to be sung, and they appear so in the book as a challenge to the reader's ingenuity in devising a workable tune.

We urge you to *sing the songs as you read through the book.* Folk songs lie dead on the printed page, and come to life only when the words are wed to the music. If you are shy, you have our permission to sing the songs silently to yourself as you read; if you have the aplomb, sing the songs aloud to whoever is near. You already know the melodies to nearly every song in this book. If you are a skillful singer, start with "Joe's Got a Head Like a Ping-Pong Ball"; if your abilities are modest, start with "Bring Back My Neighbors to Me." But sing you must!

Like a folk song itself, this book has been a communal creation which has passed through many hands to reach its current form. Thanks, then, to our indefatigable production assistant and researcher, Rosalie Miller, and to our hawkeyed word processor, Nina Thorsen, who deciphered the handwritings on all those letters and songs. Thanks to Garrison Keillor and to the staff of "A Prairie Home Companion" who collected and kept the songs safe: Margaret Moos, Jennifer Howe, Ilene Zatal, Helen Edinger, and Kate Gustafson. Thanks to the music departments of the St. Paul Public Library and the Minneapolis Public Library and Information

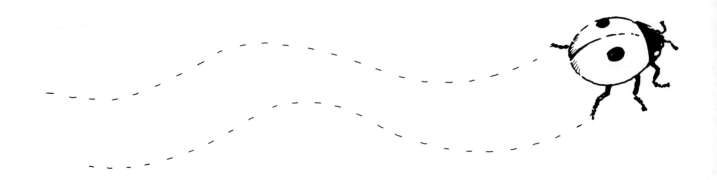

Center. Thanks to the University of Minnesota Libraries and specifically to Richard Rohrer, Patricia Turner, Joseph Branin, Richard Kelly, Don Kelsey, Dave Ashley, Nancy Tufford, Karen Kopacek, and Sharon Folk for assistance and support. Thanks also to Ellen Levine, Kathryn Court, Arne Fogel, Gail Heil, and Stephen A. Peterson for assistance.

And, at the end of our ballad, thanks to the listeners of "A Prairie Home Companion" whose wit and love of old songs, animals, kids, and each other sings from every page of this book.

—Marcia and Jon Pankake
Minneapolis
January 1988

Chapter 1

Somewhere Overindulgence

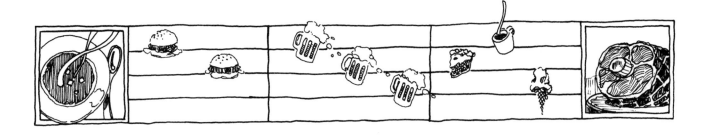

Older collections of folk songs contain a very high proportion of love songs and ballads which portray people and their actions. Our rural forebears were largely poor people with little prospect for material wealth, and they seldom celebrated food and drink in their songs. Some older folk songs about food ironically extol the supposed virtues of mean foods actually eaten out of necessity, such as "Turnip Greens" and "Goober Peas." And few folk songs celebrate the joys of the grape. Songs mentioning liquor most commonly betray the influence of the nineteenth-century temperance movement, and exist only to equate liquor with drunkenness.

In contrast, "A Prairie Home Companion" listeners sent in a great many songs about food, clothing, and other consumer products. In modern America, our problem is not having to eat mean foods but having to choose among seventy-five brands of cereals for breakfast. Our excessive choices have even generated new vocabularies for our gustatory behaviors, from the facetious ("chocoholism") to the tragic (anorexia nervosa and bulimia). One song received by the Department, "I Love to Go A-Gorging," could be the perfect theme of the constantly munching couch potato, a song which would sound odd indeed to any American of the nineteenth century other than Diamond Jim Brady.

Consumerism is of course driven by advertising, which has in its ubiquity become an element of contemporary folklore. The first songs many children learn are commercials from television, and we note that some of the recently composed songs in this chapter are themselves constructed on the models of singing commercials. "Milkshake," for example, insistently repeats its image to a terrific and wildly incongruous melody, creating a whole that is more surprising and memorable than the sum of its parts, just like the broadcast commercial.

The last part of this chapter contains "anti-commercials" which could be subtitled "The Consumer's Revenge." Advertisers should particularly note the collective nastiness of these parodies, the legacy of sales jingles repeated just one time too often, enough to send some resentful mind right over the edge.

We lead off with the wonderful "Somewhere Overindulgence," in which "a land that I heard of once in a nursery rhyme" is of course the America of material surfeit depicted in commercials, whose cheerfully dreamlike images float through the song to reassure us, as does the TV sales pitch, that despite our gorging "no one will draw the line." Intentional or not, this song betrays an irony far more dreadful than that in "Turnip Greens."

Somewhere Overindulgence

Somewhere overindulgence is just fine
In a land that I heard of once in a nursery rhyme
Where lemon drops fall from the sky
And ice cream clouds go floating by above me
Where earth is made of chocolate cake
And mud pies just taste really great
Is where you'll find me
Somewhere overindulgence is just fine
You can eat all you want to, no one will draw the line.

(TUNE: "Somewhere Over the Rainbow," 1938.)

I Want a Beer Just Like the Beer

I want a beer, just like the beer
That pickled dear old Dad
It was the first and the only beer
That Daddy ever had
It was a great big frosty beer with lots of foam
Took six men to carry Daddy home

I want a beer, just like the beer
That pickled dear old Dad.

(TUNE: "I Want a Girl Just Like the Girl That Married Dear Old Dad," 1911.)

Beer, Beer, for *** High

Beer, beer, for [school name] High
You bring the whiskey, I'll bring the rye
Send old [principal's name] out for gin
Don't let a sober senior in

Sometimes we stagger but we never fall
We sober up on wood alcohol
As our loyal faculty
Lies drunk on the barroom floor.

(TUNE: "Cheer, Cheer for Old Notre Dame.")

The Beer Was Spilled on the Barroom Floor

Oh, the beer was spilled on the barroom floor
The bar was closed for the night
A mouse came out of his hole in the wall
And sat in the pale moonlight.
He lapped up the beer on the barroom floor
And back on his haunches he did sit
And all you could hear for the rest of the night was
"Bring on the goldurned cats!"

Rye Whiskey

It's beefsteak when I'm hungry
Rye whiskey when I'm dry
A greenback when I'm hard up
Go to heaven when I die.

Chorus: It's whiskey, oh, whiskey
          Rye whiskey I cry
          If I don't get rye whiskey
          I surely will die.

If the ocean was whiskey
And I was a duck
I'd dive to the bottom
And never come up.

Chorus

But the ocean ain't whiskey
And I ain't a duck
So I'll play Jack o' diamonds
And trust to my luck.

Chorus

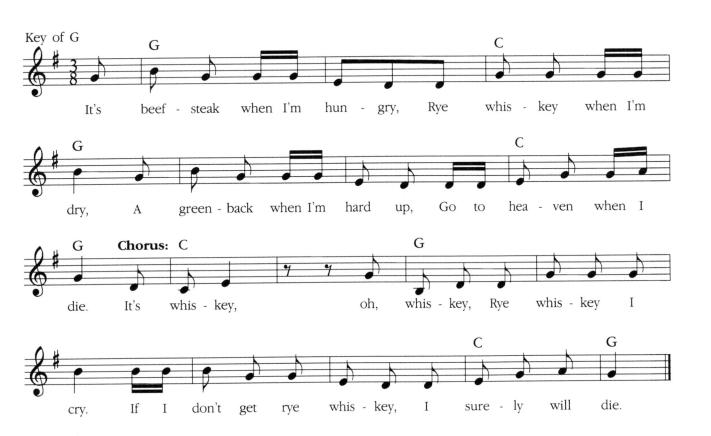

Away with Rum

Oh, we don't eat fruitcake because it has rum
And one little bite turns you into a bum
Oh, can you imagine a sorrier sight
Than a man eating fruitcake all night to get tight?

Chorus: Away, away with rum, by gum,
            With rum, by gum, with rum, by gum,
            Away, away, with rum, by gum,
            The cry of the Salvation Army.

Oh, we don't eat cookies because they have yeast
And everyone knows that turns men into beasts
A man who eats fruitcake's a public disgrace
Sprawled in the gutter with crumbs on his face.

Chorus

We don't use tobacco, because we do think
That people who use it are too apt to drink
We're coming, we're coming, our brave little band
On the right side of heaven in temperance we stand.

Chorus

Key of D

Oh, we don't eat fruit-cake be - cause it has rum, And one lit - tle bite turns you in - to a bum. Oh, can you im - a - gine a sor - ri - er sight, Than a man eat - ing fruit-cake all

Chorus:

night to get tight? A - way, —— a - way, —— with rum, by gum, With rum, by gum, with rum, —— by gum, A - way, —— a - way, —— with rum, by gum, The cry of the Sal - va - tion Ar - my.

Collard Greens

Collard greens, I've got the nicest mess of collard greens
Just throw some fatback on those collard greens, collard greens
My stomach's getting thinner
I guess it's time for dinner
Collard greens, just have a helping and you'll know just what I mean
Oh Lord, I'd really love to have a sandwich of
Those good old collard greens.

(TUNE: "Baby Face," 1926.)

The Mushroom

The mushroom is a vegetable
To select it few are able
You won't know them when you meet them
You won't know them 'til you eat them
If in heaven you awaken
You will know you were mistaken
And the ones that you have eaten
Weren't the ones you should have et.

Onions

Onions, onions, O-U-N-I-O-N-S
Onions, onions, O-U-N-I-O-N-S
Eat 'em at home and buy 'em in the park
Feed 'em to your children so you'll find them in the dark
Onions, onions, O-U-N-I-O-N-S.

(TUNE: "Ja-Da," 1918.)

Turnip Greens

Atmore girls are beauties
As clearly can be seen
'Cause the glamorous, amorous beauty queens
Are fed on turnip greens.

Atmore boys are cuties
As clearly can be seen
'Cause the rootin' tootin' kiddies
Are fed on turnip greens.

Chorus: Oh turnip greens, turnip greens
Good old turnip greens
Cornbread, bacon, and buttermilk
And good old turnip greens.

Chorus

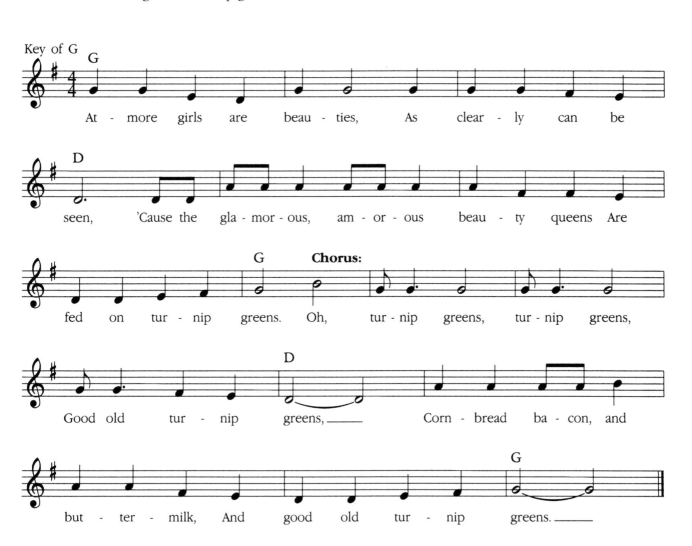

At - more girls are beau - ties, As clear - ly can be
seen, 'Cause the gla - mor - ous, am - or - ous beau - ty queens Are
fed on tur - nip greens. Oh, tur - nip greens, tur - nip greens,
Good old tur - nip greens, _____ Corn - bread ba - con, and
but - ter - milk, And good old tur - nip greens. _____

Goober Peas

Sitting by the roadside on a summer day
Chatting with my messmates, passing time away
Lying in the shadow underneath the trees
Goodness, how delicious, eating goober peas.

Chorus: Peas, peas, peas, peas, eating goober peas
Goodness, how delicious, eating goober peas!

Just before the battle, the General hears a row
He says, "The Yanks are coming, I hear their rifles now."
He turns around in wonder, and what d'you think he sees
The Michigan Militia eating goober peas.

Chorus

When a horseman passes, the soldiers have a rule
To cry out at their loudest, "Mister, here's your mule."
But another pleasure enchantinger than these,
Is wearing out your grinders eating goober peas.

Chorus

I think my song has lasted almost long enough
The subject's interesting, but rhymes are mighty rough
I wish the war was over, when free from rags and fleas
We'd kiss our wives and sweethearts and gobble goober peas.

Chorus

Chicken Sandwich

When I go in a restaurant, oh, this is what I cry,
"Give me a chicken sandwich, cup of coffee, piece of pie."
And these will be my final words until the day I die,
"Give me a chicken sandwich, cup of coffee, piece of pie."

Glory, glory, what's it to you
Glory, glory, what's it to you
Glory, glory, what's it to you
If I have a chicken sandwich, cup of coffee, piece of pie?

(TUNE: "Battle Hymn of the Republic," 1862.)

Coming Through the Rye

Don't be stingy with the cold cuts
Pile the cold cuts high
Customers should see salami
Coming through the rye.

(TUNE: "Coming Through the Rye," traditional Scots air.)

Hymn to Cheeses

What a food we have in cheeses
Mozzarella, cheddar, Swiss
Bleu and Limburger's sweet breezes
Lingering like a lover's kiss
Humble milk's apotheosis
Muenster, Provolone, Brie
Damn cholesterol's thrombosis
Cheese is Gouda stuff by me!

Heed the U.S. Dairy Council
Keep the Gruyère on the shelf
Even just a tiny ounce'll
Give you Vitamin B-12
Gather, pilgrims, at the deli
Buying Edam and Havarti
Wedges moist and cold and smelly
Bring home lots and have a party!

(TUNE: "What a Friend We Have in Jesus," 1876.)

Soup

Soup, soup, we all like soup
Dip your bowl and drain it
Let your whiskers strain it
Hark! Hark! The funny noise
Listen to the gurgling boys.

(TUNE: "Hail, Hail, the Gang's All Here," 1917.
Derived from Verdi's "Anvil Chorus.")

Coffee

C-O-F-F-E-E
Coffee is not for me
It's a drink some people wake up with
That it makes them nervous is no myth
Slaves to a coffee cup
They can't give coffee up.

Key of G

C - O - F - F - E - E, Cof-fee is not ___ for ___ me. ___

It's a drink some peo-ple wake ___ up ___ with,

That it makes them ner-vous is ___ no ___ myth.

Slaves to a cof-fee cup, They can't give cof-fee up.

Dunk! Dunk! Dunk!

Drink! Drink! Drink!

Some men like their wine, while others think whiskey is fine

Dunk! Dunk! Dunk!

When I want a shot I call for the old coffee pot

Stollen and streusel and raisin and pound

Dip them in, dip them in, stir them around

Don't use layer cake when soaking up

Because of the frosting, it sticks to the cup.

Dunk! Dunk! Dunk with a will

Dunking never will kill

Dunk! Dunk! Dunk!

You'll never get tight, though you dunk every night.

Let's dunk!

(TUNE: "Drinking Song" from *The Student Prince* ["Drink! Drink! Drink!"], 1924.)

'Neath the Crust of the Old Apple Pie

'Neath the crust of the old apple pie
There is something for you and for I
It may be a pin that the cook has dropped in
Or it may be a dear little fly.

It may be an old rusty nail
Or a piece of dear puppy dog's tail
But whatever it be, it's for you and for me
'Neath the crust of the old apple pie.

The Pie Dream

"I'm hungry," she said with a sigh
"I'm so hungry I feel I shall die.
They don't realize that a girl of my size
Requires a great deal of pie."

"What's that?" she heard someone demand.
She never could quite understand
Stare hard as she could, before her there stood
A Prince, with a pie in his hand.

He promised if she'd be his wife
She could eat custard pie with a knife
She could help herself twice to everything nice
And do nothing but eat all her life.

So they rode 'til they came to a gate
With a legend upon a brass plate:
"You should not put away what you might eat today."
So she ate and she ate and she ate.

She ate 'til she grew like a ball
Her eyes they grew dreadfully small
She grew out of her clothes and as for her nose
She didn't have any at all.

They set out on a wondrous plight
And arrived at her home after night
And her father said, "Ben, there's a pig out again."
And she woke with a terrible fright.

(TUNE: "Blest Be the Tie That Binds.")

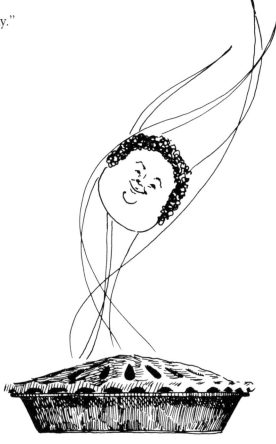

Gooseberry Pie

They may boast if they like of their bacon and greens
They may tell of roast turkey and game
They may sing loud the praises of Boston baked beans
They may all be just what they claim.
Roast beef and plum pudding may answer for some
And oysters in stew or a fry
Though I relish them all my greatest delight
Is a big piece of gooseberry pie.

Chorus: Oh, there's nothing like gooseberry pie, says I
Oh there's nothing like gooseberry pie
Since the time of the Flood, there's been nothing so good
So delicious as gooseberry pie.

As my teeth gently press through its lovely brown crust
And the moisture it holds is set free
How it sends through my frame such a thrill of delight
Oh, it's luscious as luscious can be.
There's a girl here that's taken a fancy to me
I can tell by the glance of her eye
But the girl that I marry must first understand
How to make a good gooseberry pie.

Chorus

Bos - ton baked beans, They may all be just what they___

claim. Roast beef and plum pud - ding may an - swer for some, And

oy - sters in stew or a fry; Though I re - lish them all my___

great - est de - light Is a big piece of goose - ber - ry

pie. Oh, there's no - thing like goose - ber - ry pie, says I, Oh, there's

no - thing like goose - ber - ry pie, Since the time of the Flood, there's been

no - thing so good, So de - li - cious as goose - ber - ry pie.

17

Mother's Cookies

Mother takes her rolling pin
Cuts the spicy dough quite thin
Cuts the cookies out with care
Some are round and some are square
Cookies must not bake too fast
Mother takes them out at last
They are crispy, warm, and sweet
Oh, how good they are to eat.

Hymn for Syttende Mai: Ole, Ole, Ole!

Happy, happy holiday
It's the seventeenth of May
Norskies all around the world
Are kicking up their heels
Time to eat and celebrate
I can hardly stand the wait
Lutefisk and rommegrot
Oh, how good it feels.

Eating Hilda's apple pie
Boy, that sure delights a guy
Mrs. Olson's caramel rolls
Are really tasty too
Hot dish, sild, and gammelost
Guess I like this mush the most
Milk and Kool-Aid tops it off
What a happy crew!

Spring Grove, Westby, and Duluth
They all know the gospel truth
Celebrating on this day
Is good for one and all
Time to shed those winter blues
Go without your overshoes
Even lots of preachers answer
Quickly to this call.

(TUNE: "The Doxology," or "Old Hundredth," or "Praise God from Whom All Blessings Flow," 1551.)

Deck the Halls with Lefse Slices

Deck the halls with lefse slices, fa la la la la la la uffda
Do not check on what the price is, fa la la la la la la uffda
Might be thought a strange creation, fa la la la la la la la la
But it's great as insulation, fa la la la la la la uffda.

Lefse's sure to be the fate-o, fa la la la la la la uffda
Of each old and cold potato, fa la la la la la la uffda
Mix with lard, there is no waste, fa la la la la la la la la
Also notice there's no taste, fa la la la la la la uffda.

Lefse is a Christmas treat, fa la la la la la la uffda
All the Scandinavians eat, fa la la la la la la uffda
Notice how a Norskie flaunts it, fa la la la la la la la la
Even though nobody wants it, fa la la la la la la uffda.

(TUNE: "Deck the Halls.")

Lefse

The lefse's round, with spots of brown
Oh yah you betcha, uff da!
The lutefisk is such a risk
Oh yah you betcha, uff da!

The pickled herring is so daring
Oh yah you betcha, uff da!
My belly hurts from all those burps
Oh yah you betcha, uff da!

(TUNE: "Deep in the Heart of Texas," 1941.)

Lutefisk, O Lutefisk

Lutefisk, O lutefisk
How fragrant your aroma
Lutefisk, O lutefisk
You put me in a coma
You smell so strong, you look like glue
You taste just like an overshoe
But lutefisk, come Saturday
I think I'll eat you anyway.

Lutefisk, O lutefisk
I put you in the doorway
I wanted you to ripen up
Just like they do in Norway
A dog came by and sprinkled you
I hit him with my overshoe
O lutefisk, now I suppose
I'll eat you while I hold my nose.

Lutefisk, O lutefisk
How well I do remember
On Christmas Eve how we'd receive
Our big treat of December

It wasn't turkey or fried ham
It wasn't even pickled Spam
My mother knew there was no risk
In serving buttered lutefisk.

Lutefisk, O lutefisk
Now everyone discovers
That lutefisk and lefse make
Norwegians better lovers
Now all the world can have a ball
You're better than that Geritol
O lutefisk, with brennevin*
You make me feel like Errol Flynn.

Lutefisk, O lutefisk
You have a special flavor
Lutefisk, O lutefisk
All good Norwegians savor
That slimy slab we know so well
Identified by ghastly smell
Lutefisk, O lutefisk
Our loyalty won't waver.

(TUNE: "O Tannenbaum.")

*Norwegian brandy.

Turkey Dinner

Turkey dinner, turkey dinner
Gather 'round, gather 'round
Who will get the drumstick?
Yummy yummy yumstick!
All sit down, all sit down.

Cornbread muffin, chestnut stuffing
Pumpkin pie, one foot high
All of us were thinner
'Fore we came to dinner
Me oh my, me oh my!

(TUNE: "Frère Jacques," a traditional French song dating to as early as 1811.)

Next Thanksgiving

Next Thanksgiving, next Thanksgiving
Save some bread, save some bread
Stuff it in your turkey, stuff it in your turkey
Eat the bird, eat the bird.

(TUNE: "Frère Jacques.")

Glory, Glory, Pork Superior

Mine eyes have seen the slaughter
And the coming of the lard
We have hacked apart and rendered
The old Duroc in the yard
We have used the sausage secrets
From our Grandma's recipe card
While cracklings sizzle on.

Glory, glory, pork superior
Sliced and ground is his interior
Bacon, roasts, and chops superior
While cracklings sizzle on.

(TUNE: "Battle Hymn of the Republic.")

One Fish Ball

A little man walked up and down
To see what he could find in town

He chanced upon a swell affair
And sat himself upon a chair

He took his purse from pocket hence
And found he had but two half-pence

He scanned the menu through and through
To see what two half-pence would do

The only thing 'twould do at all
Would be to order one fish ball

He called the waiter down the hall
And said, "I'll order one fish ball."

The waiter bellowed down the hall,
"This gentleman here wants one fish ball!"

The people then turned one and all
To see who'd ordered one fish ball

The little man now ill at ease
Said, "I'll have bread, sir, if you please."

The waiter bellowed down the hall,
"We don't serve bread with one fish ball!"

The little man soon went outside
And shot himself and so he died

There is a moral to it all
Don't order bread with one fish ball.

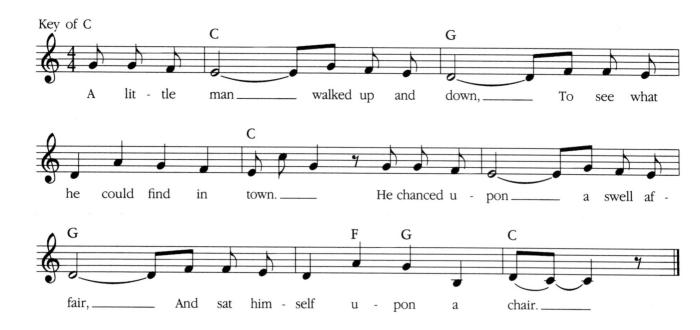

Key of C

A lit-tle man ___ walked up and down, ___ To see what he could find in town. ___ He chanced u-pon ___ a swell af-fair, ___ And sat him-self u-pon a chair. ___

I Went to Cincinnati

I went to Cincinnati and I walked around the block
And I walked right into a bakery shop
I picked up a doughnut and I wiped off the grease
I gave the lady a five-cent piece.

Well, she looked at the nickel and she looked at me
She said, "This nickel's no good to me,
There's a hole in the middle and it's all the way through."
Says I, "There's a hole in the doughnut, too.
Thanks for the doughnut, good-bye."

(TUNE: "Turkey in the Straw," or "Old Zip Coon," traditional tune, possibly Irish in origin, published in 1834.)

Waiter, Waiter

Waiter, waiter, waiter, won't you wait on me?
Waiter, waiter, I'm as hungry as can be
Oh, bring me a little chicken or some other kind of stuff
I'm so doggone hungry I could eat a powder puff
Hey, waiter, waiter, won't you wait on
Waiter, won't you wait on
Waiter, won't you wait on me.

(TUNE: "Ja-Da," 1918.)

Over There

The taters they grow small, over there
The taters they grow small, over there
The taters they grow small
They plant them in the fall
And eat them tops and all, over there.

I wish I were a geese, all forlorn
I wish I were a geese, all forlorn
I wish I were a geese
I'd live and die in peace
And accumulate much grease
Eating corn.

They had a clam pie, over there
They had a clam pie, over there
They had a clam pie
The crust was made of rye
You must eat it or else die, over there.

Today Is . . .

Today is Monday, today is Monday
Monday bread and butter
All you hungry children
We wish the same to you.

Today is Tuesday, today is Tuesday
Tuesday string beans
Monday bread and butter
All you hungry children
We wish the same to you.

Today is Wednesday, today is Wednesday
Wednesday soup
Tuesday string beans
Monday bread and butter
All you hungry children
We wish the same to you.

Today is Thursday, today is Thursday
Thursday roast beef
Wednesday soup
Tuesday string beans
Monday bread and butter
All you hungry children
We wish the same to you.

Today is Friday, today is Friday
Friday fish

Thursday roast beef
Wednesday soup
Tuesday string beans
Monday bread and butter
All you hungry children
We wish the same to you.

Today is Saturday, today is Saturday
Saturday payday
Friday fish
Thursday roast beef
Wednesday soup
Tuesday string beans
Monday bread and butter
All you little children
We wish the same to you.

Today is Sunday, today is Sunday
Sunday church
Saturday payday
Friday fish
Thursday roast beef
Wednesday soup
Tuesday string beans
Monday bread and butter
All you little children
We wish the same to you.

MON.   TUE.   WED.   THUR.   FRI.   SAT.   SUN.

The Lollipop Song

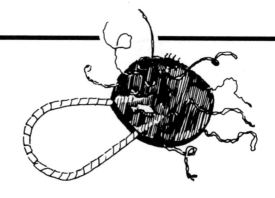

Oh, I'd rather suck on a lemon drop
Than try my luck with a lollipop
'Cause a lollipop I always drop
And it gets all over, icky.

Oh, it makes me sick the way it smears
It gets all over my hair and ears
With a jelly bean I'm always clean
But a lollipop, ooh, icky.

I've tried and tried, but I still can't find
A lollipop that's halfway refined.

So I'd rather suck on a lemon drop
Than try my luck with a lollipop
'Cause a lollipop I always drop
And it gets all over, icky,
Ooh, icky, ooh, icky, icky, icky, ooh.

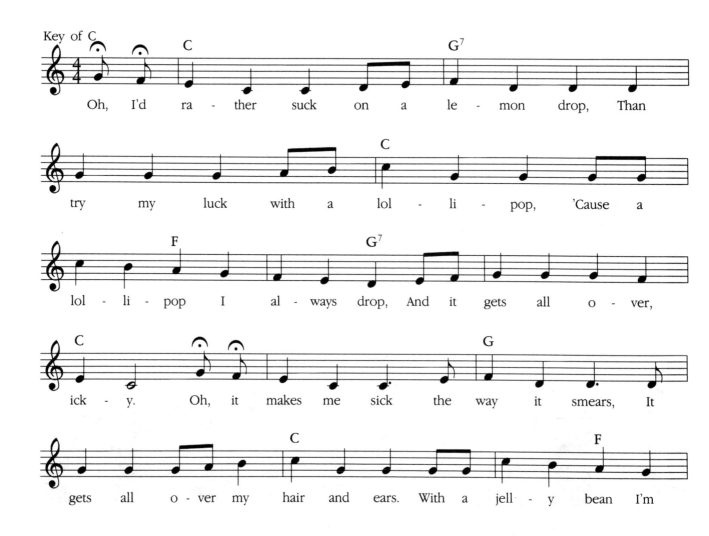

Key of C

Oh, I'd ra - ther suck on a le - mon drop, Than
try my luck with a lol - li - pop, 'Cause a
lol - li - pop I al - ways drop, And it gets all o - ver,
ick - y. Oh, it makes me sick the way it smears, It
gets all o - ver my hair and ears. With a jell - y bean I'm

al - ways clean, But a lol - li - pop, ooh, ick - y. I've
tried and tried, but still I can't find, A lol - li -
pop [Pop] that's half - way re - fined. So I'd ra - ther suck on a
le - mon drop, Than try my luck with a lol - li - pop, 'Cause a
lol - li - pop I al - ways drop, And it gets all o - ver,
ick - y, Ooh, ick - y, ooh, ick - y, ick - y, ick - y, ooh. [Spoken]

Milkshake

I like tea, coffee, milk, and whiskey too,
But most of all I like a milkshake,
Milkshake, milkshake, I like a milkshake,
Milkshake, I like a malted milk.

(TUNE: "Fugue in G Major," by Bach.)

Found a Peanut

Found a peanut, found a peanut
Found a peanut last night
Last night I found a peanut
Found a peanut last night.

Cracked it open, cracked it open
Cracked it open last night
Last night I cracked it open
Cracked it open last night.

It was rotten, it was rotten
It was rotten last night
Last night it was rotten
It was rotten last night.

Ate it anyway, ate it anyway
Ate it anyway last night
Last night I ate it anyway
Ate it anyway last night.

Got a stomachache, got a stomachache
Got a stomachache last night
Last night I got a stomachache
Got a stomachache last night.

Called the doctor, called the doctor
Called the doctor last night
Last night I called the doctor
Called the doctor last night.

Appendicitis, appendicitis
Appendicitis last night
Last night appendicitis
Appendicitis last night.

Operation, operation
Operation last night
Last night an operation
Operation last night.

Died anyway, died anyway
Died anyway last night
Last night I died anyway
Died anyway last night.

Went to heaven, went to heaven
Went to heaven last night
Last night I went to heaven
Went to heaven last night.

Met St. Peter, met St. Peter
Met St. Peter last night
Last night I met St. Peter
Met St. Peter last night.

Didn't like him, didn't like him,
Didn't like him last night
Last night I didn't like him
Didn't like him last night.

Went the other way, went the other way,
Went the other way last night
Last night I went the other way
Went the other way last night.

Met the devil, met the devil
Met the devil last night
Last night I met the devil
Met the devil last night.

Shoveling coal, shoveling coal
Shoveling coal just now
Just now I'm shoveling coal
Shoveling coal just now.

Found a peanut, found a peanut
Found a peanut just now
Just now I found a peanut
Found a peanut just now.

Cracked it open, cracked it open
[Repeat song ad infinitum] . . .

(TUNE: "Oh, My Darling Clementine," 1884.)

O'Dooley's First Five O'Clock Tea

O'Dooley got rich on a aqueduct job
And he made a considerable pile
His neighbors with envy regarded the scene
To see him assuming such style.
O'Dooley himself was as bad as the rest
With diamonds he dazzled the day
But affairs reached their height when there came an invite
To O'Dooley's first five o'clock "tay."

Chorus: Sure, is it one lump or two lumps?
Permit me to pass you the cream
Sure, Missus McCarthy, that dress you have on is a dream
The whole entertainment was governed by etiquet-"tay"
And a high-toned social event was O'Dooley's first five o'clock "tay."

Now McManus the butcher he envied such style
And he vowed he would end the restraint
He'd a bottle of whiskey concealed on his hip
Which he carried in case he felt faint.

When no one was looking he pulled out the cork
Just as stealthy and sly as could be
And he emptied the bottle of booze that he'd brought
In the kettle of five o'clock "tea."

Chorus

Now you know what a drink to the Irish will do
When a hold of their feelings it's ketched
First old Mrs. Dempsey attempted to sing
"The Night Before Larry Got Stretched"
The widow McCann hootchie-kootchied around
Just as undignified as could be
And O'Dooley's son Mike rode down stairs on his bike
At that fabulous five o'clock tea.

Chorus

Now O'Dooley himself was amazed at the sight
Especially to see his own wife
Attempting to steal Sergeant Henley's chapeau
A woman at her time of life.
He soon smelled a rat, to the kettle he ran
He sniffed and "Begorra!" cried he,
"I'll make it bad news for the man who put booze
In the kettle of five o'clock tea."

Chorus

Key of D

O' - Doo - ley got rich on an a - que - duct job, And he made a con - sid - era - ble pile._____ His neigh - bors with en - vy re -

gard - ed the scene, To see him as - sum - ing such style.____ O' -

Doo - ley him - self was as bad as the rest, With

dia - monds he daz - zled the day.____ But af - fairs reached their height when there

came an in - vite, To O' - Doo - ley's first five o' - clock

Chorus:

"tay." Sure, is it one lump or two lumps? Per -

mit me to pass you the cream. Sure, Mis - sus Mc -

Car - thy, that dress you have on is a dream.__ The whole en - ter -

tain - ment was gov - erned by et - i - quet - "tay,"____ And a high - toned

so - cial e - vent was O' - Doo - ley's first five o' - clock "tay."____

31

I Love to Go A-Gorging

I love to go a-gorging
Amid great gobs of food
And as I do my abdomen
Continues to protrude.

Chorus: Calorie, calorah
        Calorie, calorah-ha-ha-ha-ha-ha-ha
        Calorie, calorah,
        My body is obese.

Italian food with all its cheese
And thick tomato paste
It never seems to pass on through
But hangs around my waist.

Chorus

French cuisine inspires me
To even greater heights
An eight-course meal is quickly done
In seven standard bites.

Chorus

A German meal is all I need
To make my day complete
It's hard to keep account of all
The strudel that I eat.

Chorus

At hot dog stands and burger joints
To make my power play
They bring it in a wheelbarrow
Instead of on a tray.

Chorus

(TUNE: "The Happy Wanderer" [I Love to Go A-Wandering], 1954.)

Toys, Beautiful Toys

Oh give me a bike with a ring-ding I like
And a dolly that hollers "Mama!"
A boat that can toot and an astronaut suit
And electrical trains for my Pa.

Chorus: Toys, beautiful toys
        That turn on and make lots of noise
        That rattle and bang and go clangety-clang
        Beautiful, beautiful toys.

Oh give me a ball I can bounce down the hall
And a drum that goes boom-a-boom-boom
A high-flying jet and a xylophone set
And a record-cassette for my room.

Chorus

Oh give me a bat, a mechanical cat
A whistle that tweedle-dee-dees
A monster that walks and screeches and squawks
And also a flying trapeze.

Chorus

(TUNE: "Home on the Range," 1872.)

Bye, Bye, Longjohns

I have lost my underwear
I don't care, I'll go bare
Bye, bye, longjohns
They were very dear to me
Tickled me, hee, hee, hee
Bye, bye, longjohns.

When you see that little trap door behind me
Then you'll know just where that you can find me,

I have lost my underwear
I don't care, I'll go bare
Longjohns, bye, bye.

(TUNE: "Bye Bye Blackbird," 1926.)

My Pink Pajamas

1.

I wear my pink pajamas in the summer when it's hot
And I wear my flannel nightie in the winter when it's not
And sometimes in the balmy spring and sometimes in the fall
I jump right in between the sheets with nothing on at all.

Glory, glory for the summer
Glory, glory for the fall
Glory, glory for the springtime
With nothing on at all.

2.

We wear our silk pajamas in the summer when it's hot
We wear our woolen undies in the winter when it's not
And sometimes in the springtime and sometimes in the fall
We jump between the covers with nothing on at all.

Glory, glory, what's it to ya
Glory, glory, what's it to ya
Glory, glory, what's it to ya
We jump between the covers with nothing on at all.

(TUNE: "Battle Hymn of the Republic.")

Black Socks

Black socks, they never get dirty
The longer you wear them the stronger they get.
Sometimes I think of the laundry
But something keeps telling me don't wash them yet.

Black socks, they ne-ver get dir-ty, The long-er you wear them the strong-er they get. Some-times I think of the laun-dry, But some-thing keeps tell-ing me don't wash them yet.

O'Brien O'Lin

O'Brien O'Lin had no britches to wear
He got him a sheepskin and made him a pair
"With the hairy side out and the skinny side in,
Nice, light, and cool," said O'Brien O'Lin.

O'Brien O'Lin had no shirt to put on
He got him a goat skin and made him one
He planted the horns right under his chin
"They'll answer for pistols," said O'Brien O'Lin.

O'Brien O'Lin had no watch to wear
He got him a turnip and scooped it out fair
He caught him a cricket and put it therein
"It'll do for a ticker," said O'Brien O'Lin.

O'Brien O'Lin, his wife and her mother
They all went over the bridge together
His wife's mother sneezed and the bridge it fell in
"We'll go home by water," said O'Brien O'Lin.

Shovel

S is for the Spuds we get for breakfast
H is for the Ham we never see
O is for the Onions that they feed us
V is for this Verse composed by me

E is for the End of my Enlistment
L is for the Last you'll see of me
Put them all together, they spell SHOVEL
The emblem of the CCC.*

(TUNE: "M-O-T-H-E-R," 1915.)

*Civilian Conservation Corps.

I'm Looking Under a Pile of Lumber

I'm looking under a pile of lumber
Where I must have lost my gum
First it was Dentyne and then it was cloves
Then it was spearmint, nine days old
No use explaining, the one remaining
Was my dear old bubble gum
I'm looking under a pile of lumber
Where I must have lost my gum.

(TUNE: "I'm Looking Over a Four-Leaf Clover," music by Harry Woods, 1927.)

Pepsi-Cola Hits the Spot

Pepsi-Cola hits the spot
In your stomach it will rot
Tastes like beer, smells like wine
Oh my gosh! it's turpentine!

(TUNE: "Pepsi-Cola Hits the Spot," copyright 1940 by Pepsi-Cola Company and based on traditional tune from England, John Peel.)

Bosco

I hate Bosco, it is no good for me
My mommy puts it in my milk to try to poison me
I fooled Mommy, I put it in her tea
Now there is no Mommy to try to poison me.

(TUNE: "I Love Bosco," music by Joan Edwards and Lyn Duddy, 1951.)

Fleischmann's Yeast

Uncle Mert and Auntie Mabel
Fainted at the breakfast table
This should be sufficient warning
Never do it in the morning
Fleischmann's Yeast has set them right
Now they do it every night
Uncle Mert is hoping soon
They can do it in the afternoon.

(TUNE: "Hark, the Herald Angels Sing.")

Beecham's Pills

Hark! the herald angels sing
Beecham's Pills are just the thing
Peace on earth and mercy mild
Two for adults and one for a child
Joyful all ye nations rise
Medicate when you arise
With th'angelic host proclaim
They are worthy of acclaim
Hark! the herald angels sing
Beecham's Pills are just the thing.

(TUNE: "Hark, the Herald Angels Sing," music by Felix Mendelssohn, 1855.)

Comet

Comet!

It makes your teeth turn green

Comet!

It tastes like gasoline

Comet!

It makes you vomit

So buy some Comet

And vomit today!

(TUNE: "Colonel Bogey March," music by Kenneth J. Alford, 1916.)

McDonald's

McDonald's is your kind of place

Hamburgers in your face

French fries up your nose

Mustard between your toes

The last time that I went there

They stole my underwear

McDonald's is the place for me.

(TUNE: "Down by the Riverside," traditional American spiritual.)

While Shepherds Washed Their Socks

While shepherds washed their socks by night

All seated round the tub

A bar of Sunlight Soap came down

And they began to scrub

And they began to scrub.

(TUNE: "While Shepherds Watched Their Flocks by Night.")

Chew, Maiden, Chew

Chew, maiden, chew

Grape-Nuts are good for you

Though they are like little stones

They are good for building bones, so

Chew, maiden, chew

Chew, maiden, chew.

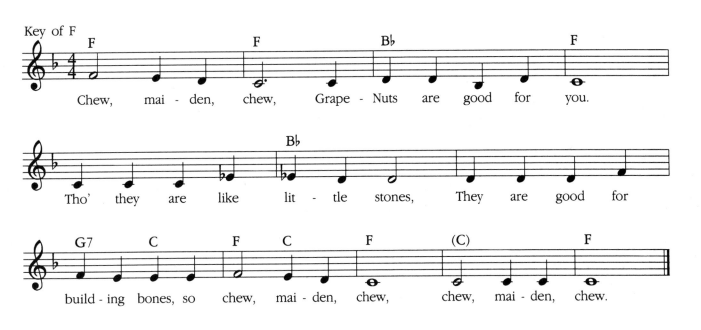

( ) = opt. change

Chapter 2

We Sing of the Polar Bear and Other Creatures

We think of animals on many levels, from pets who live with us to livestock we care for, from game animals we hunt to wild animals we don't eat, and on to mythic beasts that exist only in our imaginations, that are "good to think," as American Indians say. How we classify an animal depends mainly upon our feelings about that creature. A dog may be Old Shep padding alongside us but may sound like the Hound of the Baskervilles to someone hearing him baying across the moors.

Similarly, songs and tales about animals rarely present factual information about an animal, but often use the animal to represent some human concern in amusing, instructive, or memorable images, as do the Uncle Remus stories, or Native American animal tales, or even the old Warner Brothers and Walt Disney movie cartoons.

"A Prairie Home Companion" listeners sent us a rich array of animal songs depicting creatures from worms to whales, with a surprisingly heavy emphasis on songs about livestock and non-game wild animals. Some songs, such as "The Bear Went Over the Mountain" and "Be Kind to Your Web-Footed Friends," are favorite schoolyard songs familiar to most of us. Other fun-to-sing tunes, such as "Papa's Billy Goat" and "Whoa, Mule, Whoa," have long histories traceable through hillbilly recordings to their origins in long-ago minstrel shows.

While none of these animal songs are clearly mythic in the manner of the old ballad of "Bangum and the Boar," or Faulkner's "The Bear," some do evoke in us the complex feelings with which we characteristically respond to depictions of mythic animals—those that haunt our dreams. At one level, "It's a Long Way from Amphioxus" was carpentered together by someone eager to teach arcane zoological vocabulary. Yet, the song of this tiny, primitive beast with its will to survive and prevail evokes the somber spirit of the Darwinian theory.

And what, exactly, is the talking animal of "The Other Day I Met a Bear"? As in a dream or fairy tale, he stands for a fear that we somehow can't name but seem occasionally to need in order to make leaps we didn't know we could make, to force us to "trust our luck," as the song puts it. Inevitably, we magically discover the "luck" was within us all along. It's a fine song, and, of course, it's not really about bears at all.

We Sing of the Polar Bear

We sing of the polar bear fearless and bold
He never gets hot and he never gets cold
For where he lives summer never occurs
And the rest of the year he wears polar bear furs.

The crocodile lives in the tropical belt
With never the heat nor the cold ever felt
For in the winter his summer begins
And the rest of the year he wears crocodile skins.

While we poor unfortunates live in a clime
That calls for at least three full suits at a time
A thick one and thin one for days cold and hot
And a medium-weight for the days that are not.

(TUNE: "Sweet Betsy from Pike," music first printed in 1853; may date from 1840 or earlier.)

The Bear Went Over the Mountain

The bear went over the mountain
The bear went over the mountain
The bear went over the mountain
To see what he could see.

And what did he see there?
And what did he see there?

The other side of the mountain
The other side of the mountain
The other side of the mountain
Was all the bear could see.

(TUNE: "For He's a Jolly Good Fellow," music first published 1783 but may date from as early as the Crusades.)

The Other Day I Met a Bear

The other day   (the other day)
I met a bear   (I met a bear)
Out in the woods   (out in the woods)
Away out there   (away out there)
The other day I met a bear   (I met a bear)
Out in the woods away out there.

He looked at me   (he looked at me)
I looked at him   (I looked at him)
He sized up me   (he sized up me)
I sized up him   (I sized up him)
He looked at me, I looked at him (I looked at him)
He sized up me, I sized up him.

He said to me   (he said to me)
"Why don't you run?   (why don't you run?)
I see you don't   (I see you don't)
Have any gun."   (have any gun)
He said to me "Why don't you run? (why don't you run)
I see you don't have any gun."

I said to him   (I said to him)
"That's a good idear   (that's a good idear)
Come on now, feet   (come on now, feet)
Let's get out of here."   (let's get out of here)
I said to him, "That's a good idear (that's a good idear)
Come on now, feet, let's get out of here."

And so I ran   (and so I ran)
Away from there   (away from there)
But right behind   (but right behind)
Me, came that bear   (me, came that bear)
And so I ran away from there   (away from there)
But right behind me came that bear.

44

And then I saw   (and then I saw)
Ahead of me   (ahead of me)
A great big tree   (a great big tree)
Oh, glory be!   (oh, glory be!)
And then I saw ahead of me   (ahead of me)
A great big tree, oh, glory be!

The lowest branch   (the lowest branch)
Was ten feet up   (was ten feet up)
I'd have to jump   (I'd have to jump)
And trust my luck   (and trust my luck)
The lowest branch was ten feet up   (was ten feet up)
I'd have to jump and trust my luck.

And so I jumped   (and so I jumped)
Into the air   (into the air)
But missed the branch   (but missed the branch)
Away up there   (away up there)
And so I jumped into the air   (into the air)
But missed the branch away up there.

But don't you fret   (but don't you fret)
And don't you frown   (and don't you frown)
I caught that branch   (I caught that branch)
On the way down   (on the way down)
But don't you fret and don't you frown   (and don't you frown)
I caught that branch on the way down.

That's all there is   (that's all there is)
There ain't no more   (there ain't no more)
Unless I see   (unless I see)
That bear once more   (that bear once more)
That's all there is, there ain't no more   (there ain't no more)
Unless I see that bear once more.

(TUNE: Sipping Cider Through a Straw)

In the Blue Ridge Mountains

In the Blue Ridge Mountains of Virginia
Stood a cow on the railroad tracks
She was a good old cow, with eyes so fine
But you can't expect a cow to read a railroad sign
She stood
In the middle of the track
And the train
Hit her square in the back
Now her horns hang on the Blue Ridge Mountains
And her tail's on the railroad track.

In the jackpine woods of Minnesota
Stood a steer on Route 89
He was a good old steer with eyes so fine
And had often stopped to read a well-known highway sign
So he stood
In the middle of the route
And a car, Beep! Beep!
Hit him right in the snoot.
Now his horns adorn a steakhouse in Bemidji
And his tail's on a tall jackpine.

(TUNE: "On the Trail of the Lonesome Pine," 1913.)

The Bulldog and the Bullfrog

Oh, the bulldog on the bank and the bullfrog in the pool
Oh, the bulldog on the bank and the bullfrog in the pool
Oh, the bulldog on the bank and the bullfrog in the pool
The bulldog called the bullfrog a green ol' water fool.

Chorus: Singing tra la la la la la la la
Tra la la la la la la la
Tra la la la la la la la
Tra la la la la la

Oh, the bulldog stooped to catch him but the snapper caught his paw
Oh, the bulldog stooped to catch him but the snapper caught his paw
Oh, the bulldog stooped to catch him but the snapper caught his paw
The pollywog died laughing to see him wag his jaw.

Chorus

Said the monkey to the owl, "Oh, what'll you have to drink?"
Said the monkey to the owl, "Oh, what'll you have to drink?"
Said the monkey to the owl, "Oh, what'll you have to drink?"
"Why, since you are so very kind, I'll take a bottle of ink."

Chorus

(TUNE: "Battle Hymn of the Republic.")

Froggie Went A-Courting

Froggie went a-courting and he did ride, uh huh
Froggie went a-courting and he did ride, uh huh
Froggie went a-courting and he did ride
Sword and a pistol by his side, uh huh.

He rode up to Miss Mousie's den, uh huh
He rode up to Miss Mousie's den, uh huh
He rode up to Miss Mousie's den
Says he, "Miss Mousie, are you within?" uh huh.

He got down and he went in, uh huh
He got down and he went in, uh huh
He got down and he went in
To see Miss Mousie card and spin, uh huh.

He took Miss Mousie up on his knee, uh huh
He took Miss Mousie up on his knee, uh huh
He took Miss Mousie up on his knee
Says he, "Miss Mousie, will you marry me?" uh huh.

"Oh no, oh no, I can never do that," uh huh
"Oh no, oh no, I can never do that," uh huh
"Oh no, oh no, I can never do that,
Without the consent of Uncle Rat," uh huh.

Uncle Rat came lumbering home, uh huh
Uncle Rat came lumbering home, uh huh
Uncle Rat came lumbering home
"Who's been here since I've been gone?" uh huh.

"A fine young man of high degree," uh huh
"A fine young man of high degree," uh huh
"A fine young man of high degree,"
Says he, "Miss Mousie, will you marry me?" uh huh.

Uncle Rat went back to town, uh huh
Uncle Rat went back to town, uh huh
Uncle Rat went back to town
To buy his niece a wedding gown, uh huh.

"Oh where shall the wedding supper be," uh huh
"Oh where shall the wedding supper be," uh huh
"Oh where shall the wedding supper be?
Down in the meadow in a hollow tree," uh huh.

"Oh what shall the wedding supper be," uh huh
"Oh what shall the wedding supper be," uh huh
"Oh what shall the wedding supper be?
Two brown beans and a black-eyed pea," uh huh.

'Twas the handsomest couple that ever was seen, uh huh
'Twas the handsomest couple that ever was seen, uh huh
'Twas the handsomest couple that ever was seen
Her dress was gray and his was green, uh huh.

At last they got the young couple to bed, uh huh
At last they got the young couple to bed, uh huh
At last they got the young couple to bed
And the frog kicked the featherbed over his head, uh huh.

The ancient book lays on the shelf, uh huh
The ancient book lays on the shelf, uh huh
The ancient book lays on the shelf
If you want any more you may sing it yourself, uh huh.

O Tom the Toad

O Tom the Toad, O Tom the Toad,
Why did you hop up on the road?
O Tom the Toad, O Tom the Toad
Why did you hop up on the road?
You were my friend and now you're dead
You bear the marks of tire tread
O Tom the Toad, O Tom the Toad
Why did you hop up on the road?

O Tom the Toad, O Tom the Toad
Why did you hop up on the road?
O Tom the Toad, O Tom the Toad
Why did you hop up on the road?
You did not see yon passing car
And now you're stretched out on the tar
O Tom the Toad, O Tom the Toad
Why did you hop up on the road?

O Tom the Toad, O Tom the Toad
Why did you hop up on the road?
O Tom the Toad, O Tom the Toad
Why did you hop up on the road?
You hopped out on the yellow line
And turned into a streak of slime
O Tom the Toad, O Tom the Toad
Why did you hop up on the road?

O Tom the Toad, O Tom the Toad,
Why did you hop up on the road?
O Tom the Toad, O Tom the Toad
Why did you hop up on the road?
It's clear to all you're in a rut
We all did see your gushing gut
O Tom the Toad, O Tom the Toad
Why did you hop up on the road?

O Tom the Toad, O Tom the Toad
Why did you hop up on the road?
O Tom the Toad, O Tom the Toad
Why did you hop up on the road?
There was a loud and awful crash
For poor old Tom had just got smashed
O Tom the Toad, O Tom the Toad
Why did you hop up on the road?

(TUNE: "O Tannenbaum.")

Froggie He Am a Queer Bird

Poor froggie he am a queer bird
He ain't got no tail almost hardly.
He run when he yump, when he yump he sit down
Where he ain't got no tail almost hardly.

I know how ugly I are
I know my face ain't no star
But I don't mind it because I'm behind it
The fellow in front gets the jar.

(TUNE: "Blest Be the Tie That Binds.")

50

Little Furry Caterpillar

Little furry caterpillar, soft and slow
Feeling sleepy, thought that he to sleep would go
With his blanket closely wrapped, on a twig he lay
Little furry caterpillar dozed away.

Then one day he wakened when the sun was bright
Slipped out of his blanket feeling fine and right
Then unfolded wings of gauze carried him on high
Little furry caterpillar was a butterfly!

Lit - tle fur - ry ca - ter - pil - lar, soft and slow,

Feel - ing sleep - y, thought that he to sleep would go,

With his blan - ket close - ly wrapped, on a twig he lay,

Lit - tle fur - ry ca - ter - pil - lar dozed a - way.

The Thousand-Legged Worm

"Tell me," said the thousand-legged worm,
"Has anybody seen a leg of mine?
For if it can't be found I shall have to squirm around
On the other nine hundred ninety-nine.

"Squirm around, squirm around
On the other nine hundred ninety-nine
If it can't be found I shall have to squirm around
On the other nine hundred ninety-nine."

(TUNE: "Polly Wolly Doodle," traditional minstrel song published in 1880.)

Beetles

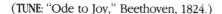

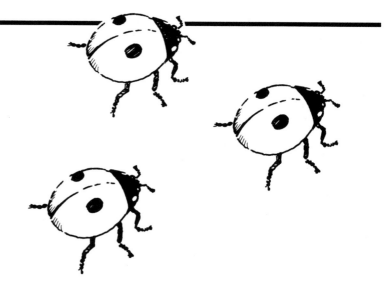

Beetles are not dirty bugs
Spiders, scorpions, or slugs
Heroes of the insect realm
They sport winged, burnished helms
They are shining and divine
They are lovely and just fine
Beetles do not bite or sting
They love almost everything.

(TUNE: "Ode to Joy," Beethoven, 1824.)

Be Kind to Your Web-Footed Friends

Be kind to your web-footed friends
For a duck may be somebody's mother
Be kind to your friends in the swamp
Where the weather is very cold and damp
You may think that this is the end
Well, it's not, because there's one more chorus
Be kind to your friends in the swamp
Where the weather is very cold and damp.

(TUNE: "The Stars and Stripes Forever," 1897.)

See These Young Ducks at Play

See these young ducks at play
All on the Sabbath day
See how they swim
Just see them teeter-totter
All across the shining water
Don't you think they hadn't oughter
On the Sabbath day?

(TUNE: "Come, Thou Almighty King," 1757.)

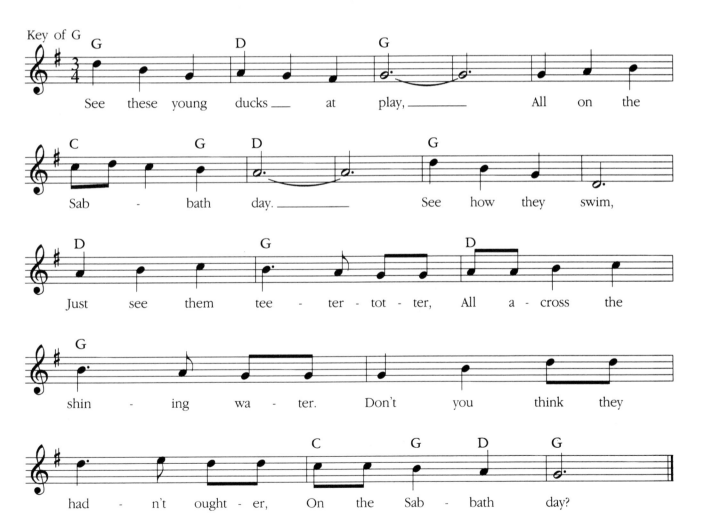

Oh, I Had a Little Chicken

Oh, I had a little chicken but it wouldn't lay an egg
So I poured hot water up and down its leg
And the little chicken hollered and the little chicken begged
And the little chicken laid me a hard-boiled egg.

Oh, I had a little duck that had a webbed foot
She built her nest in a mulberry root
Pulled the grass around her for to keep herself warm
And another little drink won't do us any harm.

(TUNE: "Turkey in the Straw.")

Papa's Billy Goat

Papa bought him a great big billy goat
Ma she washed 'most every day
Hung her clothes out on the line
And that old billy goat came that way.

He et up Pa's red flannel undershirt
You ought to have heard those buttons crack
But I'll get even with that old goat
Gonna tie him to the railroad track.

Well, I tied him to the railroad track
And the train was coming at a powerful rate
But that old goat, he gave three groans,
Coughed up that shirt, and flagged the freight.

I went to the depot and I bought me a ticket
I walked right in and I sat right down
Stuck the ticket in the brim of my hat
But that old wind blew it out on the ground.

Conductor came along, said, "Give me your ticket,
You'll have to pay again or get left on the track."
But I'll get even with that old man
I bought a round-trip ticket but I ain't coming back.

Key of C

Pa - pa bought him a great big bil - ly goat,
Ma she washed 'most ev - er - y day, Hung her clothes out
on the line, And that old bil - ly goat came that way.

Groundhog

Picked up my gun and whistled for my dogs
Picked up my gun and whistled for my dogs
Come on, boys, let's catch a groundhog
Hmm, groundhog!

Here comes Sam with a ten-foot pole
Here comes Sam with a ten-foot pole
Gonna roust that groundhog outa his hole
Hmm, groundhog!

Here he comes all in a whirl
Here he comes all in a whirl
The biggest groundhog in all the world
Hmm, groundhog!

Well, I love my groundhog, stewed and fried
Well, I love my groundhog, stewed and fried
Little bowl of soup sittin' by his side
Hmm, groundhog!

Watch me, boys, I'm about to fall
Watch me, boys, I'm about to fall
I've et 'til my pants won't button at all
Hmm, groundhog!

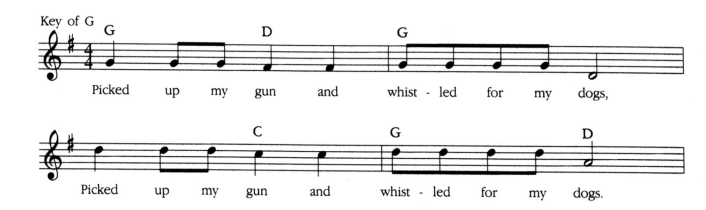

Come on, boys, let's catch a ground-hog, Hmm, ground-hog!

Groundhog Medley

1.

Oh, you must have been a beautiful groundhog
You must have been a beautiful pup
When you were only startin' to dig the flower garden
I'll bet you showed the other pups up
And when it came to casting a shadow
To tell if spring were coming or not
If you stood upon your toes then your lovely nose arose
Those must have been some wonderful times
Oh, you must have been a beautiful groundhog
'Cause tonight you're ringing my chimes.

(TUNE: "You Must Have Been a Beautiful Baby," 1938.)

2.

Groundhoggy, waiting for the spring
And all the things that spring will bring
Our groundhoggy on ground soggy
The rain and the snow make a mud-shadow show
We're loyal, with you we'll search the sky
Waiting 'til those clouds roll by
We're after the same skies of blue
Our February crew, groundhoggy, and you.

(TUNE: "Moon River," 1961.)

3.

Who foretells the coming spring
And bids the winter bye?
G-R-O-U-N-D-H-O-G-G-Y
So bow your heads and cross your hearts
And lift your glasses high
G-R-O-U-N-D-H-O-G-G-Y
Groundhog's Day, Groundhog's Day
The robin's not so very far away, hey
Who foretells the coming spring
And bids the winter bye?
G-R-O-U-N-D-H-O-G-G-Y

(TUNE: "Mickey Mouse March," 1955.)

4.

The dogs' heads sway, the chickens lay
They're waitin' for the groundhog
The turkeys pray, the kittens stray
They're waitin' for the groundhog
The whales play, the cows eat hay
They're waitin' for the groundhog
Hip hip hurray, it's Groundhog's Day
We're waitin' for the groundhog.

(TUNE: "Deep in the Heart of Texas," 1941.)

She, a Jersey Cow

They strolled the lane together
The night was studded with stars
They reached the gate in the meadow
He lifted for her the bars.
She raised her brown eyes to him
There was nothing between them now
For he was just a country boy
And she a Jersey cow.

(TUNE: "Mighty 'Lak a Rose," 1901.)

Key of G

They strolled the lane to-geth-er, The night was stud-ded with stars, They

reached the gate in the mea - dow, He lift - ed for her the bars. She

raised her brown eyes to him, There was no - thing be - tween them now, For

he was just a coun - try boy, and she a Jer - sey cow.

The Frenchman's Cow

I found her there behind the house
So dark I could not see
And as I whispered soft sweet words
I drew her close to me.

I could not speak her language
And she could not speak mine
But with her eyes she gave consent
Which suited me just fine.

I knew I should not do it but
I knew darned well I would
Oh yes, I milked that Frenchman's cow
And gosh, that milk was good.

(TUNE: "Amazing Grace.")

The Red Fox

A red fox ran away
He ran far far away
His mother had no telephone
Had no telephone
And he was far from home.

Poor Reddy, sad was he
So far away to be
He sat upon a log to cry,
"Dear, dear, where am I?"
He cried, "Oh, where am I?"

A big bear passing by
Turned when he heard the cry
He dried his tears and led him home
Led the red fox home
No more will Reddy roam.

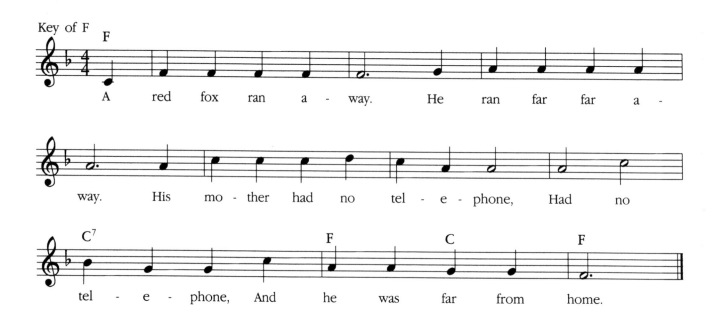

Take It Out, Take It Out, Remove It

Oh, I stuck my head in a little skunk's hole
The little skunk said, "Upon my soul,
Take it out! Take it out! Take it out! Remove it!"

Well, I didn't take it out, and the little skunk said,
"If you don't take it out, you will wish you were dead.
Take it out! Take it out! Sssssssst!" I removed it!

(TUNE: "Dixie," 1860.)

The Whale Song

In Frisco Bay there lives a whale
And she eats peanuts by the pail
And washtubs, and bathtubs, and sailboats, and schooners.

Her name is Sara and she's a peach
But don't leave food within her reach
Or babies, or nursemaids, or chocolate ice cream sodas.

She loves to smile, and when she smiles
You can see her teeth for miles and miles
And her tonsils, and her spare ribs, and things too fierce to mention.

She knows no games, so when she plays
She rolls her eyes for days and days
She vibrates and yodels and breaks the Ten Commandments.

Now what you gonna do in a case like that?
There's nothing to do but sit on your hat
Or your toothbrush, or your best friend, or anything else that's useless.

(TUNE: "Dixie.")

Whoa, Mule, Whoa

There was a man in our town
His name was Simon Slick
He had a very good old mule
But how that mule could kick
He kicked a streak of lightning
He had an iron jaw
Just the thing to have around
To tame your mother-in-law.

He kicked a cannonball around
And kicked it out of sight
He kicked a skating-rink apart
At nine o'clock at night
The skaters standing on their heads
A-gasping for their breath
He kicked his hind legs down his throat
And kicked himself to death.

Chorus: Whoa, mule, whoa
Whoa, mule, whoa
Every time that old man looked around
It was whoa, mule, whoa.

Chorus

law. Whoa, mule, whoa, Whoa, mule, — whoa, Ev - ery
time that old man looked a - round, It was whoa, mule, — whoa.

The Old Grey Mare

The old grey mare went
Phhft! down the Delaware
Phhft! down the Delaware
Phhft! down the Delaware
The old grey mare went
Phhft! down the Delaware
Many long years ago.

Chorus: Many long years ago, many long years ago
The old grey mare went
Phhft! down the Delaware
Many long years ago.

The old grey mare went
Phhft! on the whiffletree
Phhft! on the whiffletree
Phhft! on the whiffletree
The old grey mare went
Phhft! on the whiffletree
Many long years ago.

Chorus

(TUNE: "The Old Grey Mare, [She Ain't What She Used to Be]," drawing on "Down in Alabam'" of 1858. The listener who submitted this specified that the "Phhft!" should be a juicy raspberry.)

Donkey Riding

Were you ever in Quebec
Stowing timber on the deck
Where there's a king with a golden crown
Riding on a donkey?

Chorus: Hi, ho, away we go
       Donkey riding, donkey riding
       Hi, ho, away we go
       Riding on a donkey.

Were you ever off the Horn
Where it's always nice and warm
See the lion and the unicorn
Riding on a donkey?

Chorus

Were you ever in Cardiff Bay
Where the folks all shout, "Hooray!
Here comes Johnny with his six-month pay
Riding on a donkey?"

Chorus

Were you ever in Egypt
Reading hieroglyphic script
Seeing a mummy in a crypt
Riding on a donkey?

Chorus

Were you ever in Brazil
Drinking coffee 'til you're ill
Did you have to take a pill
Riding on a donkey?

Chorus

Were you ever in New York
Eating peanuts with a fork
Off a plate that's made of cork
Riding on a donkey?

Chorus

(Although listeners submitted this as an animal song, it is actually a sea chantey and the "donkey" is the donkey-engine on a ship.)

Jiggs the Dog

Oh, I had a little doggie and his name was Mister Jiggs
I sent him to the corner store to buy a pound of figs.
He came back an hour later and this is what he said,
"The figs looked rather green, my dear, I bought a bone instead."

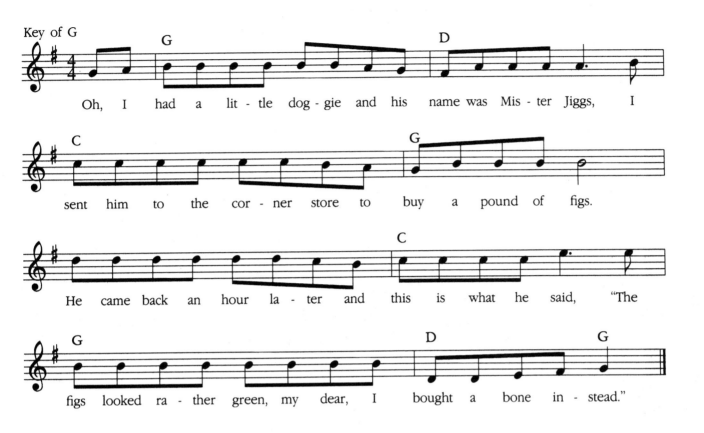

Key of G

Oh, I had a lit-tle dog-gie and his name was Mis-ter Jiggs, I

sent him to the cor-ner store to buy a pound of figs.

He came back an hour la-ter and this is what he said, "The

figs looked ra-ther green, my dear, I bought a bone in-stead."

What a Long, Long Tail

What a long, long tail our cat's got

And it's all covered with fur

But it's sure no use to fight with

And it's no use to purr

She can't wave it like a dog does

Or give the bad flies a bat

Don't laugh or cry, but tell me why

There's a tail on a long-tailed cat.

(TUNE: "There's a Long, Long Trail," 1913. Popular with British troops in World War I.)

Anybody Seen My Kitty?

Anybody seen my kitty?
Anybody seen my cat?
She's got a crook at the end of her tail
To show that she's been fighting.
Down in Dugan's alley
Up in Finnegan's flat
Kitty, kitty, kitty, kitty, kitty, kitty, kitty, kitty
Anybody seen my cat?

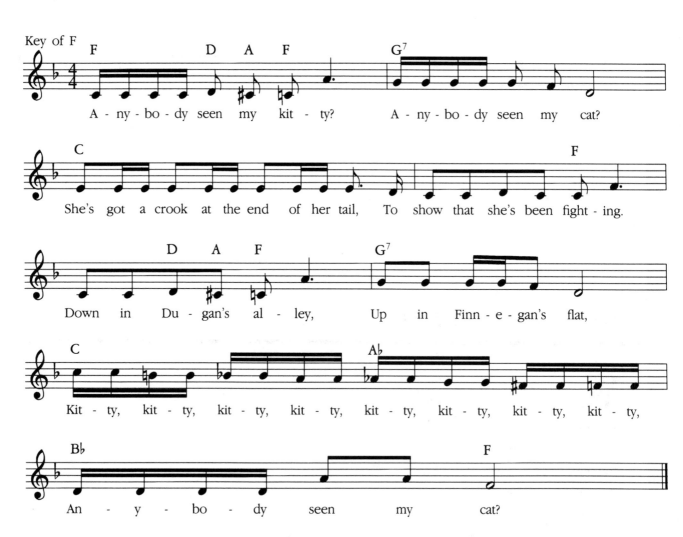

Key of F

A - ny - bo - dy seen my kit - ty? A - ny - bo - dy seen my cat?

She's got a crook at the end of her tail, To show that she's been fight - ing.

Down in Du - gan's al - ley, Up in Finn - e - gan's flat,

Kit - ty, kit - ty, kit - ty, kit - ty, kit - ty, kit - ty, kit - ty, kit - ty,

An - y - bo - dy seen my cat?

Yuck! Cats

A duck is an excellent swimmer
A monkey's both clever and shrewd
A dog loves to bring you your slippers
A cat only comes when there's food.

Chorus: Yuck! Cats! Yuck! Cats!
       Don't try to give one to me, to me
       Yuck! Cats! Yuck! Cats!
       Don't try to give one to me.

Birds chirp and twitter for hours
Rabbits make cuddly pets
Snakes can even be playful
But cats like to play hard to get.

Chorus

Donkeys are known to be stubborn
But cats are much worse, you'll agree
Try leading a cat to the water
It's easier to part the Red Sea.

Chorus

Cat lovers say, "Cats are so loving,
So diligent, loyal, and true."
But cats just know how to be sneaky,
Ignore folks, chase mice, and go "Mew."

Chorus

So cat owners, don't boast and brag so
That kitties are cute and high-class
To you cats are trusted companions
To me they're a pain in the . . .

Chorus

(TUNE: "My Bonnie Lies Over the Ocean," tune traditional from Scotland, first printed 1881.)

Pussy Willow

We had a little pussy
Its coat was silver grey
It lived down in the meadow
Not very far away.
Although it was a pussy
It'll never be a cat
'Cause it's a pussy willow
Now what do you think of that?
Meow, meow, meow, meow, meow, meow, meow, meow, scat!

(TUNE: Sing each line to one note of the ascending scale, beginning with Do, and on the last line, descend the scale and shout "Scat.")

It's a Long Way from Amphioxus

A fish-like thing appeared among the Annelids one day
It hadn't any parapods or setas to display
It hadn't any eyes or jaws or ventral nervous cord
But it had a lot of gill slits and it had a notochord.

Chorus: It's a long way from Amphioxus
It's a long way to us
It's a long way from Amphioxus
To the meanest human cuss
Goodbye, fins and gill slits
Hello, lungs and hair
It's a long, long way from Amphioxus
But we come from there.

It wasn't much to look at and it scarce knew how to swim
And Nereid was very sure it didn't come from him
The Mollusks wouldn't own it and the Arthopods got sore
So the poor thing had to burrow in the sand along the shore.

Chorus

It wiggled in the sand before a crab could nip its tail
It said, "Gill slits and myotomes are all of no avail
I've grown some metapleural folds and sport an oral hood
But all these fine new characters don't do me any good."

Chorus

It sulked awhile down in the sand without a bit of pep
Then stiffened up its notochord and said, "I'll beat 'em yet,
I've got more possibilities within my slender frame
Than all these proud invertebrates that treat me with such shame."

Chorus

Its notochord shall grow into a chain of vertebrae
As fins its metapleural folds shall agitate the sea
Its tiny dorsal nervous tube shall form a mighty brain
And the vertebrates shall dominate the animal domain.

Chorus

(TUNE: "It's a Long [, Long] Way to Tipperary," 1912.)

Chapter 3

Songs of Misrule

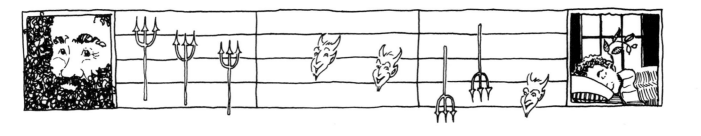

Many traditional societies observed festivals which celebrated the spirit of misrule, when for a certain prescribed time and within prescribed limits, the society's officially endorsed rules and beliefs were suspended and given over to play, freedom, and topsy-turvy reversals of custom. A lowly member of the society might be chosen as a mock bishop or king and paraded through the streets to uproarious and sometimes sacrilegious mockery. Such festivals served a healthy function of allowing a temporary release from the tensions which all civilizations impose on their citizens in the name of order and orthodoxy.

The spirit of misrule survives only faintly in our own volatile and fragile culture, most notably in an occasional festival such as Mardi Gras, or at one remove in our popular art, where comedians evoke the anarchic laughter of misrule. Such comics range from Charlie Chaplin's sublime industrial-age Puck down to his debased descendant, Pee Wee Herman, who authorizes the children watching him on television to scream and misbehave on cue.

Some of the folk songs sent to the Department explore the "musts" and "oughts" of our society, and a few preserve echoes of the spirit of misrule, testifying to the continuing burden of what Freud called the "discontents" of our civilization and our enduring need to assert our truest selves in voices of joyous rebellion. The songs probe standards of behavior from the pathetic plea to "Leave the Dishes in the Sink" to the triumphant "Ding Ding Ding Ding Ding," with interesting stops along the way with "We Come from St. Olaf" and "My Grandma's Advice," which hint at some of the oldest attractions of misrule and its celebration.

Boys Can Whistle, Girls Can Sing

Gramma Grunt said a curious thing
Boys can whistle but girls must sing.
That is what I heard her say
'Twas no longer than yesterday.

Chorus: Boys can whistle, wh, wh, wh
Girls can sing, tra-la, la, la, la.

I asked my Papa the reason why
Girls can't whistle the same as I.
He said to me, "It's the usual thing
For boys to whistle and girls to sing."

Chorus

Why can't girls whistle too, pray tell,
If they manage to do it well?
Whistling girls and crowing hens
Always come to some bad end.

Chorus

Perfect Posture

Perfect posture, perfect posture
Do not slump, do not slump
We must grow up handsome, we must grow up handsome
Hide that hump, hide that hump.

(TUNE: "Frère Jacques.")

Leave the Dishes in the Sink

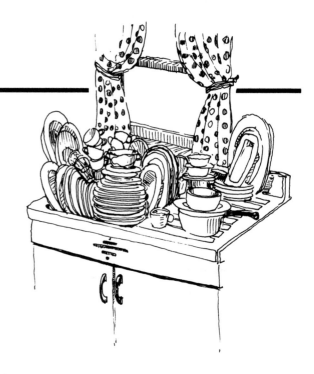

Leave the dishes in the sink
Oh, leave the dishes in the sink
Those dirty plates will have to wait
Tonight we're gonna celebrate
Oh, leave the dishes in the sink!

(TUNE: "Whistle While You Work," 1937.)

Elbows

[Person's name twice], if you're able
Get your elbows off the table.
This is not a horse's stable
But a respectable dining table.

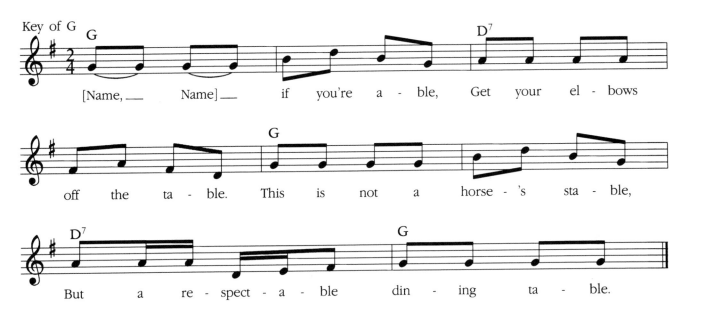

Key of G

[Name, — Name] — if you're a - ble, Get your el - bows

off the ta - ble. This is not a horse - 's sta - ble,

But a re - spect - a - ble din - ing ta - ble.

I Eat My Peas with Honey

I eat my peas with honey
And I've done it all my life
It makes the peas taste funny
But it keeps them on my knife.

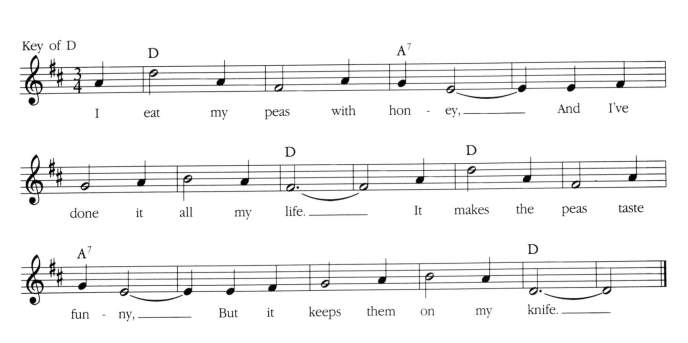

Key of D

I eat my peas with hon - ey, — And I've

done it all my life. — It makes the peas taste

fun - ny, — But it keeps them on my knife. —

Rootie-Toot-Toot

Rootie-toot-toot, rootie-toot-toot
We're the girls of the Institute
We don't drink or smoke or chew
And we don't go with the boys that do
Our class won the Bible, nyah, nyah, nyah.

(TUNE: "Did You Ever Think," and what the listeners described as "your basic nyah, nyah, nyah.")

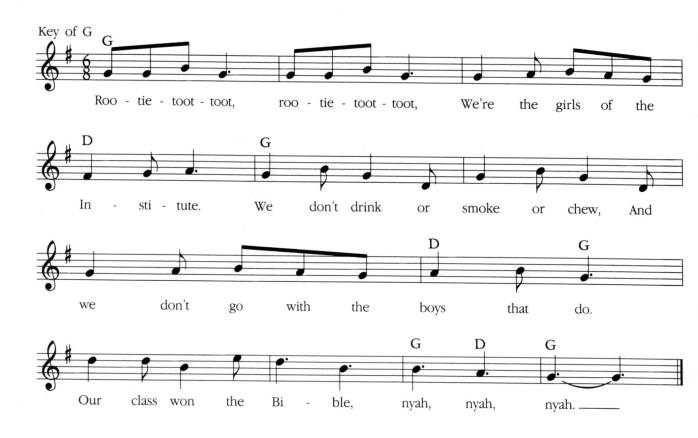

We Come from St. Olaf

We come from St. Olaf
We sure are the real stuff
We ring out and sing out
With um-ya-ya-ya
We don't smoke, we don't drink
But that's just what they think
We go out on our blankets
And we um-ya-ya!

(TUNE: "The Bells of St. Mary's," 1917.)

Respect

He asked to hold my hand
I seriously objected
I knew the feeling was grand
But I might not be respected.

He asked me for a hug
I seriously objected
I knew the feeling was snug
But I might not be respected.

He asked me for a kiss
I seriously objected
I knew the feeling was bliss
But I might not be respected.

Now I'm old and grey
My love I have rejected
They call me an old maid
But, by heck, I am respected.

I Won't Marry

Oh, I won't marry a man who's rich
For he'll get drunk and fall in a ditch
Oh, I won't marry a man who's rich
No, I won't marry at all.

Chorus: I'll take my stool and I'll sit in the shade
For I am bound to die an old maid
No, I won't marry at all, at all
No, I won't marry at all.

Oh, I won't marry a man who's poor
For he would beg from door to door
Oh, I won't marry a man who's poor
No, I won't marry at all.

Chorus

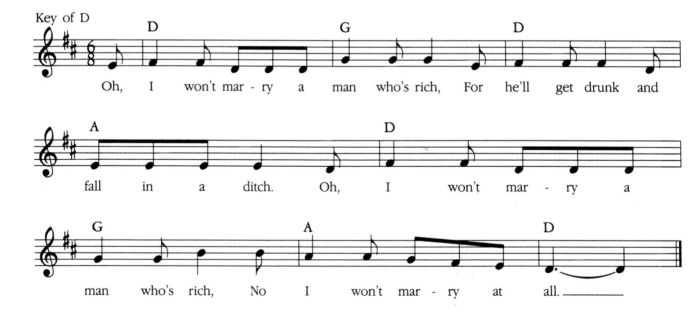

My Grandma's Advice

My grandma lived on yonder little green
As fine an old lady as ever was seen
She often cautioned me with care
Of all false young men to beware
Timmiaye, timmiumpatum, timmiumpatay
Of all false young men to beware.

The first came courting was young Johnny Green
As fine a young man as ever was seen
But the words of my grandma rang in my head
I could not tell one word that he said
Timmiaye, timmiumpatum, timmiumpatay
I could not tell one word that he said.

The next came courting was young Ellis Grove
'Twas there we met with a joyous love
With a joyous love I couldn't be afraid
Better to get married than to die an old maid
Timmiaye, timmiumpatum, timmiumpatay
Better to get married than to die an old maid.

Says I to myself, "There's some mistake
What a fuss these old folks make
If the boys and the girls had always been so afraid
Grandma herself would have died an old maid
Timmiaye, timmiumpatum, timmiumpatay
Grandma herself would have died an old maid."

Yield Not to Flirtation

Yield not to flirtation
For flirting is sin
Thy sisters will help you
Their brothers to win
Fight manfully onward
Dark lashes subdue
Don't chase after the boys, girls
Let them chase after you.

Chorus: Ask your sisters to help you
        Comfort, strengthen, and guide you
        They are willing to aid you
        They will carry you through.

(TUNE: "Yield Not to Temptation," 1868.)

Let Your Whiskers Grow

Let your whiskers grow
Let your whiskers grow
Don't waste your time in shaving.
Pull 'em out by the roots
Make laces for your boots
Look at the money you'll be saving.

Key of G

Let your whisk - ers grow, Let your whisk - ers grow,

Don't waste your time in shav - ing. Pull 'em

out by the roots, Make la - ces for your boots,

Look at the mon - ey you'll be sav - ing.

Old Dan Tucker

Old Dan Tucker was a fine old man
He washed his face in a frying pan
He combed his hair with a wagon wheel
And died with a toothache in his heel.

Chorus: So get out of the way for old Dan Tucker
He's too late to get his supper
Supper's over and dinner's cookin'
Old Dan Tucker just stand there lookin'.

I came to town the other night
I heard the noise and saw the fight
The watchman was a-runnin' 'round
Crying "Old Dan Tucker's come to town!"

Chorus

Old Dan Tucker is a nice old man
He used to ride our darby ram
He sent him whizzing down the hill
If he hadn't got up, he'd lay there still.

Chorus

Old Dan begun in early life
To play the banjo and the fife
He played the children all to sleep
And then into his bunk he'd creep.

Chorus

(TUNE: "Old Dan Tucker," 1843.)

I Ain't Gonna Grieve My Lord No More

Oh, you can't get to heaven   (oh, you can't get to heaven)

In a rocking chair   (in a rocking chair)

'Cause the Lord don't want   ('cause the Lord don't want)

No lazy folks there   (no lazy folks there)

Oh, you can't get to heaven in a rocking chair

'Cause the Lord don't want no lazy folks there

I ain't gonna grieve my Lord no more.

Chorus: I ain't gonna grieve my Lord no more

I ain't gonna grieve my Lord no more

I ain't gonna grieve my Lord no more.

Oh, you can't get to heaven   (oh, you can't get to heaven)

On roller skates   (on roller skates)

'Cause you'll roll right by   ('cause you'll roll right by)

Them pearly gates   (them pearly gates)

Oh, you can't get to heaven on roller skates

'Cause you'll roll right by them pearly gates

I ain't gonna grieve my Lord no more.

Chorus

Oh, you can't get to heaven   (oh, you can't get to heaven)

With powder and paints   (with powder and paints)

'Cause the Lord don't want   ('cause the Lord don't want)

You what you ain't   (you what you ain't)

Oh, you can't get to heaven with powder and paints

'Cause the Lord don't want you what you ain't

I ain't gonna grieve my Lord no more.

Chorus

Oh, you can't get to heaven   (oh, you can't get to heaven)

On a pair of skis   (on a pair of skis)

You'll ski right through   (you'll ski right through)

St. Peter's knees   (St. Peter's knees)

Oh, you can't get to heaven on a pair of skis

You'll ski right through St. Peter's knees

I ain't gonna grieve my Lord no more.

Chorus

Oh, you can't get to heaven   (oh, you can't get to heaven)

In a brand new suit   (in a brand new suit)

St. Peter will say   (St. Peter will say)

That you're just too cute   (that you're just too cute)

Oh, you can't get to heaven in a brand new suit

St. Peter will say that you're just too cute

I ain't gonna grieve my Lord no more.

Chorus

Oh, you can't get to heaven   (oh, you can't get to heaven)

In an automobile   (in an automobile)

The devil will grab   (the devil will grab)

That steering wheel   (that steering wheel)

Oh, you can't get to heaven in an automobile

The Devil will grab that steering wheel

I ain't gonna grieve my Lord no more.

Chorus

Oh, the deacon went down   (oh, the deacon went down)

In the cellar to pray   (in the cellar to pray)

He fell asleep   (he fell asleep)

And he stayed all day   (and he stayed all day)

Oh, the deacon went down in the cellar to pray

He fell asleep and he stayed all day

I ain't gonna grieve my Lord no more.

Chorus

Key of D

Oh, you can't get to heav-en (oh, you can't get to heav-en) In a rock-ing

chair (in a rock-ing chair), 'Cause the Lord don't

want ('cause the Lord don't want) No la-zy folks

there (no la-zy folks there). Oh, you can't get to

heaven in a rock-ing chair 'Cause the Lord don't

want no la-zy folks there. I ain't gon-na grieve my Lord no more. _____

Chorus:

I ain't gon-na grieve my Lord no more, I ain't gon-na

grieve my Lord no more, I ain't gon-na grieve my Lord no more. _____

Three Jolly Fishermen

There were three jolly fishermen
There were three jolly fishermen
Fisher, fisher, men, men, men
Fisher, fisher, men, men, men
There were three jolly fishermen.

The first one's name was Isaac
The first one's name was Isaac
I, I, saac, saac, saac
I, I, saac, saac, saac
The first one's name was Isaac.

The second one's name was Abraham
The second one's name was Abraham
Abra, Abra, ham, ham, ham
Abra, Abra, ham, ham, ham
The second one's name was Abraham.

The third one's name was Jacob
The third one's name was Jacob
Ja, Ja, cob, cob, cob
Ja, Ja, cob, cob, cob
The third one's name was Jacob.

They all went down to Amster (sh-h-h-h)
They all went down to Amster (sh-h-h-h)
Amster, Amster, (sh-h-h-h, sh-h-h-h, sh-h-h-h)
Amster, Amster, (sh-h-h-h, sh-h-h-h, sh-h-h-h)
They all went down to Amster (sh-h-h-h).

You mustn't say that naughty word
You mustn't say that naughty word
Naughty, naughty, word, word, word
Naughty, naughty, word, word, word
You mustn't say that naughty word.

We're gonna say it anyway
We're gonna say it anyway
Any, any, way, way, way
Any, any, way, way, way
We're gonna say it anyway.

They all went down to Amster-DAM!
They all went down to Amster-DAM!
Amster, Amster, DAM, DAM, DAM!
Amster, Amster, DAM, DAM, DAM!
They all went down to Amster-DAM!

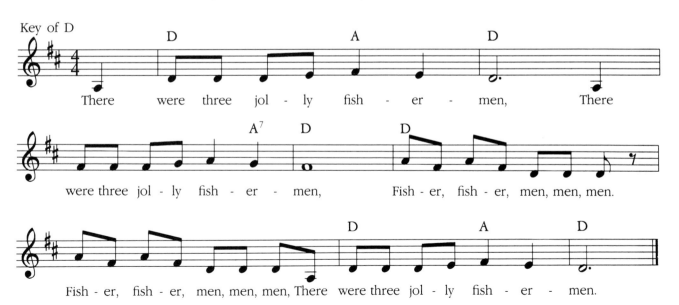

The Man Behind

When I was just a little lad, my father said to me
"Don't always be too forward, son, but act with modesty
In battle it's the man in front that fights, you'll always find
But the general gets the credit, 'cause he's the man behind

"The man behind, the man behind
He's the wisest guy that you will ever find
It's the man in front gets shot 'cause he's Johnny-on-the-spot
So always try to be the man behind."

(TUNE: "The Wearing o' the Green," traditional, from an Irish street ballad of about 1798.)

Reuben, Reuben

Reuben, Reuben, I've been thinking
What a grand world this would be
If the boys were all transported
Far across the northern sea.

Oh, my goodness gracious, Rachel
What a queer world that would be
Girls would have no boys to talk to
If we were across the sea.

Reuben, Reuben, I've been thinking
Life is sometimes awfully queer
No one knows where we are going
No one knows why we are here.

Rachel, Rachel, I've been thinking
Those are true words what you've said
We sleep all night when we're living
Sleep all day when we are dead.

(TUNE: "Reuben and Rachel," 1871.)

Chapter 4

The Burning of the School

Recent critiques of the American public educational system such as *A Nation at Risk* (1983) have sounded alarms about schools in which our children are said to experience regimented boredom alleviated only by violence and drugs, while learning little more than a hearty lifelong contempt for formal education. This depressing image carries over into Hollywood's depiction of public schools in such 1980s films as *Fast Times at Ridgemont High, Rock and Roll High School, Teachers,* and *The Principal.*

The songs about school submitted to the Department of Folk Song by "A Prairie Home Companion" listeners would appear at first glance to corroborate the formal critiques. Almost unanimously, the songs about school depict fantasies of oppressed students heaping revenge and humiliation on their hated teachers, presumably for injustices suffered but seldom specified in the songs. Also, many listeners submitted suggestions for "anti-lessons" which trivialize classic poems by setting them to comically inappropriate tunes, the sort of idle inspiration that might come to a bright but bored student half-dozing through a particularly tedious literature class.

We have met teachers who would if they could gladly put out a contract on the unknown student whose cunning mind first discovered that Emily Dickinson's poems can be sung to the tune of "The Yellow Rose of Texas" and that Robert Frost's "Stopping by Woods on a Snowy Evening" can be sung to the tune of "Hernando's Hideaway." The sure-fire guffaws evoked by singing formal verse to incongruous pop or folk tunes are guaranteed to drive out any teacher's lesson on symbolism or scansion in a sort of Gresham's Law that appeals to the eternal sophomore in many of us.

On the other hand, the songs in this chapter convey attitudes toward rather than information about their creators' school experiences, and often attitudes and experiences are at odds. The editors, for example, both of whom were conscientious and successful students who enjoyed school and liked their teachers—the modern term is, alas, "nerds"—recall dutifully chanting at the end of each school year:

> No more pencils, no more books
> No more teacher's dirty looks.

This folk rhyme conveyed nothing of our experiences with our teachers, but chanting it was *expected* of us. It was what kids did at the end of the school year, and we didn't question it.

Similarly, we suspect that most of the songs in this chapter reflect a long American tradition of schoolyard anti-intellectualism rather than genuine misery suffered by the student song-makers. These songs are what kids do in the playground. Also, entertaining invective is relatively easy to compose, and a song praising school would sound as smarmy and apple-polishing as does the schoolbookish "Cherries Are Ripe" or as hollowly boosterish as does "P.S. 52" in this chapter.

As for the giggles evoked by singing Emily Dickinson to "The Yellow Rose of Texas," we suspect that a good teacher could direct this apparent desecration into a lesson in American culture. It would be strange, after all, if one could *not* sing Dickinson's poems to a great number of popular nineteenth-century tunes, as the poems and the songs share a common tradition. Both the Amherst poet and the minstrel author of "The Yellow Rose" were soaked in the same tradition of nineteenth-century hymnody, and their creations, both the sublime and the popular, employ the standard hymn meter, itself a product of the ubiquity of tetrameter in the English language. Like the American school system, Dickinson's poems are tough enough to survive the laughter of students conforming to an old pose of academic disrespect.

Samuel Taylor Coleridge's "The Rime of the Ancient Mariner"

Our listeners advised us that the Mariner's voyage can be considerably enlivened by singing the poem to the tune of "Yankee Doodle." Try it with these verses, singing the first two to the "Yankee Doodle" stanza tune and the third to the chorus.

The fair breeze blew, the white foam flew,
The furrow followed free;
We were the first that ever burst
Into that silent sea.

Day after day, day after day,
We stuck, nor breath nor motion;
As idle as a painted ship
Upon a painted ocean.

Water, water, every where,
And all the boards did shrink;
Water, water, every where,
Nor any drop to drink.

Emily Dickinson

Listeners reported that almost any Emily Dickinson poem can be sung to "The Yellow Rose of Texas." "Because I could not stop for Death," "sung with a strong twang," states one letter, "is a hoot."

Because I could not stop for Death—
He kindly stopped for me—
The Carriage held but just Ourselves
And Immortality.

We slowly drove—He knew no haste
And I had put away
My labor and my leisure too,
For His Civility—

We passed the School, where Children strove
At Recess—in The Ring—
We passed the Fields of Gazing Grain—
We passed the Setting Sun—

Or rather—He passed Us—
The dews drew quivering and chill—
For only Gossamer, my Gown—
My Tippet—only Tulle—

We paused before a House that seemed
A Swelling of the Ground—
The Roof was scarcely visible—
The Cornice—in the Ground—

Since then—'tis Centuries—and yet
Feels shorter than the Day
I first surmised the Horses' Heads
Were toward Eternity—

In the many letters that noted ways to sing Emily Dickinson's poems, we received suggestions that "I heard a fly buzz" goes well to the tune of "America the Beautiful," "There is no frigate like a book" can be sung to "O Susannah," and one listener submitted the following list of additional tunes to which "Because I could not stop for Death" will go: "St. James Infirmary Blues," "The Marines' Hymn," "The Girl I Left Behind Me," "When Johnny Comes Marching Home," "Battle Hymn of the Republic," "Ghost Riders in the Sky," "Amazing Grace," "The Wabash Cannonball."

Henry Wadsworth Longfellow's "Excelsior!"

"This inspirational chestnut gains new life," states one listener, "when sung to the tune of Underdog's theme song."

A traveler, by the faithful hound,
Half buried in the snow was found,
Still grasping in his hand of ice
That banner with the strange device,
    Excelsior!

There in the twilight cold and gray,
Lifeless, but beautiful, he lay,
And from the sky, serene and far,
A voice fell, like a falling star,
    Excelsior!

Lewis Carroll's "Jabberwocky"

Sing this to the tune of "Greensleeves." Carroll, an amateur antiquarian, would probably have been delighted at the suggestion.

'Twas brillig, and the slithy toves
Did gyre and gimble in the wabe:
All mimsy were the borogoves,
And the mome raths outgrabe.

"Beware the Jabberwock, my son!
The jaws that bite, the claws that catch!
Beware the Jubjub bird, and shun
The frumious Bandersnatch!"

Edgar Allan Poe's "The Raven"

Some listeners recalled livening up "the jingle man's" masterpiece by singing it to the tune of "Deck the Halls." We suggest using the pattern "Once upon a midnight dreary, fa la la la la la la la la . . . ," and so forth.

Once upon a midnight dreary, while I pondered, weak and weary,
Over many a quaint and curious volume of forgotten lore—
While I nodded, nearly napping, suddenly there came a tapping,
As of some one gently rapping, rapping at my chamber door.
" 'Tis some visitor," I muttered, "tapping at my chamber door—
Only this and nothing more."

Ah, distinctly I remember it was in the bleak December;
And each separate dying ember wrought its ghost upon the floor.
Eagerly I wished the morrow:—vainly I had sought to borrow
From my books surcease of sorrow—sorrow for the lost Lenore—
For the rare and radiant maiden whom the angels name Lenore—
Nameless here for evermore.

Robert Frost's "Stopping by Woods on a Snowy Evening"

Our listeners promise that this poem takes on an entirely new dimension when sung to the tune of "Hernando's Hideaway." When you tire of that, you can go on to: "Just a Closer Walk with Thee," "The Silver Dollar Song," "When the Saints Go Marching In," "Sixteen Tons," "San Antonio Rose," "Nobody Knows You When You're Down and Out," "Johnson Rag," "Your Cheatin' Heart," "I Wish I Could Shimmy Like My Sister Kate," "Ragtime Cowboy Joe," "Casey Jones," and "The Doxology."

Whose woods these are I think I know.
His house is in the village, though;
He will not see me stopping here
To watch his woods fill up with snow.

My little horse must think it queer
To stop without a farmhouse near
Between the woods and frozen lake
The darkest evening of the year.

He gives his harness bells a shake
To ask if there is some mistake.
The only other sound's the sweep
Of easy wind and downy flake.

The woods are lovely, dark and deep,
But I have promises to keep,
And miles to go before I sleep,
And miles to go before I sleep.

Chaucer's *The Canterbury Tales*

Listeners suggested that Chaucer's archaic verse sounds more contemporary when sung to the tune of "April Showers" or "The Darktown Strutters' Ball." Both tunes require some graduate-level syllabification, however.

Whan that Aprille with his shoures soote
The droghte of March hath perced to the roote,
And bathed every veyne in swich licour
Of which vertu engendred is the flour;
Whan Zephirus eek with his sweete breeth
Inspired hath in every holt and heeth
The tendre croppes, and the yonge sonne
Hath in the Ram his halve cours yronne,
And smale foweles maken melodye,

That slepen al the nyght with open ye
(So priketh hem nature in hir corages);
Thanne longen folk to goon on pilgrimages,
And palmeres for to seken straunge strondes,
To ferne halwes, kowthe in sondry londes;
And specially from every shires ende
Of Engelond to Caunterbury they wende,
The hooly blisful martir for to seke,
That hem hath holpen whan that they were seeke.

Row, Row, Row Your Boat

Row, row, row your boat
Gently down the stream
Throw your teacher overboard
And listen to her scream.

Five days later she couldn't find her underwear
Couldn't find her underwear, didn't have a thing to wear
Ten days later she was eaten by a polar bear
And that was the end of her.

(TUNE: The first stanza is sung to "Row, Row, Row Your Boat," the second stanza to "The Old Grey Mare.")

The Great American Eagle

The great American Eagle
Flew from north to south
And as he came he carried
Miss Jessie in his mouth.

Then she started screeching
Because she was a fool
So he dropped her down in our town
And now she keeps the school.

(TUNE: "Battle Hymn of the Republic," "The Farmer in the Dell," "The Yellow Rose of Texas," or any tune that scans.)

I Shot My Poor Teacher

On top of the schoolhouse
All covered with sand
I shot my poor teacher
With a green rubber band.

I shot her with glory
I shot her with pride
I could hardly have missed her
She's forty feet wide.

I went to her funeral
I went to her grave
Some people threw flowers
I threw hand grenades.

(TUNE: "On Top of Old Smoky.")

I'm Chiquita Banana

I'm Chiquita Banana and I'm here to say
How to get rid of your teacher the easy way
Just eat a banana, throw the peel on the floor
And watch your teacher slip out the door.

(TUNE: "[I'm] Chiquita Banana," music by Len Mackenzie, Garth Montgomery, and William Wirges, 1938.)

My Hand on Myself

My hand on myself, what is dis here?
Dis is my mohawker [touch top of head]
Ya, mama, dear
Mohawker, winky dinky doo
That's what I learned in da school, yahoo!

My hand on myself, what is dis here?
Dis is my sweatboxer [touch forehead]
Ya, mama, dear
Sweatboxer, mohawker, winky dinky doo
That's what I learned in da school, yahoo!

My hand on myself, what is dis here?
Dis is my eyeblinker [touch eye]
Ya, mama, dear
Eyeblinker, sweatboxer, mohawker, winky dinky doo
That's what I learned in da school, yahoo!

My hand on myself, what is dis here?
Dis is my hornblower [touch nose]
Ya, mama, dear
Hornblower, eyeblinker, sweatboxer, mohawker, winky dinky doo
That's what I learned in da school, yahoo!

My hand on myself, what is dis here?

Dis is my boykisser [touch lips]

Ya, mama, dear

Boykisser, hornblower, eyeblinker, sweatboxer, mohawker, winky dinky doo

That's what I learned in da school, yahoo!

My hand on myself, what is dis here?

Dis is my jawbreaker [touch jaw]

Ya, mama, dear

Jawbreaker, boykisser, hornblower, eyeblinker, sweatboxer, mohawker, winky dinky doo

That's what I learned in da school, yahoo!

My hand on myself, what is dis here?

Dis is my chinchopper [touch chin]

Ya, mama, dear

Chinchopper, jawbreaker, boykisser, hornblower, eyeblinker, sweatboxer, mohawker, winky dinky doo

That's what I learned in da school, yahoo!

My hand on myself, what is dis here?

Dis is my voiceboxer [touch throat]

Ya, mama, dear

Voiceboxer, chinchopper, jawbreaker, boykisser, hornblower, eyeblinker, sweatboxer, mohawker, winky
  dinky doo

That's what I learned in da school, yahoo!

My hand on myself, what is dis here?

Dis is my ticktocker [touch chest over heart]

Ya, mama, dear

Ticktocker, voiceboxer, chinchopper, jawbreaker, boykisser, hornblower, eyeblinker, sweatboxer,
  mohawker, winky dinky doo

That's what I learned in da school, yahoo!

My hand on myself, what is dis here?

Dis is my breadbasket [touch stomach]

Ya, mama, dear

Breadbasket, ticktocker, voiceboxer, chinchopper, jawbreaker, boykisser, hornblower, eyeblinker,
  sweatboxer, mohawker, winky dinky doo

That's what I learned in da school, yahoo!

My hand on myself, what is dis here?

Dis is my kneeknocker [touch knee]

Ya, mama, dear

Kneeknocker, breadbasket, ticktocker, voiceboxer, chinchopper, jawbreaker, boykisser, hornblower,
  eyeblinker, sweatboxer, mohawker, winky dinky doo

That's what I learned in da school, yahoo!

My hand on myself, what is dis here?

Dis is my boykicker [touch foot]

Ya, mama, dear

Boykicker, kneeknocker, breadbasket, ticktocker, voiceboxer, chinchopper, jawbreaker, boykisser,
  hornblower, eyeblinker, sweatboxer, mohawker, winky dinky doo

That's what I learned in da school, yahoo!

I Love to Do My Homework

I love to do my homework, it makes me feel so good

I love to do exactly as the teacher says I should

I love to do my schoolwork, it makes me bright and gay

And I also love these men in white who are taking me away.

Key of G

I love to do my home-work, it makes me feel so good. I love to do ex-act-ly as the teach-er says I should. I love to do my school-work, it makes me bright and gay, And I al-so love these men in white who are tak-ing me a-way.

Now I Lay Me Down to Study

Now I lay me down to study
I pray, dear Lord, I won't go nutty
And if I fail to learn this junk
I pray, oh Lord, that I won't flunk
But if I do, don't pity me at all
Just lay my bones in study hall
Tell the teacher I've done my best
Then pile my books upon my chest
Now I lay me down to rest
I pray I pass tomorrow's test
If I should die before I wake
That's one less test I'll have to take.

(TUNE: "Now I Lay Me Down to Sleep," 1866.)

Study Oft on Sunday

If you study oft on Sunday
You will get no harp and wings
For you will not go to Heaven
Where they have these dandy things
But you'll go to regions balmy
On the cinder paths below
Where you'll delight in greeting
All the profs you used to know.

(TUNE: "Too-ra-loo-ra-loo-ral, That's an Irish Lullaby," 1913.)

From the Halls of School's Dark Prison

From the halls of school's dark prison
To the shores of Bubblegum Bay
We will fight our teachers' battles
With spitballs, gum, and clay.
First to fight for right to recess
Then to keep our desks a mess
We are proud to claim the title
Of "Teacher's Little Pests."

(TUNE: "The Marines' Hymn," or, "From the Halls of Montezuma to the Shores of Tripoli," 1919, based on a theme from Offenbach's *Geneviève de Brabant*, 1868.)

Deck the Halls

Deck the halls with gasoline
Fa la la la la la la la la
Light a match and watch it gleam
Fa la la la la la la la la
Watch the school burn down to ashes
Fa la la la la la la la la
Aren't you glad you played with matches?
Fa la la la la la la la la.

Cherries Are Ripe

Cherries are ripe, cherries are ripe
The robin sang one day
Cherries are ripe, cherries are ripe
It's time to start the day
Good morning, dear teacher, good morning, dear teacher
Good morning to you.

Mine Eyes Have Seen the Glory of the Burning of the School

Mine eyes have seen the glory
Of the burning of the school
We have tortured every teacher
We have broken every rule
We have marched into the office
And we killed the principal
Us kids are marching on.

Chorus: Glory, glory, hallelujah
Teacher hit me with a ruler
I met her at the door with a loaded .44
Us kids are marching on.

(TUNE: "Battle Hymn of the Republic.)

This song was submitted with more variations than any other sent to the Department of Folk Song. We include some of the variant lines below.

Lines five and six:

We have barbecued the janitor/And hung the principal
We have ransacked every office/We have shot the principal
We almost got the principal/But he got away
We have shot the secretary/And we stabbed the principal
When the principal tried to stop us/We tied him to a stool
The only principal we had/Is running like a fool
We're walking down the hall/Writing cuss words on the wall

Line seven:

The school is burning down
Our school stands there no more
Us brats are marching on
Our truth is marching on
Our troops are marching on
Oh, Stillwater, here we come!

Line ten:

I bopped her in the bean with a rotten tangerine
I shot her in the butt with a rotten coconut
I met her at the door with a baby dinosaur
I shot her from the attic with a German automatic
I hit her in the hand with a loaded rubber band
I hit her in the seater with a fifty-millimeter

Line eleven:

And that teacher won't teach no more
And I ain't seen the old goat since.

Mine Eyes Have Seen the Horror
of the Ending of the Term

Mine eyes have seen the horror
Of the ending of the term
It has poisoned all my spirits
Like an apple with a worm
It's infected all my freedom
Like an ugly cancer germ
The truth shall soon be known.

Chorus: Failure, failure, degradation,
Failure and humiliation,
Failure, failure, academia
The truth shall soon be known.

I have listened to the teachers
But the homework leaves me cold
I have never done assignments
Although many times been told
I have even missed my classes
When I was feeling bold
The truth shall soon be known.

Chorus

They are adding all my points up
And I haven't earned but few
In fact, I haven't even gotten
More than one or two
Oh, if I could only find an answer
Anything to do
The truth shall soon be known.

Chorus

On the lines of every gradebook
There is solemn news for me
The worst is yet to come when
Financial Aid ignores my plea
So I guess the only answer is
To drop my books and flee
The truth shall soon be known.

Chorus

Well, the end has finally come
And I have failed to pass a class
Though the fun and laughter, goofing off
Was really quite a gas
But I won't be in the numbers
Of the capped and gowned mass
The truth was finally shown.

Chorus

P.S. 52

Oh, 52, dear 52
We want to thank you humbly
Oh, 52, dear 52
For being very kindly

We worked so hard, we learned a lot
Oh, yes, we've toiled, but now we're smart
Oh, 52, dear 52
We want to thank you, 52.

(TUNE: "O Tannenbaum.")

School Days

School days, school days
Poker, dice, and pool days
Wrecking and necking and how-to-be-fast
Taught to the tune of a hip-pocket flask
You were my queen with dress cut low
I was your half-shot Romeo
You wrote on my slate, "You're too darn slow"
When we were a couple of kids.

(TUNE: "School Days," 1907.)

Ta Ra Ra Boom De Ay

Ta ra ra boom de ay
We have no school today
Our teacher passed away
She died of tooth decay.

We threw her in the bay
We watched her float away
The fish had lunch today
Ta ra ra boom de ay.

(TUNE: "Ta-Ra-Ra-Boom-Der-E," 1891.)

Chapter 5

Bringing in the Cows

The craft of parody is a handy shortcut to creating one's own "original" verse or song. The parodied text provides a ready-made verse form, rhyme scheme, tune, and subject upon which to elaborate. And a parody guarantees an audience response, as the shock of recognition occurs and listeners or readers make the connections between the parody and its source. Consequently, parody has been and remains a favorite form of composition with both professional and amateur authors.

Some expert parodies have surpassed and eventually displaced the originals from which they derive. Lewis Carroll's poems in the Alice books are today far better known than the obscure didactic verses Carroll parodied, and while everyone knows the folk song "She'll Be Coming 'Round the Mountain," few remember the hymn which it parodies, "The Old Ship of Zion" ("I can hear my Saviour calling as she comes . . . ."). The Carroll poems and the folk song are now simply works of art in their own right.

The parodies submitted to the Department of Folk Song should more correctly be called "burlesques," since few of them attempt to send up a serious topic or a formal poetic style, as does the true parody. Like Mark Twain's literary burlesques, the songs in this chapter take humorous liberties with popular songs and folk songs which are shopworn enough to be immediately and widely recognized. We hazard a guess that more people today sing a burlesque of "The Sheik of Araby"—adding "without no pants on" to the end of each line of the stanza and chorus—than sing the published version of the song. Only time will tell if any of our burlesques will as effectively displace their originals.

Bringing in the Cows

Bringing in the cows
Bringing in the cows
We shall come rejoicing
Bringing in the cows.

(TUNE: "Bringing in the Sheaves.")

East Side, West Side

East side, west side
All around the field
Mice and crickets are running out
From underneath the wheels
The boys are busy shocking
Shep is running along
I'm on the tractor and Dad's on the binder
All day long.

(TUNE: "The Sidewalks of New York," or "East Side, West Side," 1894.)

Onward, Christian Bedbugs

Onward, Christian bedbugs
Marching down my sheet
When you reach the bottom
Please don't bite my feet.

(TUNE: "Onward, Christian Soldiers," 1871.)

Glory, Glory, How Peculiar

Mine eyes have seen the glory of the coming of the Lord
He is wearing pink pajamas and He's riding in a Ford
He has lost the faithful drawstring of His pink pajama drawers
His pants are falling down!

Glory, glory, how peculiar
Glory, glory, how peculiar
Glory, glory, how peculiar
His pants are falling down!

Mine eyes have seen the glory of the coming of the Lord
He is coming 'round the corner in a green and yellow Ford
With one hand on the throttle and the other on a bottle
Of Old Tyme Lager Beer.

Glory, glory, hallelujah
Glory, glory, hallelujah
Glory, glory, hallelujah
It's Old Tyme Lager Beer.

The Old Chevrolet

On a hill far away stood an old Chevrolet
Its tires all tattered and torn
It just would not crank, had a leak in its tank
Someday I'll exchange for a Ford.

How I cherish the old Chevrolet
With its fenders so rusty and scored
I will cling to the old Chevrolet
And exchange it someday for a Ford.

(TUNE: "The Old Rugged Cross," 1913.)

Blest Be the Tie That Binds

Blest be the tie that binds
My collar to my shirt
For underneath its silken folds
Is half an inch of dirt.

Blest be the tie that binds
My collar to my shirt
It makes me look tidy
It covers my nightie
It also covers the dirt.

I know that my face is no star
I know I'm not lovely by far
But then I don't mind it
Because I'm behind it
It's them that's out front gets the jar.

I'd rather have eyes than a nose
I'd rather have fingers than toes
And as for my hair
I'm glad it is there
I'll be sorry when all of it goes.

Blest be the tie that binds
My collar to my shirt
And catches the gravy
From my vest
And saves it for dessert.

Nero, My Dog, Has Fleas

Nero, my dog, has fleas
Nero has fleas
Nero, my dog, has fleas
Nero has fleas

That's not a swarm of bees
Nero, my dog, has fleas
Nero, my dog, has fleas
Nero has fleas.

(TUNE: "Nearer, My God, to Thee," music based on the hymn "Bethany," 1859.)

I'm Screaming at a White Sheepdog

I'm screaming at a white sheepdog
Each time he sits upon my chair
It's a thing I'm dreading
The way he's shedding
And coats everything with hair
I'm screaming at a white sheepdog
And may he visit you some night
May his bark be worse than his blight
And may all your furniture be white.

(TUNE: "White Christmas," 1942.)

She's a Grand Old Cat

She's a grand old cat
She's a high-flying cat
And long may her proud tail wave
It's the emblem of
The cat we love
So handsome and clever and brave
Oh, the black and white
It's a horrible sight
If you happen to be a rat
May old acquaintance ne'er be forgot
Keep your eye on the grand old cat.

(TUNE: "You're a Grand Old Flag," 1906.)

The Cat That Chewed My New Shoes

Pardon me, Roy, is that the cat that chewed my new shoes?
Well, Gabby did good, just like we knew that he would
He grabbed the cat, and tied a bowline in the tail that's
Still on the kitty, now hangs from a tree.

Well, Gabby could have skinned you and as likely as not
You'd wind up with the carrots in a boiling soup pot
Or a coat of tar and feathers, but I really don't know whether
You could replace my pair of patent leathers.
Let this be a lesson to those who would feel
Hush Puppies by the davenport are something to steal
Just as in the fables, we may turn the tables
And you'll wind up the entrée for the midday meal.

Soleful, you could have been a bowl of ragout stew
So cat that chewed my new shoes, here's a lesson for you
Cat that chewed my new shoes, you're now on life number two.

(TUNE: "Chattanooga Choo Choo," 1941.)

Casey Jones the Rooster

Come all you rounders if you want to hear
The story of a brave Chanticleer
Now Casey Jones was this rooster's name
And at fighting other roosters, boys, he won his fame.

Chorus: Casey Jones ruffled up his feathers
         Casey Jones skidded when he stopped
         Casey Jones bumped the bantam's feathers
         And his carburetor flooded when his gizzard popped.

Along come a bantam called Indian Red
Cauliflower comb on the top of his head
Wings like the fenders on a Ford sedan
And he slammed old Casey to the Promised Land.

Chorus

(TUNE: "Casey Jones," 1909.)

Hang Your Head Over

Down in the valley
The valley so low
Hang your head over
And suck your big toe.

Suck your big toe, dear
Suck your big toe
Hang your head over
And suck your big toe.

(TUNE: "Down in the Valley," or "Birmingham Jail," traditional mountain song circa 1845 but not published until 1917.)

Down by the Old Garbage Slough

Down by the old (not the new but the old)
Garbage slough (not the slum but the slough)
Where I first (not the last but the first)
Smelled you (not me but you)
With your eyes (not your ears but your eyes)
So black (not brown but black)
Dressed in an old (not a new but an old)
Gunny sack (not a sock but a sack)
It was there (not here but there)
I knew (not know but knew)

That you smelled (not smiled but smelled)

Me too (not thee but me)

You were sixteen (not seventeen)

My Garbage Queen (not the King but the Queen)

Down by the old (not the new but the old)

Garbage slough (not the slum but the slough).

(TUNE: "Down by the Old Mill Stream," 1910.)

On Top of Old Smoky

On top of old Smoky

All covered with grass

I saw Davy Crockett

He fell on his . . .

Now don't get excited

Now don't get alarmed

I saw Davy Crockett

He fell on his arm!

On Top of My Headache

On top of my headache

I had a sore throat

My bones were all aching

I smelled like a goat.

My doctor prescribed

A trip on a boat

But alas and alack, dear

That boat will not float.

So now I am writing

From under the sea

The joke's on my doctor

How will he bill me?

(TUNE: "On Top of Old Smoky.")

There Are Germs

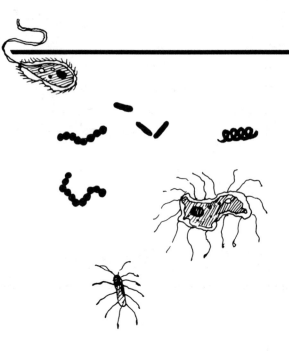

There are germs that spread diseases
There are germs most everywhere
When one coughs it brings on other sneezes
For those germs float right on through the air
So as Junior Red Cross health crusaders
All the chores to keep we all will try
And at last with our united efforts
All those bad little germs will die.

(TUNE: "Smiles," 1917.)

My Wild Irish Nose

My wild Irish nose
You'll hear it when it blows
Pugnacious and grim
It always butts in
My wild Irish nose.

My wild Irish nose
Just see how red it glows
Someday for my sake
Prohibition may take
The bloom from my wild Irish nose.

(TUNE: "My Wild Irish Rose," 1899.)

Eight Feet Tall, What a Doll

Eight feet tall
What a doll
She plays college basketball
Has anybody seen my gal?

Cauliflower ear
Guzzles beer
She could eat a half a steer
Has anybody seen my gal?

So if you run into
An eight-foot Shmoo
All covered in hair
Don't be surprised
It's not your eyes
Her mother was a grizzly bear.

She won't neck,
But what the heck,
She plays end for Georgia Tech
Has anybody seen my gal?

(TUNE: "Five Foot Two, Eyes of Blue" ["Has Anybody Seen My Girl?"], 1925.)

Don't You Call Me Sweetheart

Don't you call me sweetheart
I'm all through with you
Give me back my letter
And my kisses too
I saw you kiss another
When you said you'd be true
Don't you call me sweetheart
I'm all through with you.

(TUNE: "Let Me Call You Sweetheart," 1910.)

Let Me Call You Lizzie

Let me call you Lizzie
I'm in debt for you
Let me hear you rattle
As all good Fords do
Keep your headlights burning
And your taillights too
Let me call you Lizzie
I'm in debt for you.

(TUNE: "Let Me Call You Sweetheart.")

At the Boarding House Where I Live

At the boarding house where I live
Everything is growing old
Long grey hairs upon the butter
Everything is green with mold.

When the dog died, we had sausage
When the cat died, catnip tea
When the landlord died, I left there
Spareribs were too much for me.

(TUNE: "Silver Threads Among the Gold," 1873.)

Tinkle, Tinkle, Little Pee

Tinkle, tinkle, little pee
How I wonder where you be
In that pot so big and white
Will I flush you down tonight?
Now I have already gone
My gosh, Mommy, that was fun!

(TUNE: "Twinkle, Twinkle, Little Star," or "The Alphabet Song," music traditional from France, used as early as 1765 for "Baa, Baa, Black Sheep.")

When You Come to the End of a Lollipop

When you come to the end of a lollipop
And you sit alone with the stick
You long for the one in the candy store
And you wish for another lick
You'll never know what a lollipop
Can mean to a tired tongue
Till your lollipop is all licked and gone
And you long for another one.

(TUNE: "A Perfect Day," 1910.)

God Save the King

King George, he had a date
He stayed out very late
He was the King
Queen Mary paced the floor
King George came home at four
She met him at the door
God save the King.

(TUNE: "God Save the King," about 1619.)

We Three Kings

1.

We three kings of Orient are
Puffing on a big cigar
It was loaded, it exploded
Covering us all with tar.

2.

We three kings of Orient are
Trying to smoke a rubber cigar
It was loaded and exploded
Blowing us all afar.

(TUNE: "We Three Kings of Orient [Are]," 1857.)

Good King Wences

Good King Wences was a louse
At the feast of Stephen
Pulled his trusty pistol out
Said, "I will get even."

(TUNE: "Good King Wenceslas," music based on a Swedish melody known as early as the 1580s.)

Chapter 6

Greasy Grimy Gopher Guts

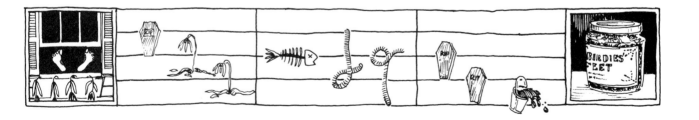

In their collective anonymity, folk song makers enjoy certain freedoms unknown to formal artists who create for the public or within the boundaries set by a market or by the mass media. Free from the need to please a broad audience, the folk song maker can follow the bidding of his psyche, quirkily creating verse that may delight only himself and his intimates. Free from the restraints of propriety, he can confront and do battle with his anxieties about his own forbidden thoughts. Free from the censorship of the market or the media, he can subvert society's verities and sacred cows without fear.

For these reasons, the most ubiquitous form of folklore is sexual: who does not know at least one off-color joke or bawdy song learned from a coworker, friend, or family member? Yet, such material has rarely found its way into folk song collections. Songmakers perhaps have offered such material to collectors only hesitantly—someone's writing down or recording the verse or song, after all, blows the artist's cover of anonymity, leaves him exposed and answerable for his creation. Then, too, those who collect or record folklore are—correctly— perceived as minions of the "official" culture, carriers of the assumptions of propriety and cultural correctness that the folk song often subverts. "Let's spare ourselves a confrontation," thinks the songmaker, "and silently pass this stuff over."

The listeners of "A Prairie Home Companion" were similarly circumspect in their submissions of songs to the Department. Knowing that their songs would be read and heard by public radio staff and evaluated for broadcast on a Family Show, they quite understandably withheld sexual material almost completely—one exception being the childishly homosexual "Whistle While You Work" variants, another being a chaste fragment of the obscene "Little Ball of Yarn" cleverly grafted onto fragments of "The Bedbugs' Baseball Game" and "The Logan County Jail" to create a laundered but still fine "new" song, "At the Jail," which discreetly omits the reason for the speaker's arrest.

Outside of sexual material, however, our listeners responded with plenty of pointedly tasteless songs. They absolutely pounced on one of our society's most circumspect and forbidden topics: death. Even though most Americans have never seen a dead body that has not been prepared for display by a mortician, we remain queasy about death, and fear it abstractly in the many forms in which it haunts us—death by atomic annihilation, death by cancer or AIDS, death by random violence on the highway or in an airliner. We then futilely try to allay our fears by distancing ourselves from death through genteel euphemism—corpses become "loved ones," their death "passing away," their burials "interment services."

The folk songs in this chapter, on the other hand, confront death directly and with an even gaze, demystifying and even ridiculing it along with the inexorable physical decay of our bodies. Indeed, some of these songs hold our death fears up and shake them like a terrier shakes a rat. Songs such as "Did You Ever Think" are brave and irreverent works of folk art in that they evoke our worst fears of death and decay in precise words and images, only to blunt the sharp edges of those fears with laughter—at least for long enough to allow us to live with our fears, as we must. In their mocking, shivering brassiness, these songs are bleak survivors of an older, more reverent American tradition of mortification of the flesh, now lost, best glimpsed in the old hymn "Oh, Lovely Appearance of Death":

> Oh, lovely appearance of death
> What sight upon earth is so fair?
> Not all the gay pageants that breathe
> Can with a dead body compare.
> In solemn delight I survey
> A corpse when the spirit is fled,
> In love with the beautiful clay,
> And longing to lie in its stead.

To which the modern folk song maker would add, "And me without a spoon!"

Bring Back My Neighbors to Me

Last night as I lay on my pillow
Last night as I lay on my bed
I stuck my feet out of the window
In the morning my neighbors were dead.

Bring back, bring back
Bring back my neighbors to me, to me
Bring back, bring back
Bring back my neighbors to me.

(TUNE: "My Bonnie Lies Over the Ocean.")

The Bathtub Song

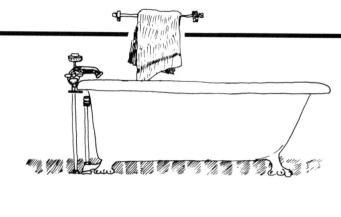

Michael, where are you going?

Upstairs to take a bath

Michael with legs like toothpicks

And a neck like a giraffe

Michael, into the bathtub,

Pulled out the plug and then

[Spoken] Oh, my goodness, oh, my soul, there goes Michael down the hole!

Michael, where are you going?

Upstairs to take a bath

Michael with legs like toothpicks

And a neck like a giraffe.

Key of C

Mi - chael, ___ where are you go - ing? ___ Up - stairs ___ to take a

bath. ___ Mi - chael ___ with legs like tooth - picks ___ And a neck like a gi -

raffe. ___ Mi - chael, ___ in - to the bath - tub, ___

Pulled out ___ the plug and then ___

[Spoken] Oh, my goodness, oh my soul,
there goes Michael down the hole!

Mi - chael ___ where are you go - ing? ___ Up - stairs ___ to take a bath. ___

Mi - chael ___ with legs like tooth - picks ___ And a neck like a gi - raffe.

A Year Ago Our Baby Died

A year ago our baby died
She died committing suicide
Of spinal meningitis
I know she died to spite us
She was a nasty old baby anyhow.

A year a-go our ba-by died.___ She died com-mit-ting
su-i-cide.___ Of spi-nal men-in-gi-tis.___ I know she
died to spite us.___ She was a nas-ty old ba-by an-y-how.___

Come Up, Dear Dinner, Come Up

My stomach is in a commotion
I'm forced to lean over the rail
I don't want to dirty the ocean
Will someone please bring me a pail?

Come up, come up
Come up, dear dinner, come up, come up
Come up, come up
Come up, dear dinner, come up!

(TUNE: "My Bonnie Lies Over the Ocean.")

I'm a-comin', I'm a-comin'
But the burps are very slow
I hear the gentle voices calling
[Spoken] Hasten, Jason, bring the basin!
          Stop! Wait! It's too late
          Urp! Slop! Bring the mop!
A sponge will do.

(TUNE: "Old Black Joe," 1860.)

McTavish Is Dead

Oh, McTavish is dead and his brother don't know it

His brother is dead and McTavish don't know it

They're both of them dead and they're lying in bed

And neither one knows that the other is dead.

(TUNE: "The Irish Washerwoman," or "The Scotch Bagpipe Melody," traditional folk dance dated at least to 1792.)

Now We Are Marching

Now we are marching

Up to the gallows

Step by step

We now approach our doom

Now dawn is breaking

Gallows are waiting

Step, step

The gallows overhead. Eek!

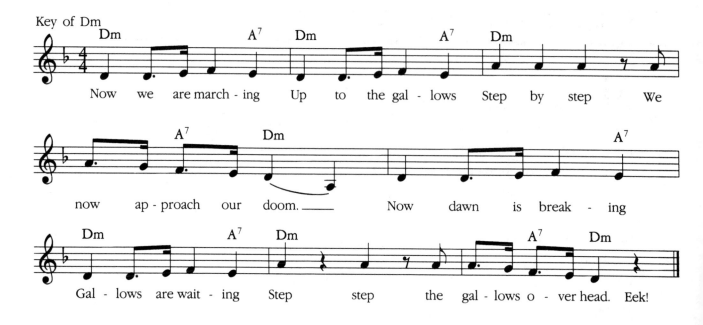

Key of Dm

Now we are march - ing Up to the gal - lows Step by step We

now ap - proach our doom. _____ Now dawn is break - ing

Gal - lows are wait - ing Step step the gal - lows o - ver head. Eek!

Casey's Coffins

Casey's coffins are so fine
Made with sandalwood and pine.

If your loved ones pass away
Let them pass the Casey way.

If your loved ones have to go
Call Columbus six-nine-oh.

Casey's customers all sing,
Death, O Death, where is thy sting!

Key of B♭

Ca - sey's cof - fins are so fine, Made with san - dal - wood and pine.

If your loved ones pass a - way, Let them pass the Cas - ey way.

If your loved ones have to go, Call Co - lum - bus six - nine - oh.

Cas - ey's cus - tom - ers all sing, Death, O Death, where is thy sting!

Whistle While You Work

1.

Whistle while you work
Hitler is a jerk
Mussolini bit his weenie
Now it doesn't squirt.

2.

Whistle while you work
Hitler was a jerk
Mussolini pulled his weenie
Just to see it squirt.

Did You Ever Think

Did you ever think
When a hearse goes by
That you may be
The next to die?

They take you out
To the family plot
And there you wither
Decay and rot.

They wrap you up
In a big white sheet
And sink you down
About six feet.

And all goes well
For about a week
And then the coffin
Begins to leak.

The worms crawl in
The worms crawl out
The ants play pinochle
On your snout!

They call their friends
And their friends' friends too
They'll make the devil of
A mess of you!

Your body turns
A slimy green
The pus runs out
Like whipping cream.
[Spoken] Darn, me without a spoon!

Your hair turns white
Your skin turns green
You start to look
Like Bishop Sheen.

Your eyes fall in
Your teeth fall out
Your liver turns
To sauerkraut.

So never laugh
When a hearse goes by
For you may be
The next to die.

(TUNE: "Did You Ever Think As the Hearse Rolls By," or, "The Worms Crawl In, the Worms Crawl Out," words and music attributed to British soldiers in the Crimean War, 1854–1856.)

National Embalming School

We live for you, we die for you
National Embalming School
We do our best to give you rest
National Embalming School
We make a coffin out of tin
Then dig a hole to put you in
We live for you, we die for you
National Embalming School!

To thee we sing, to thee we drool
National Embalming School
We stuff the corpse, we stuff the ghoul
National Embalming School
When you feel hollow deep inside
We fill you with formaldehyde
Our boys get hot when you get cool
National Embalming School!

(TUNE: "O Tannenbaum.")

Post mortem, post mortem, post mortem
Autopsy we must have
Post mortem, post mortem, post mortem
Autopsy we must have!

(TUNE: "A-Hunting We Will Go.")

Cut, slice, slash the body
We must have a reason
Gee, how this body stinks
It must be out of season.

(TUNE: "The Anvil Chorus.")

We live for you, we die for you
National Embalming School.

(TUNE: last two lines of "O Tannenbaum.")

Suffocation

Chorus: Suffocation, takes coordination
        Suffocation, what a way to go!

First you take a garden hose
Then you stick it up your nose
Turn it on, then you're gone,
Oh, oh, oh, oh!

Chorus

First you take a pillowcase
Then you stick it on your face
Tie it tight, say good night,
Oh, oh, oh, oh!

Chorus

(TUNE: "Alouette," earliest words and music published in Montreal in 1879, but probably date earlier to a traditional French-Canadian folk song.)

On Top of Old Smoky

On top of Old Smoky
All covered with blood
I met my true lover
Her face in the mud.

So I turned her over
And looked in her eyes
And they were all bloodshot
And covered with flies.

A knife in her stomach
An axe in her head
I got the impression
My lover was dead.

The Watermelon Song

Just plant a little watermelon on my grave
And let the juice seep through
Just plant a little watermelon on my grave
That's all I ask of you.
Now Southern-fried chicken sounds mighty fine
But all I ask is a watermelon vine
Just plant a little watermelon on my grave
And let the juice (slurp, slurp) seep through.

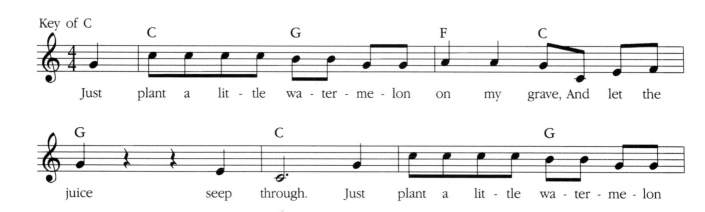

on my grave, That's all I ask of you. Now South-ern-fried chick-en sounds

might-y fine, But all I ask is a wa-ter-me-lon vine. Just

plant a lit-tle wa-ter-me-lon on my grave, And let the juice (slurp, slurp) seep through.

The Garbageman's Daughter

I'm in love with the garbageman's daughter
Who lives down by the swill
How sweet is the smell of the garbage
But her breath is sweeter still
Slop slop, slop slop!

Each night as we wade through the garbage
Her slimy hand in mine
Her greasy head on my raggedy chest
Oh, this is true love divine,
Slop slop, slop slop!

I'm in love with the gar - bage - man's daugh - ter,____ Who

lives down by the swill. How sweet is the smell of the

gar - bage,__ But her breath_ is sweet - er still. Slop slop, slop slop!

Don't Swat Your Mother, Boys

Homeward to their mother two working men did come
Weary with their honest toil and lighted up with rum
Supper was not ready, one aimed a brutal blow
When the blue-eyed baby stopped them, saying, "Brothers, don't do so!"

Chorus: Don't swat your mother, boys, just 'cause she's old
Don't mop up the floor with her dear face
Think how her love is a treasure of gold
Shining through shame and disgrace.
Don't place the rocking chair next to her eye
Don't bounce the lamp off her old bean
Angels are watching you up in the sky
Don't swat your mother, it's mean.

[Spoken] Anger was abated, the strong men bowed in tears
They were kinder to their parent
Through her few remaining years.

Chorus:

Don't swat your mo-ther, boys, just 'cause she's old, Don't mop up the floor with her dear face. Think how her love is a trea-sure of gold, _____ Shin-ing through shame and dis-grace. _____ Don't place the rock-ing chair next to her eye, Don't bounce the lamp off her old bean. _____ An - gels are watch-ing you up in the sky, Don't swat your mo-ther, it's mean. _____

[Spoken] Anger was abated, the strong men bowed in tears, They were kinder to their parent

Through her few re - main-ing years.

At the Jail

1.

I was standin' on the corner
A-doin' no harm
When along came a policeman
And took me by the arm.

He took me to a box
And rang a little bell
Then along came a patrol wagon
And took me to a cell.

I woke up Sunday morning
And looked upon the wall
The chinches and the bedbugs
Were havin' a game of ball.

The score was ten to nothing
The chinches were ahead
The bedbugs hit a home run
And knocked me out of bed.

2.

As I was walking down the street
Not doing any harm
Along comes a policeman
And grabs me by the arm.

He takes me to a little box
And rings a little bell
Along comes the wagon
And takes me to my cell.

Six o'clock next morning
I look up on the wall
The cooties and the bedbugs
Are having a game of ball.

The score is six to nothing
The bedbugs are ahead
The cooties hit a homerun
And knock me out of bed.

Seven o'clock next morning
The warden comes around
He feeds me bread and coffee
That nearly knocks me down.

The coffee tastes like turpentine
The bread is always stale
And that's the way they treat you
At the Milwaukee County Jail.

My Body Has Tuberculosis

1.

My body has tuberculosis
My body has only one lung
I spit up these big bloody hackers
I dry them and chew them for gum.

Bring back, bring back, bring back my body to me, to me
Bring back, bring back, bring back my body to me.

2.

My Bonnie has tuberculosis
My Bonnie has only one lung
She spits up that old green corruption
And rolls it around on her tongue.

Save it, save it, save it to flavor the stew, the stew
Save it, save it, save it to flavor the stew!

3.

My mother has tuberculosis
My father has only one lung
So they spat all their blood in a bucket
And froze it and sold it for gum.

Dentyne, Dentyne, froze it and sold it for gum, for gum
Dentyne, Dentyne, froze it and sold it for gum.

(TUNE: "My Bonnie Lies Over the Ocean.")

I'm a Villain

I'm a villain, a dirty little villain

I put poison in my mother's cream of wheat

My chief delight is to pick a fight

And I beat little kids on the head 'til they're dead.

'Cause I'm a villain, a dirty little villain

I leave a trail of blood where'er I go

I put a stain on the family name

And I eat—raw—meat! Pass the toothpicks!

I'm a villain, a dirty little villain

I leave a trail of woe where'er I go

I take delight in stirring up a fright

And hitting little babies on the head 'til they're dead.

I have gotten a rep for being rotten

I put poison in my mother's shredded wheat

I put the blot on the family escutcheon

I eat—raw—meat!

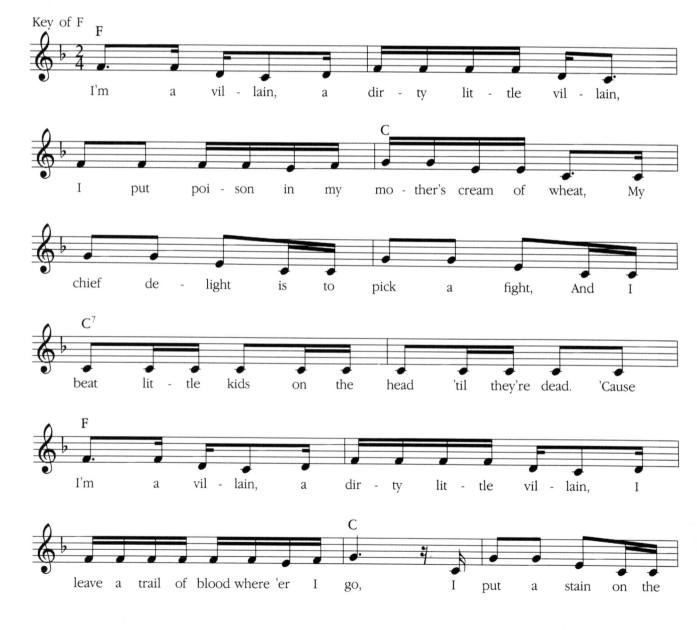

fam - ily name, And I eat raw meat! Pass the tooth - picks!

Greasy Grimy Gopher Guts

Great big gobs of
Greasy grimy gopher guts
Jubilated monkeys' meat
Concentrated birdies' feet
A great big jar of
All-purpose porpoise pus
And me without a spoon!
(I love it so.)

(TUNE: "The Old Grey Mare," with a "Good evening, friends" ending.)

Zekey Looked into the Gas Tank

Oh, Zekey looked into the gas tank
The contents of which for to see
He lit a match to assist him
Oh, bring back my Zekey to me.

Chorus: Bring back, bring back
          Bring back my Zekey to me, to me
          Bring back, bring back
          Bring back my Zekey to me.

Now Zekey had long curly tresses
And sideburns that went to his chin
And eyebrows that met in the middle
But now they are nothing but skin.

Chorus

His nose was a prominent Roman
His eyes and his teeth all in place
But the force of the gas tank's explosion
Pushed 'em all to the back of his face.

(TUNE: "My Bonnie Lies Over the Ocean.")

Little Willie I

Little Willie, full of gore
Nailed his little sister to the door
Said Willie's mother, with humor quaint,
"Careful there, Willie, or you'll spoil the paint."

Little Willie, dressed in sashes
Fell in the fireplace and burned to ashes
By and by the room grew chilly
But nobody bothered to stir up Willie.

Little Willie fell down the elevator
There they found him six months later
Willie's mother said, "Gee whiz,
What a spoiled child little Willie is."

Lit - tle Wil - lie, full of gore, Nailed his lit - tle sis - ter to the door. Said
Wil - lie's mo-ther, with hu - mor quaint, "Care-ful there, Wil-lie, or you'll spoil the paint."

Little Willie II

How well do I remember
The night that Willie died
'Twas early in the morning, just 12 o'clock at night
The cows were warbling sweetly
The bees were making hay
The sun and moon were shining dark and bright.

134

'Twas the 43rd of May
When our Willie passed away
He died harder than he'd ever died before
He was sitting in a chair
But he didn't like it there
So he got up and he died upon the floor.

You could see that he was dying
By the color of his breath
You could see the blossom nipping in the bud
And the doctor said the only thing
To save our boy from death
Was to stop the circulation of his blood.

So we filled him up with glue
In the hope 'twould bring him to
But it only brought him 8 or 9 or 10
Then he turned upon his side
Gently blew his nose and died
Then he turned and blew his nose and died again.

Now it sort of makes me sore
That our Willie is no more
'Cause of all the times he died that was the best
And it really was a shame
When that night a burglar came
And he stole the mustard plaster off his chest.

Now no more upon the mat
Will he play with pussycat
No more between his teeth will hold her tail
No more will burn his nose
On the little red-hot stove
For our darling Willie's gone and kicked the pail.

(TUNE: "Jesse James.")

I'm Looking Over My Dead Dog Rover

1.

I'm looking over my dead dog Rover
Lying on the bathroom floor
One leg is busted, another is sprained
The third got run over by my CocoPuff train
No use explaining the parts remaining
You've seen them all before
That's why I'm looking over my dead dog Rover
Lying on the bathroom floor.

2.

I'm looking over my dead dog Rover
That I overran with the mower
One leg is mangled, another is gone
The third leg is scattered all over the lawn
No use explaining the one remaining
It's stuck to the kitchen door
I'm looking over my dead dog Rover
That I overran with the mower.

(TUNE: "I'm Looking Over a Four-Leaf Clover," 1927.)

Granny's in the Cellar

Granny's in the cellar
Lordy, can't you smell her
Cooking greasy biscuits on the stove
In her eye there is some matter
That keeps dripping in the batter
And she whistles as the [sniff] runs down her nose

Down her nose, down her nose
She whistles as the [sniff] runs down her nose
In her eye there is some matter
That keeps dripping in the batter
And she whistles as the [sniff] runs down her nose.

Granpa's in the basement
And to his amazement
There is something in the wine he made last fall
And his eyes are getting redder
As his tongue is getting wetter
'Cause it's ninety-seven percent alcohol
Alcohol, alcohol
It's ninety-seven percent alcohol
His eyes are getting redder
As his tongue is getting wetter
'Cause it's ninety-seven percent alcohol.

Granny's in the laundry
And she's in a quandary
'Cause she put some starch in with her underwear
And it's gonna be disaster
When it dries as hard as plaster
But she's tough as nails and so she doesn't care
Underwear, underwear
She put some starch in with her underwear
And it's gonna be disaster when it dries as hard as plaster
But she's tough as nails so she don't care.

(TUNE: "Y'All Come.")

(One listener who submitted this advised, "Where it says [sniff] *just wind 'er up and give it a real good snort. Just don't be too long about it, and don't be too disgusting, and above all, try not to get any on you.")*

Guess I'll Eat Some Worms

Nobody loves me, everybody hates me
Guess I'll eat some worms
Long slim slimy ones, short fat juicy ones
Itsy bitsy fuzzy wuzzy worms.

First you cut the heads off, then you suck the guts out
Oh, how they wiggle and squirm
Long slim slimy ones, short fat juicy ones
Itsy bitsy fuzzy wuzzy worms.

Wiggle goes the first one, goosh goes the second one
Sure don't wanna eat these worms
Long slim slimy ones, short fat juicy ones
Itsy bitsy fuzzy wuzzy worms.

Down goes the first one, down goes the second one
Sure hate the taste of worms
Long slim slimy ones, short fat juicy ones
Itsy bitsy fuzzy wuzzy worms.

Nobody hates me, everybody likes me
Never shoulda eaten those worms
Long slim slimy ones, short fat juicy ones
Itsy bitsy fuzzy wuzzy worms.

Up comes the first one, up comes the second one
Oh, how they wiggle and squirm
Long slim slimy ones, short fat juicy ones
Itsy bitsy fuzzy wuzzy worms.

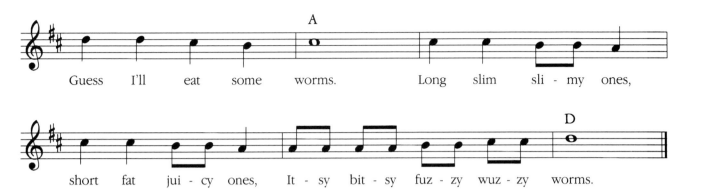

Guess I'll eat some worms. Long slim sli - my ones,

short fat jui - cy ones, It - sy bit - sy fuz - zy wuz - zy worms.

That Sausage Meat Machine

Once there was a butcher, his name was Johnny Rybeck
He made the finest sausages and sauerkraut in Speck
He made the finest sausages that ever have been seen
But one day he invented that sausage meat machine.

Chorus: Oh, Mr. Johnny Rybeck, how could you be so mean
I told you you'd be sorry for inventing that machine
Now all the neighbors' cats and dogs are nowhere to be seen
They've all been ground to sausage meat in Johnny Rybeck's machine.

One day two very little boys came walking in the store
They bought a pound of sausages, it added up to four
And while they were a-waiting, they whistled a little tune
And the sausages jumped up and down and danced around the room.

One night the darn thing busted, it wouldn't seem to go
So Johnny Rybeck climbed inside to see what made it so
His wife she had a nightmare and came walking in her sleep
And she gave the crank a helluva yank and Johnny Rybeck was meat.

Chorus

Key of G

Oh once there was a butch - er, his name was John - ny Ry - beck, ____ He made the fin - est sau - sa - ges and sau - er - kraut in Speck. ____ He made the fin - est sau - sa - ges that ev - er have been seen, ____ But one day he in - ven - ted that sau - sage meat ma - chine. ____

Chapter 7

New Songs from Old

When the folklorist John Cohen traveled to eastern Kentucky in 1959 to collect folk songs, he met the extraordinary singer Roscoe Holcomb of Daisy, Kentucky, who was to gain international recognition as an American folk musician. At their first meeting, Holcomb sang several familiar songs for Cohen and then offered a song he said he had composed, called "Across the Rocky Mountain." After hearing it, Cohen pointed out that this allegedly original song contained lines, phrases, and even entire stanzas from other traditional songs, such as "The Girl I Left Behind" and "Jackaro." Holcomb patiently replied, "Well, that's how you write a song—you take verses from other songs and put them together to make a good story."

Holcomb spoke as a true folk composer who valued not original creation but rather the creative synthesis of existing song elements—familiar tunes, common images, proven language—into "new" songs which emerge already "broken in," as recognizably belonging in the singer's culture. The notion of plagiarism has no meaning in folk tradition.

Like Holcomb's composition, the songs in this chapter have been "composed" from other songs and may be on their way to becoming wholly different works, should they circulate long enough and among sufficient numbers of singers who will subject them to their own creativity. Most of the songs appear to be recently composed, and most have "borrowed" familiar tunes to which new lyrics have been added. Often, the lyrics will retain phrasing and rhyme schemes from the original song, but a listener does not need to know the original song in order fully to enjoy the new song, as is usually the case with the parody or burlesque.

The first song in the chapter, "Poor Nellie," combines the melody of "After the Ball" with a concise recasting of the ancient (and sexist) joke of the woman removing all her artificial parts. Longer versions of this story are known in formal literature, most notably in Mark Twain's ghastly description of Old Miss Wagner in *Roughing It*, and in folklore (with a voyeuristic twist) in the ballad "The Old Maid and the Burglar."

Many of this chapter's "songs in process" will of course die the merciful death of neglect and be forgotten. Perhaps a few will someday become as powerful and elegant as Roscoe Holcomb's "Across the Rocky Mountain." Like all folk songs, they are vagabonds, forever hailing from just over the horizon and bound for parts unknown, and we make their acquaintance only on the fly.

Poor Nellie

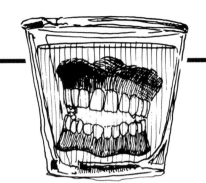

After the ball is over
Nellie takes out her glass eye
Puts her false teeth in a tumbler
Takes down her bottle of rye
Stands her wooden leg in the corner
Hangs up her hair on the wall
And the rest of poor Nellie goes bye-bye
After the ball.

(TUNE: "After the Ball," 1892.)

There Was an Old Geezer

Oh, there was an old geezer and he had a wooden leg
And they wouldn't let him ride and they wouldn't let him beg
So he got a couple spools and an old tin can
He made a little Ford and the darn thing ran.

Oh, there was an old geezer and he had a wooden leg
He had no tobacco, no tobacco could he beg
Then he met another geezer who was sly as a fox
Who always had tobacco in his old tobacco box.

Said the first old geezer, "Will you give me a chew?"
Said the second old geezer, "I'll be danged if I do.
Just save up your pennies and you'll have a lot of rocks
And you'll always have tobacco in your old tobacco box."

(TUNE: "Turkey in the Straw.")

On Top of Old Baldy

On top of Old Baldy, there's nary a hair
But only the mem'ry of hair that was there.

On top of Old Baldy so barren and neat
There's no trace of dandruff 'cause what could they eat?

A bald head's appealing when wearing a hat
But when he removes it that takes care of that.

Hair parts in the middle, hair parts on the side
But parting's a sorrow when your part gets too wide.

But nature will rob you and take all your hair
But there's false-haired lovers, so why should you care?

So come all young females and hear what I say
Make sure that his gold locks ain't really a toupee.

(TUNE: "On Top of Old Smoky.")

Mrs. Brown

I went up to see Mrs. Brown
She didn't have on any gown
I told her to slip on just any old thing
So she slipped on the stairs and came down.

(TUNE: "Blest Be the Tie That Binds," to the hymn tune "Dennis" by Hans Georg Nageli, 1845.)

Old Farmer Brown

Old Farmer Brown had an awful scare
Chased ten miles by a grizzly bear
People thought he was out of his mind
Running ten miles with a bear behind.

(TUNE: "Turkey in the Straw.")

Pile of Debris

'Twas in a pile of debris that I found her
Beneath the glow of a red neon sign
And you could smell liquor ten feet around her
When we met in that pile of debris.

Oh, I was tight, but I knew she was tighter
And we were both just as soused as could be
So I sat right down there and then to join her
Palsy-walsy on that pile of debris.

I could hear the lady mutter as she softly shed a tear,
"This is my own private gutter, what the (hic) are you doing here?"

And when the cops came around in the morning
We were still just as drunk as we could be
So they sat right down there to join us
Palsy-walsy on that pile of debris.

(TUNE: "Isle of Capri," 1934.)

That Stepladder in the Snow

You laughed when I cried
As I watched the windows slide
From the stepladder in the snow.

You were dry, I was wet
Was I mad? Oh, you bet
On that stepladder in the snow.

(TUNE: "Love Letters in the Sand," 1931.)

So I Climbed Up the Old Apple Tree

So I climbed up the old apple tree
And right out on the limb, don't you see
She stood down below with her apron held so
To catch all those apples, two, three
Just then the limb broke, holy gee
And I fell from the old apple tree
I broke seven bones and half killed Maggie Jones
In the shade of the old apple tree.

(TUNE: "In the Shade of the Old Apple Tree," 1905.)

Let Me Call You Sweetheart

Let me call you sweetheart
I'm in love with your automobile
Let me hear you whisper
That you'll pay the gasoline bill

Keep those headlights burning
And your hands upon the wheel
Let me call you sweetheart
I'm in love with your automobile.

(TUNE: "Let Me Call You Sweetheart.")

You Drove Your Buick

Oh, say, Bill, do you remember
That girl named Sally Brown
We used to chase around
She wore a gingham gown
I took her to a picnic
In my little Ford one day
And you were there and stole my girl away
You drove a great big touring car
She climbed right in with you
I'll tell you, going home that night,
Gee whiz, but I felt blue!

When you drove your Buick,
Your big yellow Buick
And I drove my little tin Ford
You both tried to guy me
As you two passed by me
But your insults I ignored
A mud hole you struck, Bill
And that's where you stuck, Bill
Your engine just puffed and roared
I had to pull out your Buick,
Your big yellow Buick
Behind my little tin Ford.

(TUNE: "When You Wore a Tulip and
I Wore a Big Red Rose," 1914.)

Two Auto Songs

1.

On a hill, far away
Stood a beat-up Chevrolet
And the fenders were touching the ground.

I opened the door
And I fell right through the floor
As the roof came a-tumbling down.

I pulled on the choke and the steering wheel broke
All I could see was smoke, smoke, smoke,

Then down came the Lord
And He gave me a Ford
And He took that old Chevy away.

(TUNE: "The Old Rugged Cross.")

2.

Over hill, over dale
As we hit the rusty nail
And those Goodyears keep rolling along.

Down the road, down the street
Through the rain and blinding sleet
And those Goodyears keep rolling along.

And it's hi-hi-hee in that auto factory
Mount up those whitewalls wide and strong,

And where'er you go
You will always know
That those Goodyears keep rolling along.

(TUNE: "The Caissons Go Rolling Along," 1918.)

After Glow Worm

1.

Down by the seashore, dimmer, dimmer
I see a figure, slimmer, slimmer
She wears false teeth and her hair's peroxided
Standing in the moonlight she looks lopsided.

Ruffles on her petticoats blowing in the breezes
Sounds like sandpaper rubbing on her kneeses
These are the things a woman can do
To lead the men astray.

2.

Down by the seashore, splatter, splatter
There sits [person's name] fatter, fatter
Teeth knocked out and hair peroxided
Tell by the moonlight she's lopsided.

Ruffles on her underpants blown by breezes
Oh, she's got those hairy kneeses
Now we know why the boys won't go
Down to the shore no more.

3.

Grow little boobies, bigger, bigger
I want a better figure, figure
All my clothes need something added
All my sweaters are slightly padded.

Grow little boobies, bigger, bigger
I want a better figure, figure
I want to look like Brigitte Bardot
So grow, little boobies, grow, grow, grow!

4.

We are the girls from Concordia College
We came here to get some knowledge
We don't smoke in public places
We don't even paint our faces.

We are truly Christian lasses
We don't cut our Doctrine classes
That is why our beauty fades
And we become old maids.

5.

We are the Smurthwaite Kewpie dollies
We don't cuss, we just say, "Golly!"
We don't smoke and we don't chew
And we don't go with the boys that do
Now you may think that we don't have fun
We don't!

(TUNE: "The Glow-Worm," first published as "Glühwürmchen," 1902.)

Put On Your New Blue Bonnet

Put on your new blue bonnet
With the U.S. Navy on it
And your brand new coat of Navy blue
We are starting on our route
To become a Navy boot
Cedar Falls, how do you do.

(TUNE: "Put On Your Old Gray Bonnet," 1909.)

We've Enlisted in the Navy

We've enlisted in the Navy
We wear the blue and gold
We've enlisted in the Navy
To preserve our peace of old
We're ambitious, we are willing
To show what we can do
We've enlisted in the service
Of the Red, White, and Blue.

Side by side we stand together
With the men who give their lives
On to victory we will push them
Don't let teardrops dim your eyes
So with courage still undaunted
We give our all in all
Onward, nothing's ever daunted
'Til the Axis does fall.

(TUNE: "I've Been Working on the Railroad," traditional American folk song.)

Parties, Banquets, and Balls

Parties, banquets, and balls
Banquets, parties, and balls
As President Truman has said before
The only way to stay out of war
Is to have lots of parties and banquets
Banquets, parties, and balls
Oh, it's parties and banquets
And banquets and parties
And balls, balls, balls!

(TUNE: "Take Me Out to the Ball Game," 1908.)

The Danube's Not Blue

The Danube's not blue   (not blue, not blue)
It's muddy as glue   (as glue, as glue)
For if you look down   (yes, just look down)
You'll see that it's brown   (yes, awfully brown)
But old Johann Strauss   (yes, Johann Strauss)
He was such a louse   (a rotten louse)
He said   (yes, he said)
What's not true   (what's not true)
That the Danube it is blue.

(TUNE: "On the Beautiful Blue Danube," 1867.)

Joe's Got a Head Like a Ping-Pong Ball

1.

Joe's got a head like a Ping-Pong ball
Joe's got a head like a Ping-Pong ball
Joe's got a head like a Ping-Pong ball, Ping-Pong Ping-Pong ball
Joe's got a head like a Ping-Pong, Ping-Pong, Ping-Pong, Ping-Pong Ping-Pong ball,
Joe's got a head like a Ping-Pong, Ping-Pong, Ping-Pong, Ping-Pong Ping-Pong ball . . . .

2.

William Tell, William Tell, see they've got your son
William Tell, William Tell, he's the only one
William Tell, William Tell, apple on his head
If you miss, he'll be dead.

William Tell, William Tell, now you take your shot
William Tell, William Tell, oh it's dead he's not
William Tell, William Tell, this is Gessler's doin'
And Rossini wrote the tune.

(TUNE: "William Tell Overture," 1829.)

The Pumpkin on the Vine

The pumpkin on the vine
The pumpkin on the vine
I picked the one that weighed a ton
And that's the one that's mine.

I made two funny eyes
A mouth that's oversize
The other gook my mother took
For baking pumpkin pies.

The pumpkin on the vine
The pumpkin on the vine
He's now a jack-o'-lantern
And you ought to see him shine.

That jack-o'-lantern—of mine!

(TUNE: "The Farmer in the Dell," traditional music based on the German children's game "Der Kirmessbauer," with a "shave and a haircut, six bits" end line.)

The Bugs Marched Down the Aisle

The mosquitoes wore tuxedos and the blackflies wore black ties
The bride she was a spider and the groom he was a snake
They were going to a wedding in my Aunt Lucy's bedding
And she was the wedding cake.

Chorus: Glory, glory, hallelujah
        You don't feel itchy, Aunty, do ya?
        Glory, glory, hallelujah
        The bugs marched down the aisle.

The little honeymooners were nice and cozy in her bloomers
And the guests all took their places in Aunt Lucy's pillowcases
The little beasts had such a feast, they danced and flew and soared
All while Aunt Lucy snored.

Chorus

(TUNE: "Battle Hymn of the Republic")

Bugs Go Wild, Simply Wild, Over Me

Bugs go wild, simply wild, over me
I'm referring to bedbugs and the fleas
Every morning, noon, and night all the bugs how they do bite
Bugs go wild, simply wild, over me.

In the morning on my pillowcase
A daddy-long-legs stares me in the face
In my underpants and shoes they assemble for a snooze
Bugs go wild, simply wild, over me.

When I sit down to rest on a hike
There are ants running left, running right
There are spiders in my hair and mosquitoes everywhere
Bugs go wild, simply wild, over me.

(TUNE: "They Go Wild, Simply Wild Over Me," 1917.)

Dakotaland

Dakotaland, Dakotaland
Upon thy frozen ground I stand
I look across the burning plains
And pray the Lord will send the rains
Our horses are the finest race
They stare starvation in the face
Our chickens are too poor to eat
They scratched the toes right off their feet.

We have no wheat, we have no oats
We have nothing at all to feed our shoats
But with a smile upon our lips
We gather in the buffalo chips
But in this land we're going to stay
We're too damn poor to move away
Dakotaland so fertile and rich
We think you are a—honey.

(TUNE: "O Tannenbaum," or "Maryland, My Maryland," 1861, music based on a twelfth-century drinking song.)

The Dogsology

Every dog must have a master
Every dog must have a bone
Every dog must have a flea
Though you bathe him frequently
Every dog will always love you
If you handle him with care
Every dog will always love you
Till you pull out all his hair.

(TUNE: "The Doxology.")

After Auld Lang Syne

1.

The fish it never cackles 'bout
Its million eggs or so
The hen is quite a different bird
One egg, and hear her crow
The fish we spurn but crown the hen
Which leads us to surmise
Don't hide your light but blow your horn
It pays to advertise.

2.

There was a man who had two sons
And these two sons were brothers
Josephus was the name of one
Bohunkus was the other
Now these two boys they had a mule

And this old mule was blind
Josephus in the saddle rode
Bohunkus rode behind
Well, these two boys they died one day
By falling in a well
Josephus up to heaven went
Bohunkus went to the other place.

(TUNE: "Auld Lang Syne," traditional melody first published in 1687.)

In the Cellar of Murphy's Saloon

Give a yell, give a cheer
For the men who drink their beer
In the cellar of Murphy's Saloon.

They are brave, they are bold
For the whiskey they can hold
In the cellar of Murphy's Saloon.

For it's hi-hi-hee, as they bring out the whiskey
Shout out the order loud and clear, "More Beer!"

As the cops break down the door
We will drink a little more
In the cellar of Murphy's Saloon.

(TUNE: "The Caissons Go Rolling Along.")

Floatin' Down the Delaware

There goes [person's name]
Floatin' down the Delaware
Holes in his underwear
Couldn't afford another pair
Three weeks later
Bitten by a polar bear
Poor old polar bear died.

(TUNE: "The Old Grey Mare.")

When It's Hogcalling Time

1.

When it's hogcalling time in the valley (Sooie! Sooie!)
I'll be calling, my darling, to you
When the cows moo moo moo in the meadow
I'll be calling, my darling, to you.

In the twilight, by the pigpen (Oink! Oink!)
All my beautiful dreams will come true
When it's hogcalling time in the valley (Sooie! Sooie!)
I'll be calling, my darling, to you.

2.

When it's hogcalling time in Nebraska
When it's hogcalling time in Nebraska
When it's hogcalling time in Nebraska
Then it's hogcalling time in Nebraska.

(TUNE: "The Red River Valley," 1896, based on "In the Bright Mohawk Valley," which was based on an earlier Canadian song. On the first repetition, all sing this straight; on the second, one person speaks the lyric while the others hum the tune; on the third, half sing and half make pig noises.)

While Shepherds Washed Their Socks

While shepherds washed their socks by night
While watching MTV
The Angel of the Lord came down
And switched to BBC
And switched to BBC.

(TUNE: "While Shepherds Watched Their Flocks.")

The Scarlet Bonnet

From off his head we take the scarlet bonnet

He wore it while in swimming and he wore it while at play

And if you ask him, "Where's the decoration?"

He'll say, "Why, I'm a swimmer, and I've swum the thing away."

Dive and swim, plunge right in

It's gone from off his head for to stay

And if you ask him, "Where's the decoration?"

He'll say, "Why, I'm a swimmer, and I've swum the thing away."

(TUNE: "She Wore a Yellow Ribbon," traditional from 1838. The listener who sent this says, "In the mid-1930s non-swimmers wore red bathing caps at Boy Scout Camp Tonkawa on Lake Minnetonka until they could swim. A noontime ceremony was held during which the red cap was taken off their heads.")

My Country's Tired of Me

1.

My country's tired of me

I come from Germany

My name is Fritz

I love my sauerkraut

It makes my ears stick out

From every mountaintop

Let sauerkraut sprout.

My country's tired of me

I went to Germany

To see the King

His name was Donald Duck

He drove a garbage truck

Here's wishing the best of luck

In Donald's reign.

2.

Can opener, 'tis of thee

Friend in emergency,

Of thee I sing

When burnt brown is the steak

And sinks the ten-pound cake

You save a tummy-ache

Oh, kitchen king!

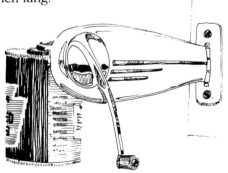

(TUNE: "America [My Country 'Tis of Thee]," 1832, based on the music of "God Save the King," 1744, which was based on an earlier melody composed for the King of Denmark.)

The Old Family Toothbrush

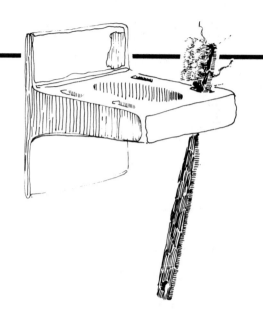

How dear to my heart is the old family toothbrush
The old family toothbrush that hung by the sink
At first it was Father's, and then it was Mother's
Now it is Brother's, but soon 'twill be mine!

The old family toothbrush, the moss-covered toothbrush
The dirty old toothbrush that hung by the sink
How dear to my heart is that old family toothbrush
The old family toothbrush that hung by the sink.

(TUNE: "The Old Oaken Bucket," 1843, based on an older Scottish air, "Jessie the Flower of Dumblane.")

My High Silk Hat

One day as I was riding on the subway
My high silk hat, my high silk hat
I laid it on the seat beside me
My high silk hat, my high silk hat
The big fat lady came and sat upon it
My high silk hat, My high silk hat
The big fat lady came and sat right on it
My high silk hat, my high silk hat.

Christopher Columbus! What do you think of that!
The big fat lady sat upon my hat
The hat she broke, now what's the joke
That big fat lady I could choke
Christopher Columbus! What do you think of that!

(TUNE: "Funiculi, Funicula," 1880. Some English variations are called "A Merry Life.")

Vive le Captain John

In the days when the savages lived in the land
Vive le Captain John!
And Indian papooses dug holes in the sand
Vive le Captain John!
A maiden was born of the cannibal race
Who delighted not in the fight or the chase
But loved to gaze on the jovial face
Of the jolly Captain John!

And now as the legend doth truly relate
Vive le Captain John!
Poor John was taken and doomed to his fate
Vive le Captain John!
He was doomed to be hung or knocked on the head
By the savage adz of the Indians red
Until at last he was dead, dead, dead
Vive le Captain John!

Now Pocahontas, hearing this vote
Vive le Captain John!
She took some birch bark and thereupon wrote
Vive le Captain John!
"If you will give your heart to me
You shall keep your head and go scot free
Together we'll live right merrily."
Vive le Captain John!

The note was taken to John that day
Vive le Captain John!
He called out loudly, "Oh, take me that way."
Vive le Captain John!
"This maid I will wed," the captain said
"She'll keep our house and make our bread
I'll live with her until I'm dead."
Vive le Captain John!

(TUNE: "Vive la Compagnie," or "Vive l'Amour," traditional French tune.)

There's a Long, Long Worm A-Crawling

1.

There's a long, long worm a-crawling
Across the roof of my tent
There's the morning bugle blowing
And it's time I went
There's the cold, cold water waiting
For me to take my morning dip
And when I return I'll find that worm
Across my pillow slip.

2.

There's a long, long nail a-grinding
Into the sole of my shoe
It grinds a little deeper
Every mile or two
There's one sweet day a-comin'
That I am dreaming about
That's the day that I can sit me down
And pull that darn nail out.

(**TUNE:** "There's a Long, Long Trail.")

D-A-V-E-N-P-O-R-T

D-A-V-E-N-P-O-R-T spells davenport
That's the only decent kind of love seat
The man who made it must have been a heart beat
D-A-V-E-N-P-O-R-T, you see
It's a hug and a squeeze
And an "Ooh, George, please!"
Davenport for me!

C-A-S-T-O-R-O-I-L spells castor oil
That's the only decent kind of medicine
The man who made it must have been an Edison
C-A-S-T-O-R-O-I-L, you see
It's a lick on a spoon
Guaranteed to kill you soon
Castor oil for me!

L-O-L-L-I-P-O-P spells lollipop
That's the only decent kind of candy

The man who made it must have been a dandy
L-O-L-L-I-P-O-P, you see
It's a lick on a stick
Guaranteed to make you sick
Lollipop for me!

(TUNE: "Harrigan," 1907.)

After Ach, Du Lieber Augustine

1.

Ach, du lieber Augustine
Slot machine run by steam
Put a nickel in the slot
Not'ing come out
Octember, Septober
No wonder I'm sober
If whiskey doesn't kill me
I'll live 'til I die.

2.

See the little angels
Ascend up, ascend up
See the little angels
Ascend up on high.
Which end up? As-cend up
Which end up? As-cend' up
See the little angels
Ascend up on high.

(The contributor of this version wrote, "My grandmother, who exemplified Victorian restraint in behavior and language, astonished the family by singing this song.")

(TUNE: "Did You Ever See a Lassie," or, "O [Ach] Du Lieber Augustine," traditional Austrian melody published as early as 1788.)

Zip Up Your Doo-Dah

Zip up your doo-dah, don't be risqué
My oh my, what a thing to display!
Plenty of people looking your way
Zip up your doo-dah, it's cold out today.

Chapter 8

Ain't We Crazy?

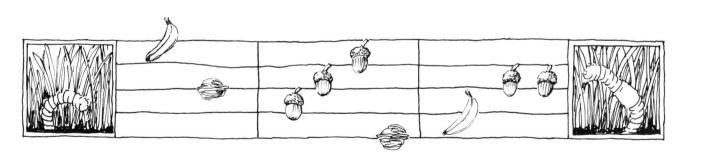

American folklore owns an ancient heritage of "nonsense" songs which intrigue us in two ways. The more sophisticated of these songs exploit the capacity of the English language to be rendered nonsensical by playing with its inherent sound-sense differences, as in puns ("the organ pealed potatoes") and in words with multiple meanings ("Can you mend the break of day?"). Other songs startle and amuse us through a basic principle of comedy, by juxtaposing incongruous images and creating outlandish metaphors, sometimes in ways which our century has come to call surrealistic.

In *Singing Family of the Cumberlands,* Jean Ritchie reports a Kentucky folk song with its roots in England, "Nottamun Town," which contains eerie examples of this unsettling folk nonsense:

> Met the King and the Queen and a company more
> A-riding behind and a-marching before;
> Come a stark naked drummer a-beating a drum,
> With his hands in his bosom come marching along . . .
>
> Set down on a hard, hot cold-frozen stone,
> Ten thousand stood around me and yet I's alone;
> Took my hat in my hand for to keep my head warm,
> Ten thousand got drownded that never was born.

This is solemn nonsense, indeed, and invokes in us an uneasy sense of ancient rituals, maze dances, and mystery plays long lost to the modern world.

In America, more typically, nonsense folk songs have allied themselves with the native love of hyperbole and tall talk epitomized by Mark Twain in his pugnacious riverboatman in *Life on the Mississippi:*

> Whoo-oop! I'm the old original iron-jawed, brass-mounted, copper-bellied corpse-maker from the wilds of Arkansaw! Look at me! I'm the man they call Sudden Death and General Desolation! Sired by a hurricane, dam'd by an earthquake, half-brother to the cholera, nearly related to the small pox on my mother's side. Look at me! I take nineteen alligators and a bar'l of whisky for breakfast when I'm in robust health, and a bushel of dead rattlesnakes when I'm ailing. I split the everlasting rocks with my glance, and I squelch the thunder when I speak! Whoo-oop! Stand back and give me room according to my strength! Blood's my natural drink and the wails of the dying is music to my ear! Cast your eye on me, gentlemen! and lay low and hold your breath, for I'm about to turn myself loose!

The humorous songs sent by PHC listeners to the Department, from which we have selected the following examples of nonsense, contain a high proportion of old folk songs, often those perpetuated by radio and recordings, but nevertheless songs learned, sung, and enjoyed down to our time for the evergreen appeal of their ingeniously crafted foolishness. Old favorites such as "Ain't We Crazy" employ outlandish puns and wordplay as well as bizarre juxtapositions of images, while "A Horse Named Bill" and "I Was Born About Ten Thousand Years Ago" carry on the Twain tradition of braggadocio exaggerated to the point of nonsense.

The latter songs were often recorded from the 1920s down through the "folk song revival" of recent years, but other songs are new to us and are perhaps recently composed.

>Do ships have eyes when they go to sea?
>Are there springs in an ocean bed?
>
>And
>
>Does six and six make nine?
>Does ice grow on a vine?
>Is old brother Joe an Eskimo
>In the good old summertime?

Such poetry continues to convey the old humor of incongruity and surprise, but beneath its sheer nonsense we can still feel some of the same uneasy doubt of "Nottamun Town," doubt that logic and rational language alone can account for the full range of our human experiences.

Ain't We Crazy?

Well, I know a little ditty, it's as crazy as can be
The guy who wrote it wanted it, so he handed it to me.
I found I couldn't use it for it sounded kind of blue
And that's the very reason why I'm handing it to you.

It's a song the alligators sing while coming through the rye
And serenade the elephants up in the trees so high.
The iceman hums this ditty as he shovels in the coal
And the monkeys join the chorus up around the Northern Pole.

Chorus: Ain't we crazy, ain't we crazy
This is the way we pass the time away, hey! hey!
Ain't we crazy, ain't we crazy
We're going to sing this song all night today.

It was midnight on the ocean, not a streetcar was in sight
The sun was shining brightly for it rained all day that night.
'Twas a summer's night in winter and the rain was snowing fast
A barefoot boy with shoes on stood a-sitting in the grass.

Chorus

'Twas evening and the rising sun was setting in the west
The little fishes in the trees were cuddled in their nest.
The rain was pouring down and the sun was shining bright
And everything that you could see was hidden from your sight.

The cows were making cowslips, the bells were wringing wet
The bumblebees were making bums and smoking cigarettes.
A man slept in a stable and came out a little hoarse
He hopped up on his golf sticks and drove all around the course.

Chorus

It was midnight on the ocean, not a streetcar was in sight
I stepped into a drugstore to get myself a light.
Well, the man behind the counter was a lady old and grey
Who used to peddle doughnuts on the road to Mandalay.

She said, "Hi there, stranger!" Her eyes were wet with tears
She stuck her head beneath her foot and stayed that way for years.
Her children six were orphans except one tiny tot
Who lived in the house across the street above a vacant lot.

Chorus

Key of G

Well, I know a lit-tle dit-ty, it's as cra-zy as can

be, The guy who wrote it want-ed it, so he

hand-ed it to me. I found I could-n't use it for it

sound-ed kind of blue, And that's the ver-y

rea-son why I'm hand-ing it to you.

Chorus: Ain't we cra - zy, ain't we cra - zy? This is the way we

pass the time a - way, hey! hey! Ain't we cra - zy, ain't we

cra - zy? We're going to sing this song all night to - day._____

169

I Was Born About Ten Thousand Years Ago

I was born about ten thousand years ago
And there isn't anything that I don't know
I saw Peter, Paul, and Moses playing ring-around-the-roses
And I'll lick the guy that says it isn't so.

I was here before the country had a king
I saw Cleopatra pawn her wedding ring
I was on a streetcar flying when George Washington stopped lying
I was there when Melba first began to sing.

I helped Brigham Young invent Limburger cheese
I taught Solomon his little ABC's
And I sailed out on the bay with Methuselah one day
To save his flowing whiskers from the breeze.

Queen Elizabeth, she fell in love with me
We were married in Milwaukee secretly
I got tired of her and shook her, then I joined with General Hooker
And we chased mosquitoes out of Tennessee.

I saw Samson when he laid the village cold
I saw Daniel tame the lions in their hold
I helped build the Tower of Babel up as high as they were able
And there's lots of other things I haven't told.

I saw Satan when he looked the garden o'er
I saw Adam and Eve driven from the door
I was behind the bushes peeking at the apple they were eating
And I swear that I'm the guy that ate the core.

I was born about ten thousand years ago
And there isn't anything that I don't know
I saw Peter, Paul, and Moses playing ring-around-the-roses
And I'll lick the guy that says it isn't so.

I Was Born One Night One Morn

I was born one night one morn
When the whistle went "Toot, toot."
You can fry a snake or bake a cake
When the mud pies are in bloom,
Does six and six make nine?
Does ice grow on a vine?
Is old brother Joe an Eskimo
In the good old summertime?
Oh, loop-de-loop in your noodle soup
Just to give your socks a shine.
I'm guilty, Judge, I ate the fudge
Three cheers for old Enzyme.
I cannot tell a lie
I hocked an apple pie
It's on a tree beneath the sea
Above the bright blue sky.
Oh, Easter eggs don't wash their legs
Their children will have ducks
I'd rather buy a lemon pie
For forty-seven bucks.
Oh, way down in Barcelona
They jump into the foamia
But that is all balonia
Paderewski, blow your horn. Toot, toot!

Golly, Ain't That Queer

We've got a cow down on our farm
Golly, ain't that queer
And she gives milk without alarm
Golly, ain't that queer.

One day she drank from a frozen stream
And froze her tail like an iron beam
And ever since she's given ice cream
Golly, ain't that queer.

My brother Bill is a fireman bold

He puts out fires

One day he went to a fire, I'm told

'Cause he puts out fires

The fire lit some dynamite

And it blew poor Bill clear out of sight

But where he's gone he'll be all right

'Cause he puts out fires.

(TUNE: "Old McDonald Had a Farm," 1917, but the tune was known as early as 1859.)

The Worm Song

The earth was wet with the dew of the dawn

As the warm scented air swept over the lawn

A big fat worm came out of the ground

To see the world and to look around

And as he gazed at the azure sky

Another little worm came up nearby.

Said he, with a wiggle, "You're a cute little worm,

Let's you and I go out for a squirm

I could easily fall in love with you

If you'll condescend to a rendezvous."

But the cute little worm just shook its head

And to the big fat worm it said,

"No rendezvous between us two

'Cause I'm the other end of you."

Key of G

The earth was wet with the dew of the dawn, As the

A Horse Named Bill

Oh, I had a horse and his name was Bill
And when he ran he couldn't stand still
He ran away, one day,
And also I ran with him.

He ran so fast he could not stop
He ran into a barber shop
And fell exhaustionized with his eyeteeth
Into the barber's left shoulder.

I had a gal and her name was Daisy
When she sang the cat went crazy
With deliriums and St. Vituses
And all kinds of cat-aleptics.

One day she sang a song about
A man who turned himself inside out
And jumped into the river
Because he was so very sleepy.

Oh, I'm going out in the woods next year
And shoot for beer, and not for deer
I am, I ain't
I'm a great sharpshootress.

At shooting birds I am a beaut
There is no bird that I can't shoot
In the eye, in the ear, in the teeth,
Or in the finger.

Oh, I went up in a balloon so big
The people on earth looked like a pig
Like a mice, like a katydid, like flieses
And like fleasens.

The balloon turned up with its bottom side higher
It fell on the wife of a country squire
She made a noise like a hound dog, like a steam whistle
And like dynamite.

Oh, what can you do in a case like that?
What can you do but stamp on your hat
And your toothbrush, and your grandmother
And anything else that's useless.

(TUNE: "Dixie.")

The Skinniest Man I Ever Knew

1.

Oh, the skinniest man I ever knew
Was a man from Hokum Pokum
If I ever told you how skinny he was
You'd think I was only jokin'.

Chorus: Oh, me, oh, my,
He couldn't catch his breath
So he fell right through the hole in his pants
And choked himself to death.

For exercise he used to dive
Through the holes of a nutmeg grater
His body was so lean and thin
His head like a sweet potater.

Chorus

2.

The thinnest man I ever saw
He lived down in Hoboken
If I told you just how thin he was
You'd think that I was joking
He's as thin as the milk in a cheap hotel
Or the peel of an Irish potato
For exercise he used to dive
Right through the nutmeg grater.

(TUNE: "Take Me Back to Tulsa," 1941.)

He never would go out at night
Nor walk the streets alone
For fear some lean and hungry dog
Would take him for a bone.

Chorus

One night when all the folks were out
The lamps were burning dimly
A bedbug got him by the seat of his pants
And rammed him up the chimney.

Chorus

I rock, you rock,
Don't you rock so hard
Every time you rock, I rock too
So don't you rock so hard.

Catalina Magdalena

There was a funny girl and she had a funny name
But she got it from her father just the same, same, same.

Chorus: Oh, Catalina Magdalena
       Hoopensheimer Wobbleheimer
       Hogan Bogan Logan was her name.

She had two teeth in her mouth
One pointed east and the other one south, south, south.

Chorus

Her feet were flat like a bathroom mat
I don't know how they got like that, that, that.

Chorus

She had two eyes in her head
One was glass and the other was lead, lead, lead.

Chorus

Her ears stuck out like sails on a boat
Her Adam's apple wobbled up and down in her throat, throat, throat.

Chorus

She had two hairs on her head
One was black and the other was red, red, red.

Chorus

She had two arms on her chest
One pointed east and the other west, west, west.

Chorus

She had two socks on her feet
One was messy and the other was neat, neat, neat.

Chorus

She had two cats in her bed
One was alive and the other was dead, dead, dead.

Chorus

A ten-ton truck hit Magdalene
The owner had to buy a new machine, chine, chine.

Chorus

Side by Side

We got married last Friday
My wife stood there beside me
Our friends had all gone
We were alone, side by side.

We were glad we were wed then
We got ready for bed then
Her teeth and her hair
She placed on the chair, side by side.

One cork leg so dainty
One glass eye so small
Her left arm she took off before me
And placed on the chair by the wall.

I stood there broken-hearted
For most of my wife had departed
So I slept on the chair
There was more of her there, side by side,
We're side by side.

(TUNE: "Side by Side," 1927.)

My Freckle-Faced Consumptive Mary Ann

Oh, she promised to meet me when the clock struck seventeen
At the stockyards a mile away from town
Where pigs' feet and pigs' ears and tough old Texas steers
Sell for sirloin steak at ninety cents a pound.

Oh, she's my darling, my daisy, she's humpbacked and she's crazy
She's knock-kneed, bow-legged, pigeon-toed, and blind
And they say her teeth are false just from drinking Epsom salts
She's my freckle-faced consumptive Mary Ann.

Key of D

Oh, she prom - ised to meet me when the clock struck sev - en -

teen At the stock - yards a mile a - way from town, _____ Where pigs'

feet and pigs' ears and tough old Tex - as steers Sell for

sir - loin steak at nine - ty cents a pound. _____ Oh, she's my

dar - ling, my dai - sy, she's hump - backed and she's cra - zy. She's

knock - kneed, bow - legged, pig - eon - toed, and blind. _____ And they

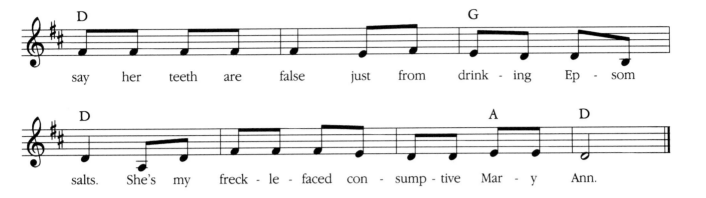

say her teeth are false just from drink - ing Ep - som

salts. She's my freck - le - faced con - sump - tive Mar - y Ann.

Ve Got Troubles

My daughter's the biggest of all of my kids
Her kneecaps stick out yust like two fruit jar lids
Her legs are so big that when she's in a rush
She puts on leg makeup vith a calcimine brush.

Chorus: Ve got troubles, vat shall ve do?
Ve got troubles, vat shall ve do?
Yumpin' Yiminy, I'm telling you
Dat ver de vorsta, vat shall ve do?

Saturday night I shampooed my wife's hair
Rinsed it in vinegar, she didn't care
It got in her ears, now she hears a lot less
She's suffering from pickled hearing, I guess.

Chorus

I crossed a swan vith a big bull moose
Came up vit a number I called a svoose
I crossed a hoot owl vit a nanny goat too
Now the yard's full of hootenannies, vat shall ve do?

Chorus

How Pleasant That Would Be

Oh, do not be offended now because I start to sing
For if I had not come out here the curtain down would ring
The man who should have sung this song inside was taken sick
As I was standing idly here they grabbed me mighty quick.
And they wanted me to take his place and do the best I could
They said, "Go on and sing your song." I told them that I would
They're standing 'round to watch me now, my actions just to see
They said, "You can't get more than killed." How pleasant that would be!

Oh, P. T. Barnum's great big show was in an awful stew
They'd lost a curiosity and didn't know what to do
It happened just a week ago, and how they wept and sighed
And through the crowd it quickly spread, the big baboon had died.
They wanted me to take his place and do the best I could
They put me in a great big cage with monkeys bad and good
They'd call me Crolly number two, let kids stick pins in me
They'd feed me candy and peanuts. How pleasant that would be!

Oh, McCody and McCroskey, they matched their dogs to fight
They posted fifty dollars each to fight on Friday night
We all went down to McCody's house, McCody he was there
But they couldn't find McCroskey or his bull pup anywhere.
They wanted me to take his place and do the best I could
They said, "Go on and win this fight!" I told them that I would
"Be sure, me boy, you lick this pup, for if you don't, you see
He'll chew you into sausage meat!" How pleasant that would be!

My sister held a policy upon her husband's life
He ran away and left her a very disappointed wife
If she could only prove him dead, his insurance she could claim
She'd go and get a coffin and thereon inscribe his name.
And she wanted me to take his place and do the best I could
She'd lock me in a coffin that was made of brass and wood
But when the mourners were all gone, she said she'd set me free
If she'd forget and leave me in, how pleasant that would be!

Key of G

G   C

Oh, do not be of - fend - ed now be - cause I start to

Am   D

sing, For if I had not come out here this cur - tain down would

G   C

ring. The man who should have sung this song in - side was ta - ken

Am   D⁷   G   D⁷

sick, As I was stand - ing id - ly here they grabbed me might - y

G   G   C

quick. And they want - ed me to take his place and do the best I

Am   D⁷

could. They said, "Go on and sing your song." I told them that I

G   G   C

would. They're stand - ing 'round to watch me now, my ac - tions just to

Am   D⁷   G   D⁷   G

see. They said, "You can't get more than killed." __ How pleas - ant that would be!

181

While Looking Out a Window

While looking out a window

A second-story window

I slipped and sprained my eyebrow on the pavement, the pavement

Go get the Listerine, sister wants a beau

And a boy's best friend is his mother, his mother.

They spanked him with a shingle

Which made his panties tingle

Because he socked his little baby brother, his brother

We feed our baby garlic so we'll find him in the dark

And who shot the sleeves off father's vest, his vest?

While looking through a knothole

In father's wooden leg

Why do they build the shore so near the ocean, the ocean

A snake's belt slips because he has no hips

And his waistline is just below his necktie, his necktie.

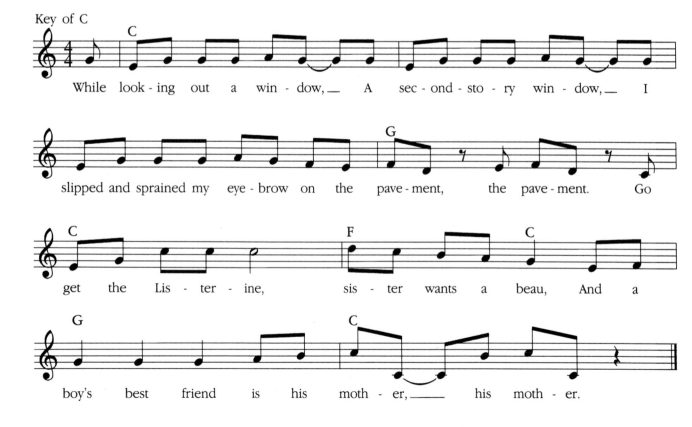

The Billboard Song

1.

As I was walking down the street one dark and dusky day
I came across a billboard with pieces blown away
It was all torn and tattered from a storm the night before
And reading all the pieces left, this is what I saw:

Smoke Coca-Cola cigarettes, chew Wrigley's Spearmint beer
Ken-L-Ration dog food will make your complexion clear
The doctors say that babies should smoke until they're three
And people over 65 should bathe in Lipton's Tea
Enjoy your next vacation in a brand new Frigidaire
Learn to play the piano in your thermal underwear
If you want to make this country a better place today
Then buy a record of this song and break it right away.

2.

As I was walking down the street a billboard caught my eye
The advertisements listed there would make you laugh and cry
The wind and rain had come last night and washed them half away
The other half remaining there would make this billboard say:

Smoke Coca-Cola, drink Camel cigarettes
See Lillian Russell wrestle with a box of Oysterettes
Pork and Beans will meet tonight in a finished fight
Philip Gibbs will lecture on Sapolio tonight
Bay Rum is good for horses, ours is the best in town
Castoria cures the measles, just pay five dollars down
Teeth extracted without pain, cost but half a dime
And Ingersolls on sale tonight a little out of time.

There Was a Rich Man Who Lived in Jerusalem

There was a rich man who lived in Jerusalem
Glory Hallelujah, hi-er-o-cherum
He wore a silk hat and he looked very
    sprucelum
Glory Hallelujah, hi-er-o-cherum.

Chorus: Hi-ro-cherum, hi-ro-cherum
         Skimadelick dee-doodle-ium
         Skimadelick dee-doodle-ium
         Glory Hallelujah, hi-er-o-cherum.

By his gate there stood a human wreckium
Glory Hallelujah, hi-er-o-cherum
He wore a bowler hat with the rim around his
    neckium
Glory Hallelujah, hi-er-o-cherum.

Chorus

The poor man asked for to have some bread
    and cheesium
Glory Hallelujah, hi-er-o-cherum
The rich man said, "I'll call the policeium."
Glory Hallelujah, hi-er-o-cherum.

Chorus

The poor man died and his soul went to
    heavenium
Glory Hallelujah, hi-er-o-cherum
He danced with the saints 'til a quarter past
    elevenium
Glory Hallelujah, hi-er-o-cherum.

Chorus

The rich man died but he didn't fare so wellium
Glory Hallelujah, hi-er-o-cherum
He couldn't go to heaven so he had to go to hellium
Glory Hallelujah, hi-er-o-cherum.

Chorus

The rich man asked for to have a consolium
Glory Hallelujah, hi-er-o-cherum
The Devil only answered, "Go shovel on some
    coalium!"
Glory Hallelujah, hi-er-o-cherum.

Chorus

The moral of the story is that riches are no jokeium
Glory Hallelujah, hi-er-o-cherum
And we'll all go to heaven 'cause we're all stony
    brokium
Glory Hallelujah, hi-er-o-cherum.

Chorus

The Biblical Baseball Game

Eve stole first and Adam second

St. Peter umpired the game

Rebecca went to the well with the pitcher

While Ruth in the field won fame

Goliath was struck out by David

A base hit made on Abel by Cain

The Prodigal Son made one home run

Brother Noah gave out checks for the rain.

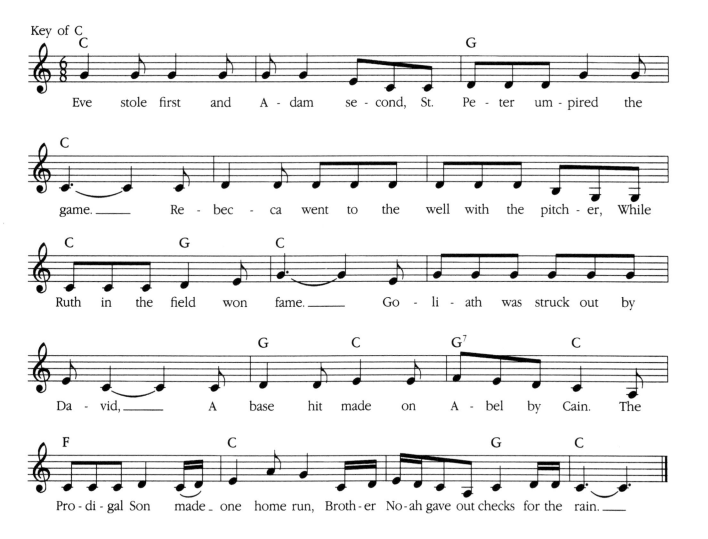

Young Folks, Old Folks (or The Silly Sunday School)

Adam was the first man, Eve she was a mother
Cain he was a wicked man because he slew his brother
Samson was a strong man, Noah built the ark
Jonah was a fisherman and was swallied by a shark.

Chorus: Young folks, old folks, ev'rybody come
        Come along to Sunday School and have a lot of fun
        Bring a stick of chewing gum and park it at the door
        And you'll hear some Bible stories that you never heard before.

God made the world in six days and rested on the seventh
According to the contract it should have been the eleventh
But the carpenters were out on strike and the masons wouldn't work
So the foremen dug a hole and they filled it up with dirt.

Chorus

When they finished with the firmament they started on the sky
They hung it overhead and left it there to dry
They studded it with stars made of pretty damsels' eyes
To give us a little light when the moon forgot to rise.

Chorus

Adam was the first man, Eve was his spouse
They started in a-keeping house
All went well 'til the baby came
And they started in a-raising Cain.

Chorus

Adam was the first man, we all do believe
He had a wife and her name was Eve
She was fair to look upon and oh, how she could dance
And her dress was made of Shredded Wheat and so were Adam's pants.

Chorus

Noah was a carpenter walking in the dark
Stumbled on a hammer and he built himself an ark

The rains came down in showers fine
And the ark sailed away on scheduled time.

Chorus

Noah became a mariner and sailed around the sea
With half a dozen wives and a whole menagerie
He tried his hand at fishing, so the Bible tale confirms
But he didn't have much luck because he only had two worms.

Chorus

There are plenty of these Bible tales, I'll tell you more tomorrow
How Lot with the wife and family fled from Sodom and Gomorrah
But his wife turned to rubber so he settled on the spot
She was fixed up for a monument and missed a happy Lot.

Chorus

Here comes Ruth looking all around
Just like the girls in this here town
Didn't wear a bustle or powder on her nose
But she got a fella as everybody knows.

Chorus

Daniel was a stubborn man who wouldn't mind the King
The King he said he'd never heard of such a funny thing
Put Daniel in the lions' den with Daniel underneath
But Daniel was a dentist and he pulled the lions' teeth.

Chorus

Salome was a dancer and she danced the hootchy-kootch
She danced before the King and he liked her very much
"But," said the King, "we must have no scandal here."
"Hell!" said Salome and she kicked the chandelier.

Chorus

Samson was a husky guy from the P.T. Barnum school
He used to lift five hundred pounds as strongman in the show
'Til a lady named Delilah got him all fixed up with gin
They caught him bald-headed and the coppers ran him in.

Chorus

But Samson wasn't satisfied, the pace got in his hair
He mooned around when the act was on and set himself a chair
He'd slain ten thousand Philistines with the jawbone of a mouse
But that weight-lift act of Samson's brought down the house.

Chorus

Elijah was a prophet, he worked the county fairs
He advertised his act with a pair of dancing bears
He held a sale of prophecies 'most every afternoon
And he went up every evening in a gaudy silk balloon.

Chorus

Ahab had a lovely wife, her name was Jezebel
While hanging out the clothes one day, down off the roof she fell.
"Your wife has gone all to the dogs," was what they told the king
But Ahab said he'd never heard of such a doggone thing.

Chorus

Jonah signed up for a transatlantic sail
He spent three days in the belly of a whale
Jonah got bored and the whale got depressed
So Jonah pushed the button and the whale did the rest.

Chorus

Goliath was a giant, also a cuss
Went around the countryside looking for a fuss
When he saw David, he laughed 'til he bust
Then David heaved a rock and socked him on the crust.

Chorus

Meshach, Shadrach, and Abednego
Told the king where he could go
He put them in the furnace and gave the door a slam
But they wore asbestos BVD's and didn't give a—hoot.

Chorus

Methuselah was crabby 'cause he couldn't take a joke
He had all the makings of an old and seedy bloke
His whiskers got so long that he couldn't see ahead
If he'd tucked in all the covers he could have used them for his bed.

Chorus

Esau was a cowboy, a wild and woolly rake
Half the ranch belonged to him, half to his brother Jake
Now Esau thought the title to the property wasn't clear
So he sold out to his brother for a sandwich and a beer.

Chorus

Moses was a prophet, they found him by a brook
He was found by Pharaoh's daughter when she went in for a dook
She took him home to father, said she found him by the shore
Pharaoh merely smiled and said, "I've heard that one before."

Chorus

189

While the Organ Pealed Potatoes

While the organ pealed potatoes
Lard was rendered by the choir
As the sexton rang the dishrag
Someone set the church on fire.

"Holy Smokes!" the preacher shouted
As he madly tore his hair
Now his head resembles heaven
For there is no parting there.

(TUNE: "Silver Threads Among the Gold.")

Questions

Do ships have eyes when they go to sea?
Are there springs in an ocean bed?
Does the jolly tar fall from a tree?
Does a river ever lose its head?
Are fishes crazy when they go in seine?
Can an old hen sing her lay?
Can you give relief to a windowpane?
Can you mend the break of day?

What vegetable is a policeman's beat?
Is a newspaper white when it's read?
Is a baker broke when he's making dough?
Is an undertaker's business dead?

Would a wallpaper store make a good hotel
On account of the borders there?
Would you paint a rabbit on a bald man's head
Just to give him a little hare?

If a grass widow married a grass widower
Would their children all be grasshoppers?
Can you give a policeman a silver coin
For silver wasn't made for coppers?
If you ate a square meal, would the corners hurt?
Could you dig with an ace of spades?
Would you throw a rope to a drowning lemon
Just to give a little lemon aid?

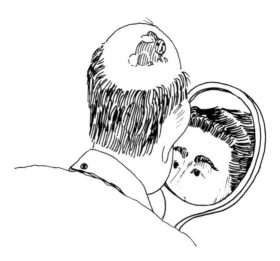

Key of A

Do ships have eyes when they go to sea? Are there springs in an o - cean
bed? Does the jol - ly tar fall from a tree? Does a
riv - er ev - er lose its head? Are fish - es cra - zy when they
go in seine? Can an old hen sing her lay?_____ Can you
give re - lief to a win - dow pane? Can you mend the break of day?

Ain't It Great to Be Crazy?

Way down south where bananas grow
A flea stepped on an elephant's toe
The elephant cried with tears in his eyes
[Spoken] "Why don't you pick on somebody your own size!"

Chorus: Boom, boom, ain't it great to be crazy?
   Boom, boom, ain't it great to be crazy?
   Silly and foolish all day long
   Boom, boom, ain't it great to be crazy?

Horsie and flea and three blind mice
Sitting in the barnyard shooting dice
Horsie slipped and fell on the flea
[Spoken] "Oops," said the flea, "there's a horsie on me."

Chorus

Eli, Eli, he sells socks
Dollar a pair and a nickel a box
The longer you wear 'em, the stronger they get
[Spoken] Put 'em in the water and they don't get wet.

Chorus

Bought me a pair of combination underwear
Guaranteed not to rip or tear
Wore 'em three months without hesitation
[Spoken] I couldn't get 'em off because I lost the combination.

Chorus

Chapter 9

Fun with Words and Sounds

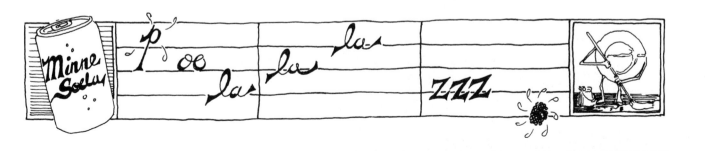

Most of the readers of this book will experience during their lifetimes a shift from relying on the printed page for information and entertainment to a new reliance on video and the computer, just as earlier generations experienced a shift from the oral tradition to reading and writing. Despite the five-hundred-year history of print, its hegemony over oral tradition has occurred fairly recently, within the last few generations. Well into this century, many Americans educated and entertained themselves with spoken and sung words and sounds which they created themselves or had learned from people rather than books.

In 1928, The Blue Ridge Corn Shuckers, a pioneer hillbilly band headed by Ernest Stoneman of Galax, Virginia, recorded for RCA Victor a charming skit entitled "Possum Trot School Exhibition" in which the band members impersonate schoolchildren competing in their yearly recital. The musicians are very likely demonstrating oral techniques of learning recalled from their own school days around the turn of the century. Their brief "readings" all rhyme, their spelling recital is an archaic chant which cumulatively syllabifies* the word as it is spelled, and their "speeches" resonate with a love of diction and the musical capabilities of the voice.

In addition to using song and rhyme as mnemonic devices for learning, country people were skilled at using the voice as a substitute for musical instruments in providing rhythmic accompaniment for dancing or games called "play parties," which substituted for dances in some religious communities. Wordless field hollers, animal imitations, tongue-twisters, and flights of fanciful rhetoric additionally testified to the delight people with an oral tradition took in savoring language and the sound of the human voice.

Most readers will recall some experience of this tradition, if no more than learning their ABC's by singing the alphabet to the tune of "Twinkle, Twinkle, Little Star." PHC listeners recalled and sent to the Department a fund of similar lore, much of it remnants of traditional ways of learning and amusement. The books of the Bible and the list of prepositions sung as mnemonic devices appear here, as well as a series of comic rhetorical exercises translating simple verse into highfalutin verbiage, a vocabulary-stretching form of entertainment dating at least to the nineteenth-century minstrel stage.

From jump rope rhymes to tongue-twisters to good-natured raspberries, this chapter rejoices in noises and words that one hopes will not disappear completely from a world increasingly dominated by sounds no more entertaining than the computer's beep and rhetoric no more joyous than the hollow jargon of pop music and television advertising.

---

*"Incomprehensibility: I-N in, I-N-C-O-M incom, I-N-C-O-M-P-R-E incompre, I-N-C-O-M-P-R-E-H-E-N incomprehen, I-N-C-O-M-P-R-E-H-E-N-S-I-B-I-L incomprehensibil, I-N-C-O-M-P-R-E-H-E-N-S-I-B-I-L-I-T-Y." (This long sentence is quickly and musically chanted and comes out sounding like an auctioneer's chant.)

The King of the Cannibal Islands

1.

We sailed from the port the other day
Intending to stop at Botany Bay
But it happened that we were cast away
Among the Cannibal Islands.

Chorus: Hokey pokey okey-o
Portikiki kapalar kung
Winguree wungeree chingaree chung
The King of the Cannibal Islands.

The King invited us up to tea
His name was Chirochirokee
And we were as thick as thick could be
Among the Cannibal Islands.

Chorus

Said the King, "Will you be my son-in-law
And marry the Princess Wishiwaw?"
Said I, "Will His Majesty hold his jaw!"
To the King of the Cannibal Islands.

Chorus

2.

Chorus: Hokey pokey winky wam
Billy McGee and Billy McGam
Hangery wangery chingery chong
The King of the Cannibal Islands.

Woman pudding and baby sauce
Little boy pie for the second course
He swallowed them all without remorse
The King of the Cannibal Islands.

Chorus

The end of my story remains to be told
About this monarch so brave and bold
He died of eating his clergyman cold
The King of the Cannibal Islands.

Chorus

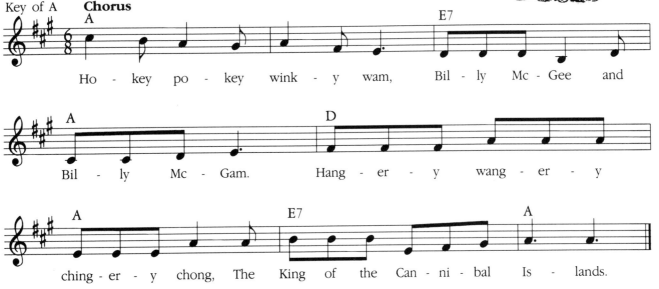

Key of A   **Chorus**

Ho - key po - key wink - y wam, Bil - ly Mc - Gee and

Bil - ly Mc - Gam. Hang - er - y wang - er - y

ching - er - y chong, The King of the Can - ni - bal Is - lands.

There Was a Little Rooster

Oh, there was a little rooster
In our little country store
And he phfft! on the counter
And he phfft! on the floor
And he phfft! in the sugar
And he phfft! on the bread
And if I hadn't ducked
He'd have phfft! on my head.
(Somebody catch that darn thing!)

(TUNE: "Turkey in the Straw," with "shave and a haircut, six bits" tag. One listener who sent a version of this song explains, "The *phfft!* is the sound you make when you pucker your lips and blow air through them. I'm not sure how to spell it—it's a pooping sound, you know.")

If I Were As High

If I were as high   If I were as low
As the moon in the sky   As a morsel of snow
I would look down at you   I would look up at you
And go [raspberry]!   And go [raspberry]!

Love to Be in Copenhagen

Love to be in Copenhagen
In the morning, in the morning
Love to be in Copenhagen
In the morning, ya, ya.

We climb the church steeple
And spit at the people
Love to be in Copenhagen
In the morning, ya, ya.

(TUNE: "Did You Ever See a Lassie," or "Ach, Du Lieber Augustine." Two listeners sing this as a duet in which "one singer must make a raspberry sound [poop] by sticking out his or her tongue and vibrating it, followed by two falsetto *eee-eee* squeaks. Another person must sing the verses to that accompaniment.")

Have You Ever Seen?

Have you ever seen a horse fly, a horse fly, a horse fly?
Have you ever seen a horse fly? Now you tell us one.

Have you ever seen a shoe box, a shoe box, a shoe box?
Have you ever seen a shoe box? Now you tell us one.

Have you ever seen a chimney sweep, a chimney sweep, a chimney sweep?
Have you ever seen a chimney sweep? Now you tell us one.

Have you ever seen a dish mop, a dish mop, a dish mop?
Have you ever seen a dish mop? Now you tell us one.

(TUNE: "Did You Ever See a Lassie," or "Ach, Du Lieber Augustine." One listener recalls, "We used to sing this in college, between dinner and dessert on some rowdy nights. One table group would start by singing a verse, another table would sing a second verse, and so on; the object was to keep the song going as long as possible and be the group to come up with the last possible verse. The endless verses were made up on the spot.")

Down at the Station

Down at the station, early in the morning
See the little pufferbellies all in a row
See the stationmaster pull the little handle
Puff, puff, toot, toot, off we go!

My Name Is Solomon Levi

My name is Solomon Levi
My store's on Salem Street
That's where to buy your coats and vests
And everything that's neat.

Second-handed ulsterettes
And overcoats so fine
For all the boys that trade with me
At One-Hundred-and-Forty-Nine.

Oh, Solomon Levi, poor Solomon Levi
Oh, Solomon Levi, la la la la la.

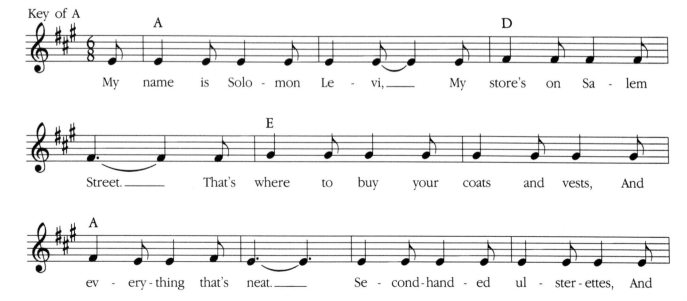

o - ver - coats so fine, ———— For all the boys that

trade with me, At One - Hun - dred - and - For - ty - Nine.————

Oh, Sol - o - man Le - vi, poor Sol - o - mon Le - vi.

Oh, Sol - o - mon Le - vi, la la la la la.————

John Jacob Jingleheimer Schmidt

John Jacob Jingleheimer Schmidt
That's my name too
Whenever I go out, the people always shout
"There goes John Jacob Jingleheimer Schmidt!"
La la la la la la la!

Too Much of a Name

Some people are anxious for honor and fame
And they strive all their lifetime in getting a name
But too much of a name is a possible thing
And this you will say when you hear what I sing
Now my father and mother were excellent folks
But they both had a weakness for practical jokes
So when I was born they were both of one mind
They said I should have all the names they could find.

Chorus: For there were Jonathan Joseph Jeremiah
       Timothy Titus Obadiah
       William Henry Walter Sim
       Reuben Rufus Solomon Jim
       Nathaniel Daniel Abraham
       Roderick Frederick Peter Sam
       Simon Timon Nicholas Pat
       Christopher Dick Jehosephat.

I was sent to be christened before I could speak
So I might not object to this curious freak
There were two other babies that morning as well
And for those two babies it turned out a sell
The reason was that I was first of the three
So the parson began operations on me
And it took him so long for my titles to call
That these two other babies got no names at all!

Chorus

When I came to be married the case was as bad
The parson stared at me as if he were mad
He started his task but he found very soon
That the job was too great to be finished by noon
Said he, "My dear sir, 'tis a very great shame
That your parents denied you a sensible name
But since you are here without reason or rhyme
You'll have to get married one name at a time."

Chorus

Michael Finnigan

There once was a man named Michael Finnigan
He grew whiskers on his chinnigan
The wind came out and blew them innigan
Poor old Michael Finnigan! Beginnigan!

There once was a man named Michael Finnigan
He got drunk from too much ginnigan
And so he wasted all his tinnigan
Poor old Michael Finnigan! Beginnigan!

There once was a man named Michael Finnigan
He kicked up an awful dinnigan
Because they said he must not sinnigan
Poor old Michael Finnigan! Beginnigan!

There once was a man named Michael Finnigan
He went fishing with a pinnigan
Caught a fish but he dropped it innigan
Poor old Michael Finnigan! Beginnigan!

There once was a man named Michael Finnigan
Climbed a tree and barked his shinnigan
Took off several yards of skinnigan
Poor old Michael Finnigan! Beginnigan!

There once was a man named Michael Finnigan
He grew fat and he grew thinnigan
Then he died and we have to beginnigan
Poor old Michael Finnigan! Beginnigan!

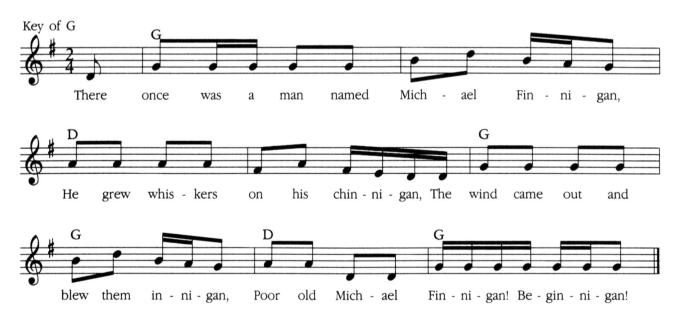

I Saw Esau

I saw Esau sitting on a seesaw
I saw Esau with my girl
I saw Esau sitting on a seesaw
Giving her a merry whirl
When I saw Esau he saw me
And I saw red and got so sore
So I took a saw and I sawed Esau
Off that old seesaw, hey!
I took a saw and I sawed Esau
Off that old seesaw.

The Mule

On mules we find two legs behind
And two we find before
We stand behind before we find
What the two behind be for
When we're behind the two behind
We find what these be for
So stand before the two behind
And behind the two before.

(TUNE: "Auld Lang Syne.")

The Posture Song

Are you a camel, or aren't you a camel?
And say, have you got a hump, hump, hump?
Do you sit at the table just as straight as you're able
Or are you always in a lump, lump, lump?

202

Are you a flopper, a flip-floppy flopper

Without any starch in your spine?

If you are a flopper, a flip-floppy flopper

Please go somewhere else to recline.

(TUNE: "When You Wore a Tulip and I Wore a Big Red Rose.")

The Preposition Song

With on for after at by in

Against instead of near between

Through over up according to

Around among beyond into

Until within without upon

From above across along

Toward before behind below

Beneath beside during under.

(TUNE: "Yankee Doodle.")

No L

A-B-C-D-E-F-G

H-I-J-K-M-N

O-P-Q-R-S-T

U-V-W-X-Y-Z

No L, no L, no L, no L

No L, no L, no L, no L.

(TUNE: "The First Noël," 1833.)

Books of the Old Testament

Genesis, Exodus, Leviticus, Numbers, Deuteronomy
Joshua, Judges, Ruth, and First and Second Samuel
First and Second Kings, and First and Second Chronicles
Ezra, Nehemiah, Esther, Job, and now the book of Psalms.

Proverbs, Ecclesiastes, Song of Solomon
Isaiah, Jeremiah, Lamentations, Ezekiel, Daniel, Hosea
Joel, Amos, Obadiah, Jonah, Micah, Nahum, Habakkuk
Zephaniah, Haggai, Zechariah, Malachi.

Books of the New Testament

Matthew and Mark and Luke and John, Acts, Romans
First and Second Corinthians, Galatians, Ephesians
Philippians, Colossians, First and Second Thessalonians.

First Timothy, Second Timothy, Titus, Philemon and
Hebrews, James, First Peter, Second Peter
Three Johns, Jude, and Revelation.

The States Song

What did Io-way, boys, what did Io-way?
I'm asking you now as a personal friend, what did Io-way?

She weighed a Washing-ton, boys, she weighed a Washing-ton
I'm telling you now as a personal friend, she weighed a Washing-ton.

What did Ida-ho, boys, what did Ida-ho?
I'm asking you now as a personal friend, what did Ida-ho?

She hoed her Mary-land, boys, she hoed her Mary-land
I'm telling you now as a personal friend, she hoed her Mary-land.

How did Flori-die, boys, how did Flori-die?
I'm asking you now as a personal friend, how did Flori-die?

She died in Missou-ri, boys, she died in Missou-ri
I'm telling you now as a personal friend, she died in Missou-ri.

How did Connecti-cut, boys, how did Connecti-cut?
I'm asking you now as a personal friend, how did Connecti-cut?

He cut with his Arkan-saw, boys, he cut with his Arkan-saw
I'm telling you now as a personal friend, he cut with his Arkan-saw.

Where has Ore-gone, boys, where has Ore-gone?
I'm asking you now as a personal friend, where has Ore-gone?

She's taking Okla-home, boys, she's taking Okla-home
I'm telling you now as a personal friend, she's taking Okla-home.

Where else has Ore-gone, boys, where else has Ore-gone?
I'm asking you now as a personal friend, where else has Ore-gone?

She went to pay her Texas, she went to pay her Texas
I'm telling you now as a personal friend, she went to pay her Texas.

What did Dela-wear, boys, what did Dela-wear?
I'm asking you now as a personal friend, what did Dela-wear?

She wore her New Jersey, boys, she wore her New Jersey
I'm telling you now as a personal friend, she wore her New Jersey.

What else did Dela-wear, boys, what else did Dela-wear?
I'm asking you now as a personal friend, what else did Dela-wear?

She wore her North Da-coat, boys, she wore her North Da-coat
I'm telling you now as a personal friend, she wore her North Da-coat.

What did Tenne-see, boys, what did Tenne-see?
I'm asking you now as a personal friend, what did Tenne-see?

She saw what Arkan-saw, boys, she saw what Arkan-saw
I'm telling you now as a personal friend, she saw what Arkan-saw.

What did Missi-sip, boys, what did Missi-sip?
I'm asking you now as a personal friend, what did Missi-sip?

She sipped her Minne-soda, boys, she sipped her Minne-soda
I'm telling you now as a personal friend, she sipped her Minne-soda.

How did Wiscon-sin, boys, how did Wiscon-sin?
I'm asking you now as a personal friend, how did Wiscon-sin?

She stole a New-brass-key, boys, she stole a New-brass-key
I'm telling you now as a personal friend, she stole a New-brass-key.

(TUNE: "It Ain't Gonna Rain No Mo'.")

Overeducated Nursery Rhymes

Row, Row, Row Your Boat

Propel, propel, propel your craft
Smoothly down the liquid solution
Ecstatically, ecstatically, ecstatically, ecstatically
Existence is merely an illusion.

Three Blind Mice

1.

Three decrepit rodents, three decrepit rodents
Observe how they motivate, observe how they motivate
They all pursued the agriculturist's spouse
Who cut off their appendages with a culinary cleaver
Have you ever witnessed such a phenomenon in your existence
As three decrepit rodents?

2.

Three myopic rodents, three myopic rodents
Observe how they perambulate, observe how they perambulate
They all circumnavigated the agriculturist's significant other
Who amputated their extremities with a carving utensil
Did you ever observe such an occurrence in your existence
As three myopic rodents?

3.

Three rodents with serious visual impairments, three rodents with serious visual impairments
Notice the manner in which they perambulate, notice the manner in which they perambulate
They all pursued the agriculturist's spouse
Who dissected their caudal appendanges with a carving utensil
Have you previously witnessed a spasm of events in your era
Similar to three rodents with serious visual impairments?

Twinkle, Twinkle, Little Star

Scintillate, scintillate, globule aurific
Fain would I fathom thy nature specific
Loftily poised in the ether capacious
Strongly resembling a gem carbonacious
Scintillate, scintillate, globule aurific
Fain would I fathom thy nature specific.

Indicate the Way

Indicate the way to my habitual abode
I'm exhausted, I desire to retire
I had a little drink sixty minutes ago
And it went right to my cerebellum
No matter where I may perambulate
My feet won't take me to my domicile
You can always hear me singing this song
Indicate the way to my habitual abode.

(TUNE: "Show Me the Way to Go Home," 1925.)

She Waded in the Water

She waded in the water till she got her toes all wet
She waded in the water till she got her toes all wet
She waded in the water till she got her toes all wet
But she didn't get her [clap, clap] wet yet!

(TUNE: "Battle Hymn of the Republic." Repeat, progressing to feet, ankles, shins, calves, knees, thighs, at which point the song ends with the last line, "She finally got her bathing suit wet." A listener pointed out that the song "is designed to make people who haven't heard it before a trifle uncomfortable, especially in mixed company. She finally gets her bathing suit wet on thighs or hips, depending on the situation.")

Susie Had a Steamboat

Susie had a steamboat, the steamboat had a bell
Miss Susie went to heaven and the steamboat went to
Hello operator, give me number nine
And if you disconnect me I'll kick you in the
Behind the 'frigerator there was a piece of glass
Miss Susie sat upon it and broke her little
Ask me no more questions and I'll tell you no more lies
The boys are in the girls' room, zipping down their
Flies are in the country, bees are in the park
Miss Susie's in the bedroom, kissing in the D-A-R-K, dark.

Key of C

Su - sie had a steam - boat, the steam - boat __ had a bell. Miss
Hell - o, op - er - a - tor, _____ give me __ num - ber nine. And
Be - hind the friger - a - tor _____ There was a piece of glass. Miss
Ask me no more ques - tions and I'll tell you no more lies. The
Flies are in the coun - try, _____ bees are __ in the park. Miss

Su - sie went to heav - en, the steam - boat went to
if you dis - con - nect me, I'll kick you in the
Su - sie sat up - on it and broke her lit - tle
boys are in the girls' room, __ zip - ping down their
Su - sie's in the bed - room, __ kiss - ing in the

D - A - R - K, dark.

Do Your Ears Hang Low?

Do your ears hang low?   [singer dangles hands from ears]
Do they wobble to and fro?   [waves dangling hands to and fro]
Can you tie 'em in a knot?   [mimes tying a large knot]
Can you tie 'em in a bow?   [mimes tying a bow at throat]

Can you throw 'em over your shoulder?   [hands over one shoulder]

Like a continental soldier?   [marches in place stiffly]

Do your ears hang low?   [dangles hands from ears]

Do your ears hang high?   [singer lifts hands up]

Do they wave up in the sky?   [waves hands above head]

Do they crinkle when they're wet?   [hands droop and wave]

Do they straighten when they're dry?   [arms straight overhead]

Can you wave 'em at your neighbor?   [waves hands at audience]

With a minimum of labor?   [waves only fingers at audience]

Do your ears hang high?   [singer finishes with hands up]

(TUNE: "Turkey in the Straw.")

Junior Birdman

Up in the air, Junior Birdman

Up in the air upside down

Is it a bird, plane, or Superman?

No, it's Junior Birdman upside down!

When you hear the great announcement

That his wings are made of tin

Then you will know that Junior Birdman

Has sent his box tops in.

'Cause it takes five box tops, four bottle bottoms

Three labels, two wrappers, and one thin dime

To become a Junior Birdman upside down!

(A listener who learned this at Girl Scout camp explains: "The secret to the Junior Birdman song is that throughout the song, whenever the words *Junior Birdman* are sung (or simply whenever you please) you put on your Junior Birdman mask. To make the mask you form circles with your thumbs and index fingers, holding the ends of your fingers together. Now locate the two outstretched fingers on each hand which are not your pinkies, and put the tips of these fingers under your jawbone palm side to the jaw. Now lift the eyeholes up to your eyes and your mask is complete. It was quite a feat when I was at camp.")

My Hat It Has Three Corners

My hat it has three corners
Three corners has my hat
And if it had not three corners
It would not be my hat.

(TUNE: "The Carnival of Venice," 1854. A listener included these instructions: "The first time through, sing as written. Next time, omit the word *hat* and point to your head. The third time, omit *hat*, point to your head, and omit *three* and hold up three fingers. The last time, omit *hat* and point to your head, omit *three* and hold up three fingers, and omit *corners* and draw a corner in the air with your index finger.")

Bingo

There was a farmer had a dog
And Bingo was his name
B-I-N-G-O
B-I-N-G-O
B-I-N-G-O
And Bingo was his name.

There was a farmer had a dog
And Bingo was his name
B-I-N-G-*
B-I-N-G-*
B-I-N-G-*
And Bingo was his name.

There was a farmer had a dog
And Bingo was his name
B-I-N-*-*
B-I-N-*-*
B-I-N-*-*
And Bingo was his name.

There was a farmer had a dog
And Bingo was his name
B-I-*-*-*
B-I-*-*-*
B-I-*-*-*
And Bingo was his name.

There was a farmer had a dog
And Bingo was his name
B-*-*-*-*
B-*-*-*-*
B-*-*-*-*
And Bingo was his name.

There was a farmer had a dog
And Bingo was his name
--*-*-*
--*-*-*
--*-*-*
And Bingo was his name.

(At the * marks, claps or other appropriate noises replace the letters.)

Jump Rope Rhyme

Sister had a baby
She called it Tiny Tim
She put it in the bathtub
To see if it could swim
He drank up all the water
He ate up all the soap
He tried to eat the bathtub
It wouldn't go down his throat
Mother, Mother, I am ill
Call the doctor over the hill
Mother, Mother, will I die?
Yes, my darling, bye and bye

Mother called the doctor
Doctor called the nurse
The nurse she called the lady
With the alligator purse
In came the doctor
In came the nurse
In came the lady
With the alligator purse
"Measles" said the doctor
"Mumps" said the nurse
"Nothing" said the lady
With the alligator purse.
1-2-3-4-5-6-7-8-9-10

Two players turn the rope for a jumper, keeping time with the spoken rhythm of the verse. At the end of the stanzas, the turners double the speed of the rope, counting to ten. Only the most skillful jumper will keep up with the increased rhythm and continue to clear the rope until the count of ten.

Glub, Glub, Glub Your Boat

Glub, glub, glub your boat
Underneath the stream
Ha, ha, fooled you
I'm a submarine!

(TUNE: "Row, Row, Row Your Boat.")

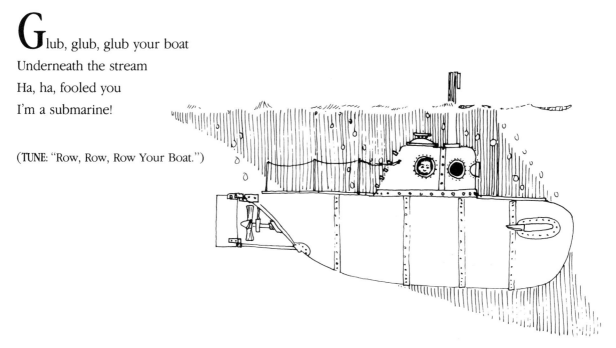

Nonsense Rhymes

1.

One zollom, two zollom
Zigga-zigga zam
Bobtailed tiger
And a tallow lump of tan
Harum-scarum, birds in the airum
Crack-a-bone, eat your meat
Go to bed with dirty feet
Hocka-bocka-ginger blue
Hands and never die.

Ma-hee, ma-hie, ma-hoe
Ma-rum-stum pumpadiddle
Soup-bag pilliwinckle
Sing-song polly
Mitch-a-kime-ee-o.

One re-orey ickery-am
Fillesey follisey Nicholas-John
Queevey-quavey English Navy
Stinkum, stankum, buck!

2.

Sweet Susie Sapple
Cheeks like an apple
Sweet Susie Sapple
Yodely yodely yo!

One-ery two-ery tickery tory
Ala-ma-crackery, crackery majory
Wishy-go-happy, merry-go-lee
Humpty dumpty ninety-three.

Ince swy dry
A lisha lush lie
A lisha lusha poddletusha
Ince swy dry.

Thistle-Sifting

The successful thistle-sifter
In sifting a sieve full of unsifted thistles
Thrust not three thousand thistles through the thick of his thumb.

See that thou in sifting a sieve full of unsifted thistles
Thrust not three thousand thistles through the thick of thy thumb.
Success to the successful thistle-sifter!

Louisiana Rainstorm

One listener sent to the department instructions for an aural activity to be performed by a leader and an audience of about thirty or more participants. The leader shows the audience how to make four different kinds of sounds with hands and feet and then divides them into four groups. Then, in turn, each group produces the sound signaled by the leader and continues to do so until cued by the leader to change to the next sound. As the leader blends and builds the sounds to progressively louder, then progressively softer, levels, the effect is that of hearing a rumbling rainstorm approach and depart. "Louisiana Rainstorm" was performed by the World Theatre audience during one broadcast of the Department of Folk Song, undoubtedly this activity's only radio performance.

"First you show the audience the four actions or sounds, because they are really the performers in this one. Action 1 is for each person to rub the open hands together briskly—that's the sound of the wind. Action 2 is to pat hands on your legs—that's the patter of the rain beginning. Action 3 is to tap with both hands on the back of the seat in front of you (or on any hard surface)—that's the pouring rain. Action 4 is to continue that tapping but to stomp both feet on the floor at the same time—that's the sound of heavy rain and thunder. Alone, these actions sound odd, but together it's great.

"Now that the audience knows what to do, divide them into four groups and just have one group at a time follow the leader. Then, without any words that would spoil the sound of the storm, the leader on stage gives hand signals directing the audience through the storm. During the action, you may pantomime that you cannot hear, and they'll get louder; or you can pantomime 'sh-sh-sh,' and they'll get softer. This also sustains it. Start with group 1 doing Action 1, and keep them doing it while you move on to start each following group, until you come back to group 1 again, and so on, until the storm has passed as quietly as it came. This has worked really well at the University of Virginia and a camp."

Chapter 10

The Peanut Gallery

Folk songs are created and preserved by people who belong to singing communities in which work and play provide opportunities for shared music making. In America's rural past, workers sang outdoors on the job and generations of the extended family sang as they worked together on the farm and in the home. Older collections of folk songs testify to the richness of these singing communities of miners, or lumberjacks, or railroad men, or cowboys, and document songs often handed down for several generations within families.

Our modern world has sadly lost these conditions for creating folk songs. The desk, the cash register, the computer terminal, the truck cab—few workplaces now provide an environment friendly to workers sharing songs. And the mobile, fragmented urban nuclear family appears to share less and less time, apart from staring at the television screen that has replaced the family hearth.

The playground has long been a fertile garden for folk song, however, and on the evidence of songs sent to the Department of Folk Song, it remains so. Children grouped in their schools, teams, and summer camps may even be our last vestige of communities who share time, tasks, and interests sufficient to foster communal music such as singing rounds. Children ten and under sent a surprisingly large number of songs to the Department, and many adults sent songs they recalled from their own childhoods. Consequently, the playground and the summer camp may be the most common social environments represented by the songs in this book.

While children do compose their own songs, probably most "children's songs" were originally made up by adults for children. In this chapter, for instance, "How Do You Like to Go Up in a Swing?" is a fragment of a Robert Louis Stevenson poem. Many songs betray themselves by their diction: what self-respecting child would compose a line such as "I've picked a pretty nosegay," which appears in "This Is My Dolly's Birthday."

But children select, embellish, alter, and pass on to other children only those songs that strongly appeal to them, and so the songs here have passed through a rigorous process of selection which we feel has transformed even the most coy adult creations into folk art representative of children's tastes and needs.

One senses the child's love of drollery in such songs as "I Have a Little Dog" and "Oh My Monster, Frankenstein" and a fascination with mischief in "Four Little Angels," "The Butcher's Legs," "Oh, I Wish I Was A . . . ," and "Once I Went in Swimmin'," the latter four songs apparently devised to test the limits of adult authority figures such as parents and school bus drivers. "Wait for the Wagon," elementary as it is, interestingly pinpoints the very common and specific childhood fear of being eaten up.

The finest and most charming of our childhood songs, though, are the lullabies with which we end the chapter. Alan Lomax has said that the best song makers for children "are

218

the folk, whose rhymes are rubbed clean and hard against the bone of life," and "whose fantasies are heart-warming and fertile because they rise out of billions of accumulated hours of living with and caring for children." In these deceptively simple songs lie the last remnants of the family song tradition, in which the generations collaborate to create and remember tender, vivid images of what William Blake called Innocence and Experience. "Dreamland opens here," sings the Innocence of the lullaby, to which its Experience counters, "In the canebrake the wildcat cries." A child raised on such images will be wise indeed.

Oh My Monster, Frankenstein

In a castle, near a mountain
Near the dark and murky Rhine
Dwelt a doctor, the concoctor
Of the monster, Frankenstein.

Chorus: Oh my monster, oh my monster
Oh my monster, Frankenstein
You were built to last forever
Dreadful scary Frankenstein.

In a graveyard near the castle
Where the moon refused to shine
He dug for noses and for toeses
For his monster, Frankenstein.

Chorus

(TUNE: "Oh, My Darling Clementine.")

Four Little Angels

Four little angels all dressed in white

Tried to get to heaven on the end of a kite

The kite string broke and down the angels fell

Instead of going to heaven they went to

Three little angels dressed in white

Tried to get to heaven on the end of a kite

The kite string broke and down the angels fell

Instead of going to heaven they went to

Two little angels dressed in white

Tried to get to heaven on the end of a kite

The kite string broke and down the angels fell

Instead of going to heaven they went to

One little angel dressed in white

Tried to get to heaven on the end of a kite

The kite string broke and down the angel fell

Instead of going to heaven she went to

Don't get excited, don't lose your head

Instead of going to heaven they went to bed.

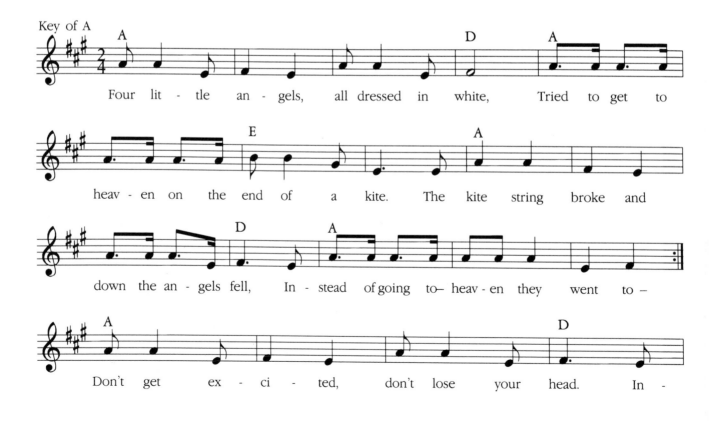

stead   of going   to   heav - en   they   went   to   bed.

The Butcher's Legs

We walked into the butcher's
Where the meat was hung on pegs
The fat old butcher kept shouting out,
"I've got some lovely legs!"

So we all walked into the shop
To shelter from the rain
We lifted his apron and looked at his legs
And we all walked out again.

Key of D

We   walked in - to   the   bu - tcher's, Where   the   meat   was   hung   on

pegs. ____   The   fat   old bu - tcher kept   shout - ing   out,   "I've

got   some love - ly   legs!" ____   So   we   all   walked in - to   the

shop ____   To shelt - er from   the   rain. ____   We   lift - ed his   a - pron and

looked at   his   legs, And   we   all   walked out   a - gain. ____

This Is My Dolly's Birthday

This is my dolly's birthday
She is just one year old
I've picked a pretty nosegay
Which I shall give her to hold
There'll be a birthday party
For which she's written this note:
"Please come to my birthday party,
Yours truly, Dolly," she wrote.

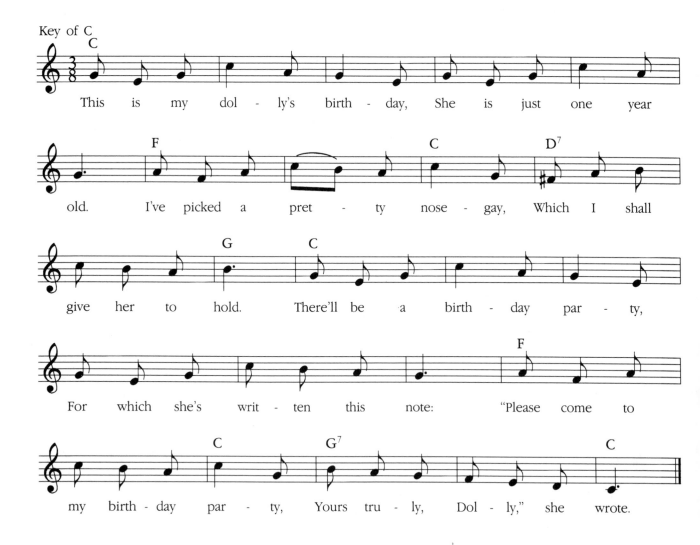

Dolly and Teddy

My dear little dolly
Her eyes are bright blue
She can open and shut them
And she smiles at me too.

Teddy Bear, don't go there
Under Johnny's rocking chair
Teddy Bear, don't go there
You will get an awful scare.

The Dreidel Song

I had a little dreidel
I made it out of clay
And when it's dry and ready
Oh, dreidel I will play
Oh, dreidel, dreidel, dreidel
I made it out of clay
And when it's dry and ready
Oh, dreidel I will play.

All the Pretty Little Horses

Hushabye, don't you cry
Go to sleepy, little baby
When you wake you shall have cake
And all the pretty little horses
Black and bay, dapple and gray
Coach and six little horses.

Way down yonder over in the meadow
There's a poor little lambie
Bees and the butterflies flying 'round his eyes
Make the poor thing cry for mammy.

Mockingbird

My Pa bought me a mockingbird
Tweedle deedle dee

If that mockingbird don't sing
My Pa will buy me a diamond ring

If the diamond ring turns brass
My Pa will buy me a looking-glass

If the looking-glass gets broke
My Pa will buy me a billy goat

If the billy goat bucks me
My Pa will buy me an apple tree

If the apple tree don't bear
My Pa will buy me a Teddy bear

If the Teddy bear gets torn
My Pa will buy me a bugle horn

If the bugle horn makes too much noise
My Pa will buy me some other toys.

I Have a Little Dog

I have a little dog and her name is Candy
She is a very intelligent pup
She can stand up on her hind legs
If you hold the front ones up.

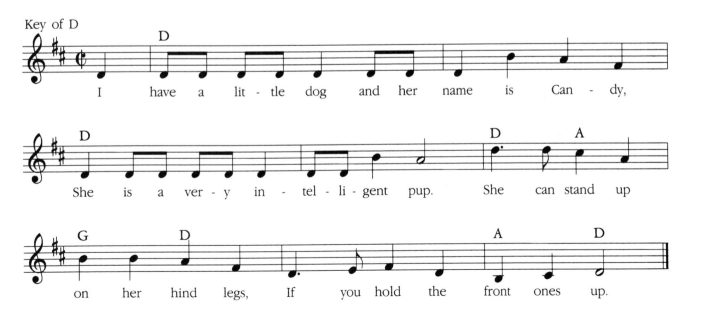

Oh, I Wish I Was A . . .

Oh, I wish I was a little piece of orange
Oh, I wish I was a little piece of orange
I'd go squirty, squirty, squirty
Over everybody's shirty
Oh, I wish I was a little piece of orange.

Oh, I wish I was a little piece of soap
Oh, I wish I was a little piece of soap
I'd go slippery, slippery, slimy
Over everybody's hiney
Oh, I wish I was a little piece of soap.

Oh, I wish I was a little beddy-bug
Oh, I wish I was a little beddy-bug
I'd go bitey, bitey, bitey
Under everybody's nightie
Oh, I wish I was a little beddy-bug.

Oh, I wish I was a little cigarette
Oh, I wish I was a little cigarette
For I'd sit up late at night
And the men would hold me tight
Oh, I wish I was a little cigarette.

Oh, I wish I was a little English sparrow
Oh, I wish I was a little English sparrow
I would sit up in the steeple
And I'd spit on all the people
Oh, I wish I was a little English sparrow.

Oh, I with I wath a wittle thugar bun
Oh, I with I wath a wittle thugar bun
I'd thlippey and I'd thlidey
Into everyone'th inthidey
Oh, I with I wath a wittle thugar bun.

Oh, I with I wath a fithy in the thea
Oh, I with I wath a fithy in the thea
I'd thwim around tho cute
Without a bathing thuit
Oh, I with I wath a fithy in the thea.

How Do You Like to Go Up in a Swing?

How do you like to go up in a swing?
Up in the air so blue?
Oh, I do think it's the pleasantest thing
Ever a child can do.

(From "The Swing," Robert Louis Stevenson, *A Child's Garden of Verses.*)

The North Wind Doth Blow

The North Wind doth blow and we shall have snow
And what will poor Robin do then, poor thing?
He'll sit in the barn to keep himself warm
And hide his head under his wing.

(Published in 1715 edition of *Mother Goose's Melodies*.)

Ring Around the Rosy

Ring around the rosy
A pocketful of posies
Ashes, ashes
We all fall down.

It's Raining, It's Pouring

It's raining, it's pouring
The old man is snoring
He bumped his head and went to bed
And couldn't get up in the morning.

Just When I'm Ready to Start on My Ears

Just when I'm ready to start on my ears
That is the time when my soap disappears
It jumps from my fingers and slithers and slides
Down to the end of the tub where it hides.

(TUNE: "Tell Me Why.")

When Pa Was a Little Boy

When Pa (when Pa), when Pa (when Pa), when Pa was a little boy like me
He used to go a-swimmin' (a-swimmin')
He used to go way up the creek
Where there was no fear of women (of women)
One day (one day), one day (one day), one day somebody came along
And stole ole Pa's apparel (apparel)
Pa stayed in the water all day long
And that night came home in a barrel (a barrel).

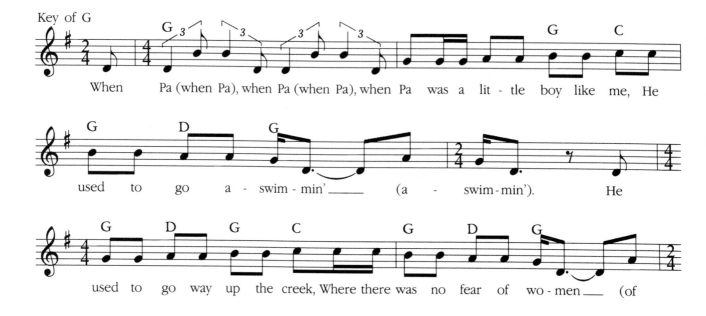

Key of G

When   Pa (when Pa), when Pa (when Pa), when Pa   was a   lit - tle   boy   like   me, He

used   to   go   a - swim - min' _____   (a -   swim-min').   He

used   to   go   way   up   the   creek, Where there was   no   fear   of   wo - men ____   (of

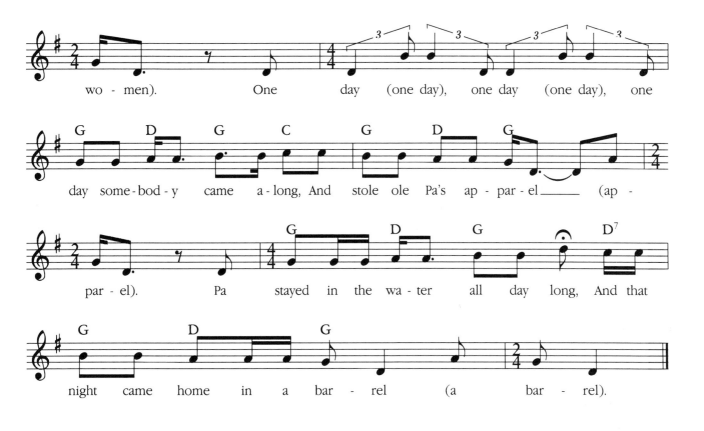

wo - men).   One   day (one day),   one day (one day),   one day some-bod-y came a-long, And stole ole Pa's ap-par-el_____ (ap - par-el).   Pa   stayed in the wa-ter all day long, And that night came home in a bar - rel   (a   bar - rel).

Wait for the Wagon

Wait for the wagon
Wait for the wagon
Wait for the wagon
And we'll all take a ride.

Wait for the dragon
Wait for the dragon
Wait for the dragon
And we'll all be inside.

(TUNE: "Wait for the Wagon," 1851. Popularly parodied during and after the Civil War.)

Wait   for   the   wag - on,   Wait   for   the   wag - on,   Wait   for   the   wag - on,   And   we'll   all   take   a   ride.

Once I Went in Swimmin'

Once I went in swimmin'
Where there were no women
Down beside the sea.

Seeing no one there
I hung my underwear
Upon a willow tree.

Dove into the water
Just like Pharaoh's daughter
Dove into the Nile.

Someone saw me there
And stole my underwear
And left me with just a smile.

What Do You Do with a Dirty Family?

What do you do with a dirty brother?
What do you do with a dirty brother?
What do you do with a dirty brother,
Early in the morning?
Throw him in the lake and wait 'til he's washed up
Throw him in the lake and wait 'til he's washed up
Throw him in the lake and wait 'til he's washed up
Early in the morning.

What do you do with a dirty sister?
Dunk her in the river and dry her with a beach towel.

What do you do with a dirty mommy?
Put her in the washer and push "Full Cycle."

What do you do with a dirty daddy?
I don't know, I've never seen one!

(TUNE: "What Shall We Do with the Drunken Sailor?" published 1891, but the tune was known as early as 1800.)

Ho-Hum, Nobody's Home

Ho-hum, nobody's home
Eat nor drink nor money have I some
When will we be me-eh-eh-ery?

(To be sung as a round.)

Life Is But a Melancholy Flower

Life is but a, life is but a
Melancholy flower, melancholy flower
Life is but a melan, life is but a melan
Choly flower, choly flower.

(TUNE: "Frère Jacques." To be sung as a round.)

One Bottle Pop

One bottle pop, two bottle pop
Three bottle pop, four bottle pop
Five bottle pop, six bottle pop
Seven, seven bottle pop.

Fish and chips and vinegar
Vinegar, vinegar
Fish and chips and vinegar
Pepper, pepper, pepper pot.

Don't throw your junk in my back yard
My back yard, my back yard
Don't throw your junk in my back yard
My back yard's full.

(To be sung as a round.)

Key of G

One bot-tle pop, two bot-tle pop, Three bot-tle pop, four bot-tle pop,

Five bot-tle pop, six bot-tle pop, Sev-en, sev-en bot-tle pop.

Fish and chips and vin-e-gar, Vin-e-gar, vin-e-gar,

Fish and chips and vin-e-gar, Pep-per, pep-per, pep-per pot.

Don't throw your junk in my back yard, My back yard, my back yard,

Don't throw your junk in my back yard, My back yard's full.

My Dame's Crane

My dame has a lame, tame crane

My dame has a crane that is lame

Pray, gentle Jane, may my dame's lame, tame crane

Drink from your well again?

(A round from England.)

Shoo Shoo Shoo Reparoo

Shoo shoo shoo reparoo

Shoo repparum scum

Fillapeppa too

Rats in the skelligan

Zittalatta ling

Zittalatta lingo

BANG-O! [Playfully spank child on bottom.]

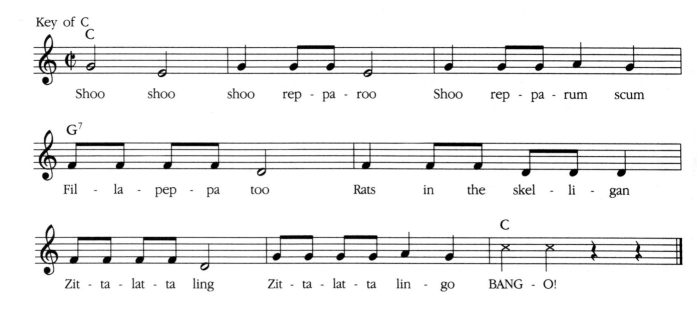

Key of C

Shoo   shoo   shoo   rep - pa - roo   Shoo   rep - pa - rum   scum

Fil - la - pep - pa   too   Rats   in   the   skel - li - gan

Zit - ta - lat - ta   ling   Zit - ta - lat - ta   lin - go   BANG - O!

Charlie, Won't You Rock the Cradle?

Whatcha gonna do with the baby-o?

Whatcha gonna do with the baby-o?

Whatcha gonna do with the baby-o?

Take it to its mammy-o.

Chorus: Charlie, won't you rock the cradle?

Charlie, won't you rock the cradle?

Put him in the cradle and rock him fast
If he won't go to sleep, just smack his face
Put him in the cradle and rock him slow
If he won't go to sleep just let him go.

Chorus

Wrap him up in a tablecloth
Throw him up in the stable loft
If that baby starts to cry
Stick your finger in the baby's eye.

Chorus

Key of D

D

What - cha gon - na do with the ba - by - o?

What - cha gon - na do with the ba - by - o?
Take _____ it _____ to its _____ mam - my - o.

Chorus:

D   A   D

Char - lie, won't you rock the cra - dle? Char - lie, won't you rock the cra - dle?

Go to Sleepy, Little Baby

Go to sleepy, little baby
Go to sleepy, little baby
And when you awake
You will patty-pattycake
Bright and shining in the morning.

Bye, Baby, Bye

The sun has gone from the shining sky
Bye, baby, bye
The flowers are closing their sleepy eyes
Bye, baby, bye
The stars are lighting their lamps to see
That baby and birdie and squirrels all three
Are fast asleep as they all should be
Bye, baby, bye.

The squirrel's dressed in a coat of grey
Bye, baby, bye
He wears it by night as well as by day
Bye, baby, bye
The robin's dressed in feathers and down
With warm red breast and wings of brown
But baby's dressed in a little nightgown
Bye, baby, bye.

The squirrel sleeps in a hole in a tree
Bye, baby, bye
And there he sleeps as snug as can be
Bye, baby, bye
The robin's nest is high overhead
Where leafy boughs of the maple spread
But baby's nest is a little white bed
Bye, baby, bye.

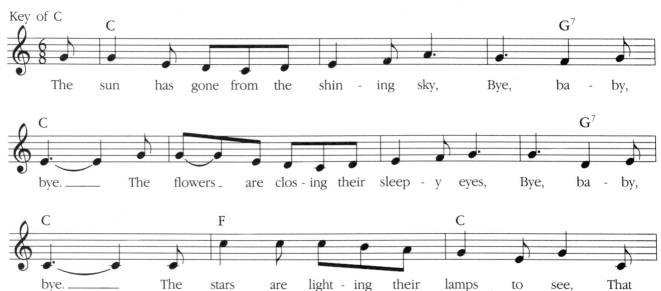

Key of C

The sun has gone from the shin - ing sky, Bye, ba - by,

bye. _____ The flowers _ are clos - ing their sleep - y eyes, Bye, ba - by,

bye. _____ The stars are light - ing their lamps to see, That

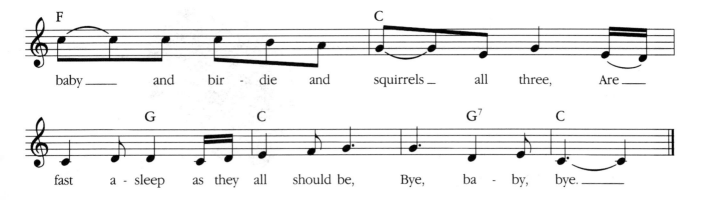

baby ____ and bir - die and squirrels _ all three, Are ____

fast a - sleep as they all should be, Bye, ba - by, bye. ____

My Little Owlet

Rockabye, my little owlet
In thy mossy swaying nest
With thy little woodland brothers
Close thine eyes and take thy rest.

Hushabye, my little owlet
Many voices sing to thee
"Hushabye," the water whispers
"Hush," replies the tall pine tree.

Sleep, oh, sleep, my little owlet
Through our tent the moon shines bright
Like a great eye it will watch thee
Sleep 'til comes the morning light.

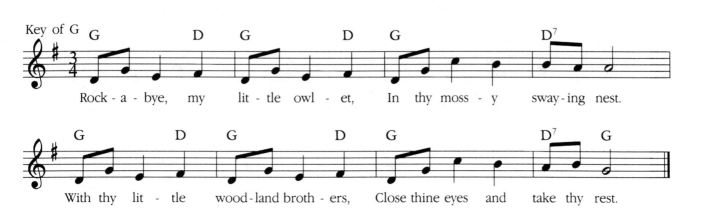

Rock - a - bye, my lit - tle owl - et, In thy moss - y sway - ing nest.

With thy lit - tle wood-land broth - ers, Close thine eyes and take thy rest.

Sail, Baby, Sail

Baby's boat the silver moon
Sailing in the sky
Sailing o'er the sea of sleep
While the clouds float by.

Chorus: Sail, baby, sail
Out upon the sea
Only don't forget to sail
Back again to me.

Baby's fishing for a dream
Fishing near and far
Her line a silver moonbeam is
Her bait a silver star.

Chorus

(Words by Alice C. D. Riley, 1899.)

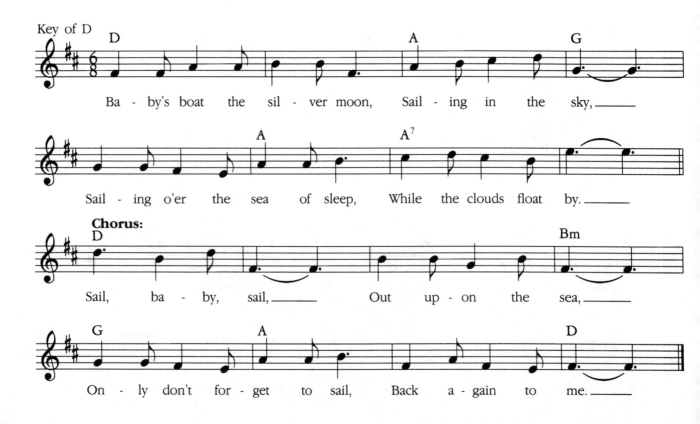

Key of D

Ba - by's boat the sil - ver moon, Sail - ing in the sky,_____

Sail - ing o'er the sea of sleep, While the clouds float by._____

Chorus:

Sail, ba - by, sail,_____ Out up - on the sea,_____

On - ly don't for - get to sail, Back a - gain to me._____

Rock Me to Sleep

Rock me to sleep on a cradle of dreams
Sing me a lullaby of song
Tuck a cloud up under my chin
Lord, blow the moon out, please.

Louisiana Lullaby

Dreamland opens here
Sweep the dream-path clear
Listen, child, dear little child
To the song of the crocodile
To the song of the crocodile.

Dreamland opens here
Sweep the dream-path clear
Listen, child, now close your eyes
In the canebrake the wildcat cries
In the canebrake the wildcat cries.

Dreamland opens here
Sweep the dream-path clear
Listen, child, now listen well
What the tortoise may have to tell
What the tortoise may have to tell.

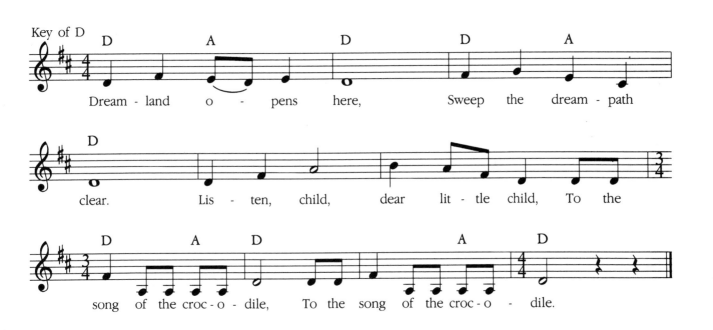

The Little Ole

The little Ole with his umbrella
All children love him, the friendly fellow
He comes unseen and he makes no noise
He puts to bed little girls and boys.

This strange umbrella he spreads above them
It's full of pictures and children love them
And when the child into dreamland sails
He tells them wonderful fairy tales.

He tells of beautiful stars that guide us
Of lovely angels that walk beside us
Of fairies dancing so merrily
That everyone would like to see.

(From a story by Hans Christian Andersen,
originally set to music by O. Jacobsen.)

And all the children who mind their mothers
And always try to be good to others
Shall under Ole's umbrella hear
Sweet angel voices so soft and clear.

When night is over and day is breaking
With rosy cheeks and a smile they waken
A kiss for Mother, a hug for Dad
And thanks to God for the dreams they've had.

Key of D

The lit - tle Ole____ with his um - brel - la, All chil - dren love him, the friend - ly fel - low. He comes un - seen and he makes no noise, He puts to bed____ lit - tle girls and boys.

240

 Chapter 11

The Grab Bag

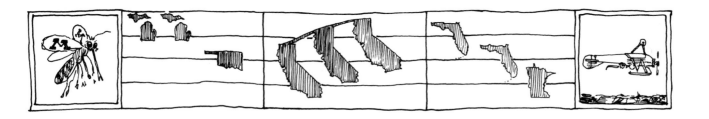

A folk song embodies a paradox in being simultaneously personal (sometimes intensely so) to the singer who learns and perpetuates it, and yet belonging ultimately to the community (or even generations of communities) of which the singer is a member. In the same paradoxical way, a folk song may be at once highly conventional in its structure or sentiments, and yet crankily idiosyncratic in its imagery or language. Thanks to these paradoxes, some songs always elude those bags of tricks played by folklorists and makers of song books: neat categories for their collections. Consequently, most folk song collections include a chapter of "miscellany," songs that seem to fit nowhere else in the scheme of the collection, but which are just too good to leave out. This chapter is our grab bag.

Several of the songs about states or places submitted to the Department follow the fine old American tradition of ridiculing a place (usually just across the nearest state line) where, according to the song, the weather is foul, the work hard, the pay low, and the citizenry none too clever. The nineteenth century produced several such songs about Arkansas, to which our listeners have added their jibes against Alaska, Iowa, Minnesota, the Dakotas, Kansas, Texas, and New Mexico. Much less effective in their vague rhetoric are the boosterish "Birmingham's My Home," "South Dakota Is the Sunshine State," and "We're from Kansas," which seem to reflect the kind of civic cheerleading current in the 1920s.

Our miscellany also includes a classic railroad folk song, "The Rummy Dummy Line," and two songs which originated as pop songs of a couple of generations ago but which may have retained some currency for their various depictions of battles in the war of the sexes, "She Sat on Her Hammock" and "Wait 'Til We Get 'Em Up in the Air, Boys." And how exactly would one categorize the unforgettable "My Pappy's Whiskers," other than as one of the more bizarre portraits of patriarchal nurturing one is likely to encounter? We couldn't decide exactly what the song is, but we certainly couldn't leave it out.

Alaska: Home on the Snow

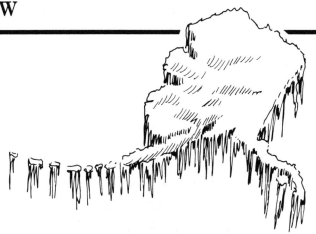

Oh, give me a home
Between Fairbanks and Nome
Where the moose and the caribou play
Where nothing will grow
'Cause it's covered with snow
From June to the following May.

Home, home on the snow
Where it's mild when it's ninety below
But the sun shines for me
By the great Bering Sea
In the life of a gay sourdough.

(TUNE: "Home on the Range," c. 1873.)

When It's Springtime in Alaska

When it's springtime in Alaska
And it's forty-five below
All the Eskimos go barefoot
Because they like the snow.

All the polar bears get sunburned
And the seals all lose their hair
When it's springtime in Alaska
And it's forty-five below up there.

(TUNE: "When It's Springtime in the Rockies," 1929.)

Cape Cod Girls

O h, Cape Cod girls, they have no combs
Heave away, heave away
They comb their hair with codfish bones.

Chorus: Heave away, heave away, heave away, you bully, bully boys
Heave away, heave away, heave away, and don't you make a noise
For we're bound for Australia.

Oh, Cape Cod boys, they have no sleds
Heave away, heave away
They slide down hill on codfish heads.

Chorus

Oh, Cape Cod cats, they have no tails
Heave away, heave away
They blew away in northeast gales.

Chorus

Oh, Cape Cod boats, they have no sails
Heave away, heave away
They sail their boats with codfish tails.

Chorus

(Traditional American sea chantey known as early as 1830.)

Oh, Cape Cod girls, they have no combs, Heave a - way, heave a - way, They

comb their hair with cod - fish bones. Heave a - way, heave a - way, heave a - way, you

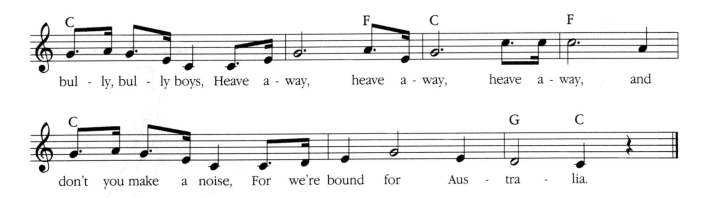

bul - ly, bul - ly boys, Heave a - way, heave a - way, heave a - way, and

don't you make a noise, For we're bound for Aus - tra - lia.

Birmingham's My Home

I'm a lover of the Southland living down in Alabam'
In the fairest of her counties in her favored Birmingham
Garden Spot of dear old Dixie, she has made me what I am
And Birmingham's my home!

Chorus: Dixie, Dixie, how I love you
Dixie, Dixie, how I love you
Dixie, Dixie, how I love you
And Birmingham's my home!

Lying in a level valley bordered by the best of farms
With her mines of coal and iron and the choicest of her charms
Birmingham's a thing of beauty, hugged by nature's rugged arms
And Birmingham's my home!

Chorus

(TUNE: "Battle Hymn of the Republic.")

245

Minnesota!

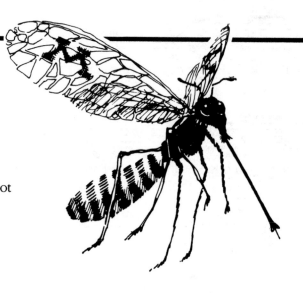

Minnesota!
Where the snoose flies thicker than the snow
And behind each weed, you'll find a Swede
And the winter's forty-two below.
Oh! by jimminy, the fish jump higher than a foot
And mosquitoes grow as big as crow
From Rochester way up to Dulut'.
You can have all your Vermonts and Maines
We got ten thousand lakes when it rains
So if you want recreation
Take your next vacation
In that beautiful land, Minnesota
Minnesota, ya sure!

(TUNE: "Oklahoma!," 1943.)

Oh, Ay Liff in Minneapolis

Oh, Ay liff in Minneapolis, da city of da Svedes
Vere efferybody talk da Svensk ven making known der needs
Vere effery time da sun does shine, it shines upon der veeds
Oh, my Minneapolis!
Minn-e-a-polis foreffer
Minn-e-a-polis foreffer
Ay vould go to Sveden neffer
From dis Minneapolis!

(TUNE: "Battle Hymn of the Republic.")

My Home's in Montana

My home's in Montana, I wear a bandana
My spurs are of silver, my pony is gray
When riding the ranges, my luck never changes
With foot in the stirrup I'll gallop away.

When far from the ranches I chop the pine branches
To heap on the campfire as daylight grows pale
When I have partaken of beans and of bacon
I whistle a merry old song of the trail.

When valleys are dusty, my pony is trusty
He lopes through the blizzard with snow in his ears
The cattle may scatter but what does it matter
My rope is a halter for pig-headed steers.

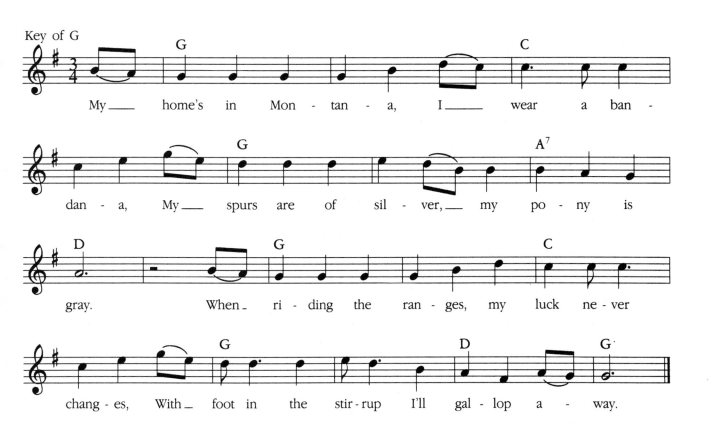

The Nose of Oklahoma Smells You

The nose of Oklahoma smells you
All the livelong day
The nose of Oklahoma smells you
You cannot get away

Always braggin' 'bout your wonders
Always shooting off your mouth
The nose of Oklahoma smells you
Our neighbors to the south.

(TUNE: "The Eyes of Texas Are upon You," published 1903, music based on "I've Been Working on the Railroad.")

Sweet Dakotaland

We've reached the land of drought and heat
Where nothing grows for man to eat
We do not live, we only stay
We are too poor to get away.

Chorus: Dakotaland, sweet Dakotaland!
As on the highest butte I stand
And look away across the plains
And wonder why it never rains
'Til Gideon blows his trumpet sound
And says the rain has gone around.

We have no grain, we have no oats
We have no corn to feed our shoats
The pigs go crying down the lane
They wonder why it never rains.

Chorus

Our horse is of the bronco race
Starvation stares him in the face
God in his mercy give us grace
The people of Dakotaland.

Chorus

Our women are all of one kind
Our women are all of one mind
With balking hands and turned-up nose
They gather chips of buffaloes.

Chorus

Key of G

We've reached the land of drought and heat, Where no - thing grows for

man to eat. We do not live, we on - ly stay, We are too poor to

get a - way. **Chorus:** Da - ko - ta - land, sweet Da - ko - ta - land! As

on the high - est butte I stand And look a - way a -

cross the plains And won - der why it ne - ver rains 'Til

Gid - eon blows his trum - pet sound And says the rain has gone a - round.

South Dakota Is the Sunshine State

South Dakota is the Sunshine State
All the people are feeling great
Sunshine and smiles are our stock in trade
Sunshine and smiles of the very best grade
South Dakota, South Dakota,
That is the Sunshine State.

I Don't Give a Darn for the Whole State of Iowa

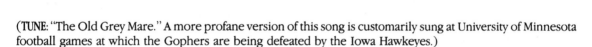

I don't give a darn for the whole state of Iowa
Whole state of Iowa, whole state of Iowa
I don't give a darn for the whole state of Iowa
'Cuz who in the heck likes corn?
Who in the heck likes corn? Who in the heck likes corn?
I don't give a darn for the whole state of Iowa
'Cuz who in the heck likes corn?

(TUNE: "The Old Grey Mare." A more profane version of this song is customarily sung at University of Minnesota football games at which the Gophers are being defeated by the Iowa Hawkeyes.)

New Mexico, We Love You

There is a land of dusty roads
Of rattlesnakes and horny toads
There is a land of dusty roads
Of rattlesnakes and horny toads
The dusty wind forever blows
It never rains, it never snows
How we survive God only knows
New Mexico, we love you.

(TUNE: "O Tannenbaum.")

We're from Kansas

We're from Kansas, dear old Kansas
Where the great big sunflowers grow
Where the girls are pretty
And when you see them smile
You know the reason
You would walk a thousand miles.

Back to Kansas, good old Kansas
Where the skies are blue
Should auld acquaintance be forgot
Kansas, we're all for you!

Key of F

We're from Kan - sas,　　dear old Kan - sas, Where the great big sun-flowers

grow.　Where the girls are pret - ty　And when you see them smile,　You

know the rea - son You would walk a thous - and miles.

Back to Kan - sas,　good old Kan - sas, Where the skies are blue.　Should

auld ac - quain - tance be for - got,　KAN - SAS, WE'RE ALL FOR YOU!

Smiles That Are Best of All

There are smiles in Pennsylvania
There are smiles in Idaho
There are smiles from Maine to California
There are smiles from north to Mexico
There are smiles all over this great nation
There are smiles where'er your footsteps fall
But the smiles you get while in _____
Are the smiles that are best of all!

There are smiles in Minnesota
There are smiles in old Virginie-o
And you'll find them down in dear old Georgia
And in every part of Ohio
There are miles of smiles in Massachusetts
And in Michigan and Tennessee
But the smiles they smile right here in _____
Are the smiles that look good to me.

(TUNE: "Smiles." Listeners who submitted this song advised singers to insert the name of their own home state in the blanks.)

There Are Ships

There are ships that carry rations
There are ships that carry mail
There are ships that carry ammunition
There are ships that only carry sail
There are ships that carry President Wilson
These are mighty giants of the foam
But I'd trade them all for just a rowboat
If that rowboat would carry me home.

(TUNE: "Smiles.")

253

The Rummy Dummy Line

Oh, across the prairie on a streak of rust
There is something coming in a cloud of dust
It rolls into the village with a wheeze and a whine
It's the five o'clock flyer on the Rummy Dummy Line.

Chorus: On the Rummy Line, on the Dummy Line
        Rise and shine and pay your fine
        Rise and shine and pay your fine
        When you're riding with the dummies on the Rummy Dummy Line.

Oh, I got on the Dummy and I couldn't pay my fare
The conductor said, "What are you doing there?"
He took me by the collar and he showed me to the door
And said, "I don't want to see you on the Dummy anymore."

Chorus

Oh, three old ladies all dressed in brown
Got on the Dummy at a little old town
"The seats are all taken," said one with a frown
So [sing a friend's name] got up and they all sat down.

Chorus

Oh, I saw a snail go a-whizzing past
A guy says, "My, this train is fast."
Says I, "Old man, that may be true
But the question is, What is it fast to?"

Chorus

I said to the conductor, "Can't you speed it up a bit?"
He said, "You can walk if you don't like it"
Says I, "Old man, I'd take your dare
But the folks don't expect me 'til the train gets there."

Chorus

Key of C

Oh, a - cross the prair - ie on a streak of rust, There is

some - thing com - ing in a cloud of dust. It

rolls in - to the vil - lage with a wheeze and a whine, It's the

five - o' - clock fly - er on the Rum - my Dum - my Line.

Chorus: On the Rum - my Line, on the Dum - my Line ____ Rise and shine and

pay your fine, Rise and shine and pay your fine, When you're

rid - ing with the dum - mies on the Rum - my Dum - my Line.

Never Go Camping on Labor Day

Fee-fi-fiddly-fay
Never go camping on Labor Day
Fee-fi-fiddly-foo
Take your raincoat if you do.

Johnny Macree

The days are short and the nights are long
And the wind is nipping cold
The tasks are hard and the sums are wrong
And the teachers often scold
But Johnny Macree, oh, what cares he
As he whistles along the way
As he whistles along the way
"It will all come right by tomorrow night,"
Says Johnny Macree today.

The plums are few and the cake is plain
And the shoes are out at toe
For coins you look in the purse in vain
They were all spent long ago
But Johnny Macree, oh, what cares he
As he whistles along the street
As he whistles along the street
"Would you have the blues for a pair of shoes
When you still have a pair of feet?"

She Sat on Her Hammock

She sat on her hammock and strummed her guitar
Strummed her guitar, strummed her guitar
She sat on her hammock and strummed her guitar
Strummed her guitar.

He sat down beside her and smoked his cigar
Smoked his cigar, smoked his cigar
He sat down beside her and smoked his cigar
Smoked his cigar.

He told her he loved her but oh, how he lied
Oh, how he lied, oh, how he lied
He told her he loved her but oh, how he lied
Oh, how he lied.

They were to be married but she up and died
She up and died, she up and died
They were to be married but she up and died
She up and died.

She went up to heaven and flip-flop she flied
Flip-flop she flied, flip-flop she flied
She went up to heaven and flip-flop she flied
Flip-flop she flied.

He went down to Hades and sizzled and fried
Sizzled and fried, sizzled and fried
He went down to Hades and sizzled and fried
Sizzled and fried.

And that's what will happen to men who have lied
Men who have lied, men who have lied
And that's what will happen to men who have lied
Men who have lied.

(TUNE: "Oh, How He Lied.")

Wait 'Til We Get 'Em Up in the Air, Boys

Sometimes you try to love a girl
And she says "No" to you
It makes you feel so blue
But there's nothing you can do
You take her for an auto ride
And start the mushy talk
And then if you get fresh with her
She'll get out and start to walk
They've fooled us ever since the world began
But listen, boys, I've got a brand-new plan:

Chorus: Wait 'til we get 'em up in the air, boys
Wait 'til we get 'em up in the air
You can make them hug and squeeze you too
For if they don't, just say you won't come down until they do
So wait 'til we get 'em up in the clouds, boys
There won't be anyone to watch you there
Now you can loop the loop 'til she can hardly get her breath
It isn't hard to reason with a girl that's scared to death
So wait 'til we get 'em up in the air, boys
Up, up, up, up, way up, up in the air.

Do you remember when you took a girlie out to dine?
You used to buy her wine 'cause it made her feel so fine
She'd always hug and kiss you 'cause she felt so light and gay
And I suppose you're worried since they took the wine away
But boys it's not as bad as you expect
An aero ride will have the same effect:

Chorus

(Words by Lew Brown, music by Albert Von Tilzer, 1919.)

Key of G

Some - times you try to love a girl, And she says "No" to you. It

makes you feel so blue, But there's noth-ing you can do. You take her for an au - to ride, And

start the mush-y talk. And then if you get fresh with her, She'll get out and start to walk. They've

fooled us ev - er since the world be - gan, But lis - ten, boys, I've got a brand - new plan:

Chorus:

Wait 'til we get 'em up in the air, boys, Wait 'til we get 'em up in the

air. You can make them hug and squeeze you, too, For

if they don't, just say you won't come down un - til they do. So wait 'til we get 'em up in the

clouds, boys, There won't be an - y - one to watch you there. Now

you can loop the loop 'til she can hard - ly get her breath. It is - n't hard to rea - son with a

259

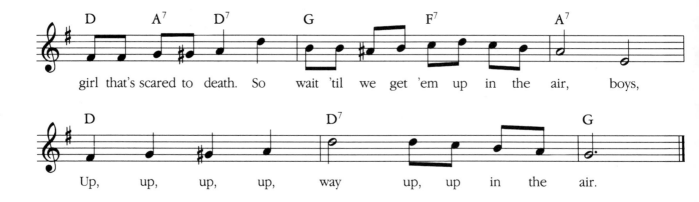

girl that's scared to death. So wait 'til we get 'em up in the air, boys,

Up, up, up, up, way up, up in the air.

When We Went to Sunday School

When your ma was teacher and my pa was preacher

We went to Sunday School

Over my hymnbook I looked at you

I caught you peeping too

When your dear old mother said, "Love one another"

We thought it a wonderful rule

But you're sweeter today than you were, dearie

When we went to Sunday School.

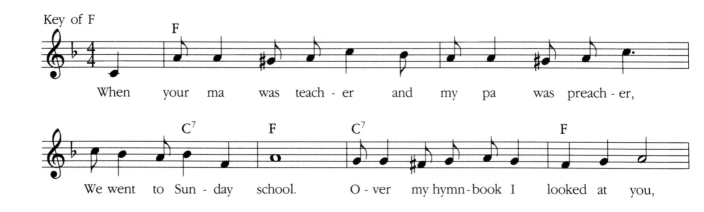

When your ma was teach - er and my pa was preach - er,

We went to Sun - day school. O - ver my hymn - book I looked at you,

I caught you peep - ing too. When your dear old moth - er said,

"Love one an - oth - er," We thought it a won - er - ful rule. But you're

sweet - er to - day than you were, dear - ie, When we went to Sun - day School.

I Ain't Got No Money

Oh, I ain't got no money
No M-O-N-E-Y
I'm busted, disgusted
Financially embarrassed
I haven't got a solitary C-E-N-T
When I think of the old folks
Lordy, how I sigh
'Cause I ain't got no money
No M-O-N-E, M-O-N-E, M-O-N-E-Y.

My Pappy's Whiskers

I have a dear old Pappy for whom I nightly pray
And he has got some whiskers that are always in the way.

Chorus: Oh, they're always in the way
The cows eat them for hay
They hide the dirt on Pappy's shirt
But they're always in the way.

And when we have our breakfast no cereal do we eat
We chew on Pappy's whiskers 'cuz they're just like shredded wheat.

Chorus

At night when we are sleeping no blankets do we need
We use our Pappy's whiskers, oh, yes we do indeed.

Chorus

Our Pappy went out walking and the wind was blowing hard
It blew his whiskers 'cross the street into the neighbor's yard.

Chorus

Our Pappy fought in Flanders but he wasn't killed you see
His whiskers looked like bushes and fooled the enemy.

Chorus

And when the bill collector my Pappy comes to see
He wraps his whiskers 'round him and imitates a tree.

Chorus

And when my little sister has nothing else to do
She sits on Pappy's whiskers to watch the old man chew.

Chorus

When Pappy's playing baseball and lands on second base
Poor old Pappy's whiskers are still in the batter's face.

Chorus

My Pappy went out sailing and the wind blew down the mast
He held his whiskers in the air, the boat went twice as fast.

Chorus

My Pappy worked in a brewery but no filters did they use
His whiskers came in handy for straining out the booze.

Chorus

Chapter 12

Sweet Sentiments and Old Favorites

Now it's time for some serious singing. We have collected in this chapter those songs sent to the Department which most readers will recognize and be able to sing, and a few others which we hope might be on their way to wider recognition.

If we knew exactly how these songs have become as widely known as they are, we would be able to write a most interesting study. Take "Oh, My Darling Clementine," for example. We would hazard three observations about this song. First, most readers of this book will be able to sing correctly from memory at least the chorus of "Clementine," and with help from the printed lyrics, will be able successfully to perform the song in its entirety on first try. Second, probably none of these readers will have ever seen Percy Montrose's original 1884 music and lyrics. Third, very few of those who can sing any part of "Clementine" will be able to say exactly where, when, how, and from whom they first heard it. Was it from that guitar-strumming counselor beside the scout camp fire, or was it in fourth grade from the class songbook? Was it at a hootenanny at college, or from the soundtrack of a John Ford western on late night TV? Or does that familiar refrain seem to echo within your bones, as though you had been born with it inside you?

Few Americans now belong to a stable community in which songs are handed down from person to person over the generations. In our media-dominated society, songs survive for long periods and gain wide currency only to the extent that they pass from circulation among amateur or "folk" musicians into circulation by the media in refurbished or refreshed versions and back again for further circulation at the folk level.

In the case of "Clementine," we know that although it perhaps was based on older material, it was first published in sheet music in 1884, a part of the self-conscious mythologizing of the West, along with the Buffalo Bill Wild West Show and Ned Buntline pulp stories. Over the years, people very likely began to sing it from memory and to pass it on to other singers. By the 1930s, country singers such as Bradley Kincaid had revived and recorded the song as part of the new phenomenon of "country and western" music, and people began to learn the song anew from the radio and from recordings. By the 1960s, the song was again revived and recorded by The Weavers and other groups as part of the hootenanny singalong craze, from which, again, people began to sing the song on their own.

We suspect that many of the songs in this chapter share histories similar to that of "Clementine," moving in and out of the streams of popular and folk musics until they attain that "in the bones" feeling of familiarity with which most of us will recognize them—certainly not the classic mother-to-daughter model of folk song transmission, but as close to a pure folk tradition as modern TV-watching, Walkman-wearing Americans are likely to get.

We close, inevitably, with "Tell Me Why," the favorite singalong of "A Prairie Home Companion" audiences in the World Theater, and a song which the broadcast has very probably revitalized in the modern "folk tradition." Exactly where and when did *you* first hear "Tell Me Why"? Was it from the guitar-strumming camp counselor beside the camp fire, or was it from an older sister as you were helping her do the dishes, or were you both doing dishes while "A Prairie Home Companion" was coming in over the kitchen radio? It really doesn't matter— sing it with us! Before you know it, the song's sweet sentiments will settle in your bones, and you will neither know nor care how they got there.

Billy Boy

"Where have you been, Billy boy, Billy boy,
Where have you been, charming Billy?"
"Oh, I've been to see my wife, she's the darling of my life,
But she's a young thing, and cannot leave her mother."

"Can she bake a cherry pie, Billy boy, Billy boy,
Can she bake a cherry pie, charming Billy?"
"She can bake a cherry pie quick as a cat can wink its eye
But she's a young thing, and cannot leave her mother."

"How old is she, Billy boy, Billy boy,
How old is she, charming Billy?"
"She is three times seven, twenty-two and eleven
But she's a young thing, and cannot leave her mother."

"Will she wed you in the spring, Billy boy, Billy boy,
Will she wed you in the spring, charming Billy?"
"We'll be married in the spring, that is why I must sing,
She'll be mine and I'll never have another."

(Traditional English folk song known as early as 1824.)

Brother John

Are you sleeping,
Are you sleeping,
Brother John,
Brother John?

Morning bells are ringing
Morning bells are ringing
Ding, dong, ding
Ding, dong, ding.

(To be sung as a round.)

White Coral Bells

White coral bells upon a slender stalk
Lilies-of-the-valley line my garden walk
Oh, don't you wish that you could hear them ring?
That will happen only when the angels sing.

(To be sung as a round.)

Old Folks at Home

Way down upon the Swanee River
Far, far away
There's where my heart is turning ever
There's where the old folks stay
All up and down the whole creation
Sadly I roam
Still longing for the old plantation
And for the old folks at home.

Chorus: All the world is sad and dreary
Everywhere I roam
Oh, brothers, how my heart grows weary
Far from the old folks at home.

All round the little farm I wandered
When I was young
There many happy days I squandered
Many the songs I sung
When I was playing with my brothers
Happy was I
Oh, take me to my kind old mother
There let me live and die.

Chorus

(Words and music by Stephen Foster, 1851.)

Little Brown Jug

My wife and I lived all alone
In a little log hut we called our own
She loved gin and I loved rum
And I tell you we had lots of fun.

Chorus: Ho, ho, ho, you and me
        Little brown jug, don't I love thee?
        Ho, ho, ho, you and me
        Little brown jug, don't I love thee?

As I go toiling o'er the farm
Little brown jug goes under my arm
Sits me down by a shady tree
No one there but you and me.

Chorus

(Words and music by Joseph E. Winner, 1869.)

Camptown Races

The Camptown ladies sing this song
Doo-dah, doo-dah!
The Camptown racetrack's five miles long
Oh, de-doo-dah-day!
I went down there with my hat caved in
Doo-dah, doo-dah!
I came back home with a pocket full of tin
Oh, de-doo-dah-day!

Chorus: Goin' to run all night
Goin' to run all day
I bet my money on the bob-tailed mare
Somebody bet on the bay.

Old muley cow come on the track
Doo-dah, doo-dah!
The bobtail fling her over her back
Oh, de-doo-dah-day!
Then fly along like a railroad car
Doo-dah, doo-dah!
Running a race with a shooting star.
Oh, de-doo-dah-day!

Chorus

See them flying on a ten-mile heat
Doo-dah, doo-dah!
Round the racetrack, then repeat
Oh, de-doo-dah-day!
I win my money on the bobtailed nag
Doo-dah, doo-dah!
I keep my money in an old tow bag.
Oh, de-doo-dah-day!

Chorus

(Words and music by Stephen Foster, 1850.)

Crawdad

You get a line and I'll get a pole, honey
You get a line and I'll get a pole, oh babe
You get a line and I'll get a pole
And we'll go down to the crawdad hole
Honey, oh baby mine.

Yonder comes a man with a pack on his back, honey
Yonder comes a man with a pack on his back, oh babe
Yonder comes a man with a pack on his back
Packin' all the crawdads he can pack
Honey, oh baby mine.

I sell my crawdads three for a dime, honey
I sell my crawdads three for a dime, oh babe
I sell my crawdads three for a dime
Your crawdads ain't so good as mine
Honey, oh baby mine.

Whatcha gonna do when the hole runs dry, honey
Whatcha gonna do when the hole runs dry, oh babe
Whatcha gonna do when the hole runs dry
Set there and watch the crawdads die
Honey, oh baby mine.

The old duck done said to the drake, honey
The old duck done said to the drake, oh babe
The old duck done said to the drake
Ain't no more crawdads in this lake
Honey, oh baby mine.

You get a line and I'll get a pole, honey
You get a line and I'll get a pole, oh babe
You get a line and I'll get a pole
And we'll go down to the crawdad hole
Honey, oh baby mine.

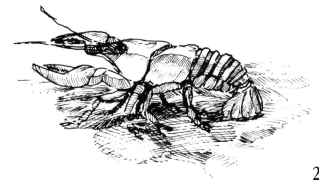

Clementine

In a cavern, in a canyon
Excavating for a mine
Dwelt a miner, forty-niner
And his daughter Clementine.

Chorus: Oh my darling, oh my darling
Oh my darling Clementine
You are lost and gone forever
Dreadful sorry, Clementine.

Light she was and like a feather
Though her shoes were number nine
Herring boxes without topses
Sandals made for Clementine.

Chorus

Drove she ducklings to the water
Every morning just at nine
Stubbed her toe upon a splinter
Fell into the foaming brine.

Chorus

In a churchyard, in a canyon
Where the ivy doth entwine
There are roses and other posies
Fertilized by Clementine.

Chorus

In my dreams she used to haunt me
Clad in seaweed wet with brine
When alive I used to hug her
Now she's dead, I draw the line.

Chorus

(Original words and music by Percy Montrose, 1884.)

Jesse James

Jesse James was a lad who killed many a man
He robbed the Glendale train
He stole from the rich and he gave to the poor
He'd a heart and a hand and a brain.

Chorus: Poor Jesse had a wife to mourn for his life
          Three children they were brave
          But that dirty little coward that shot Mr. Howard
          Has laid poor Jesse in his grave.

For it was Robert Ford, that dirty little coward
I wonder how he feels
For he ate of Jesse's bread and slept in Jesse's bed
Then he laid Jesse James in his grave.

Chorus

It was on a Wednesday night and the moon was shining bright
When they stopped the Glendale train
And the people they did say for many miles away
It was robbed by Frank and Jesse James.

Chorus

It was on a Saturday night when Jesse was at home
Talking to his family brave
Robert Ford came along like a thief in the night
And he laid poor Jesse in his grave.

Chorus

The people held their breath when they heard of Jesse's death
And wondered how he ever came to die
It was one of the gang called little Robert Ford
That shot Jesse James on the sly.

Chorus

Polly-Wolly-Doodle

Oh, I went down south for to see my gal
Sing polly-wolly-doodle all the day
My Sal, she is a spunky gal
Sing polly-wolly-doodle all the day.

Chorus: Fare thee well, fare thee well
    Fare thee well my fairy fay
    For I'm going to Louisiana for to see my Suzianna
    Sing polly-wolly-doodle all the day.

Oh, my Sal she is a maiden fair
Sing polly-wolly-doodle all the day
With curly eyes and laughing hair
Sing polly-wolly-doodle all the day.

Chorus

Behind the barn, down on my knees
Sing polly-wolly-doodle all the day
I thought I heard a chicken sneeze
Sing polly-wolly-doodle all the day.

Chorus

It sneezed so hard with the whooping cough
Sing polly-wolly-doodle all the day
It sneezed its head and tail right off
Sing polly-wolly-doodle all the day.

Chorus

Goodbye, Old Paint

Goodbye, old Paint, I'm a-leavin' Cheyenne
I'm a-leavin' Cheyenne, I'm off for Montan
I'm a-ridin' old Paint, I'm a-leadin' old Fan
Goodbye, little Annie, I'm a-leavin' Cheyenne.

Oh, hitch up your horses and feed them some hay
And seat yourself by me as long as you stay
My horses ain't hungry, they won't eat your hay
I'll ride on a little further and feed 'em on the way.

Go Tell Aunt Rhody

Go tell Aunt Rhody
Go tell Aunt Rhody
Go tell Aunt Rhody
Her old gray goose is dead.

The one she's been saving
The one she's been saving
The one she's been saving
To make a feather bed.

It died in the millpond
It died in the millpond
It died in the millpond
Standing on its head.

It died on a Friday
It died on a Friday
It died on a Friday
With a cold in its head.

She'll Be Comin' 'Round the Mountain

She'll be comin' 'round the mountain when she comes
She'll be comin' 'round the mountain when she comes
She'll be comin' 'round the mountain
She'll be comin' 'round the mountain
She'll be comin' 'round the mountain when she comes.

Subsequent stanzas:

She'll be riding six white horses when she comes
She will carry three red roses when she comes
She'll be wearing pink pajamas when she comes
She'll be hootin' and a-tootin' when she comes

I Wish I Was Single Again

I wish I was single again
I wish I was single again
For when I was single, my pockets did jingle
I wish I was single again.

I married a wife, I did
I married a wife, I did
I married a wife, she's the joy of my life
But I wish I was single again.

My wife made some bread, she did
My wife made some bread, she did
My wife made some bread, it was heavy as lead
I wish I was single again.

My wife made some pie, she did
My wife made some pie, she did
My wife made some pie, I thought I would die
I wish I was single again.

My wife made some jam, she did
My wife made some jam, she did
My wife made some jam, it wasn't worth—ten cents
I wish I was single again.

My wife she died, she did
My wife she died, she did
My wife she died and I laughed 'til I cried
Just to think I was single again.

I married another, I did
I married another, I did
I married another, she's the devils' grandmother
And I wish I was single again.

She beat me, she banged me, she did
She beat me, she banged me, she did
She beat me, she banged me, she swore she would hang me
Now I wish I was single again.

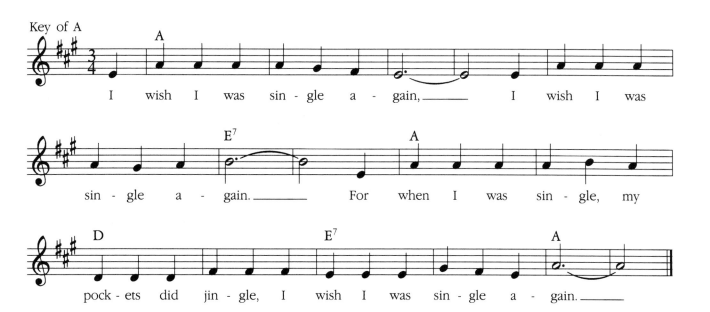

Over the River and Through the Woods

Over the river and through the woods
To Grandmother's house we go
The horse knows the way to carry the sleigh
Through the white and drifted snow
Over the river and through the woods
Oh, how the wind does blow!
It stings the toes and bites the nose
As over the ground we go.

Over the river and through the woods
To have a first-rate play
Oh, hear the bells ring, ting-a-ling-ling,
Hurrah for Thanksgiving Day!
Over the river and through the woods
Trot fast, my dapple grey
Spring over the ground like a hunting hound
For this is Thanksgiving Day.

Over the river and through the woods
And straight through the barnyard gate
We seem to go extremely slow
It is so hard to wait
Over the river and through the woods
Now Grandmother's cap I spy
Hurrah for the fun! Is the pudding done?
Hurrah for the pumpkin pie!

(Words by Lydia Marie Child.)

Long, Long Ago

Tell me the tales that to me were so dear
Long, long ago, long, long ago
Sing me the songs I delighted to hear
Long, long ago, long ago
Now you are come, all my grief is removed
Let me forget that so long you have roved
Let me believe that you love as you loved
Long, long ago, long ago.

Do you remember the path where we met?
Long, long ago, long, long ago
Ah, yes, you told me you'd never forget
Long, long ago, long ago
Then to all others my smile you preferred
Love when you spoke gave a charm to each word
Still my heart treasures the praises I heard
Long, long ago, long ago.

Though by your kindness my fond hopes were raised

Long, long ago, long, long ago

You by more eloquent lips have been praised

Long, long ago, long ago

But by long absence your truth has been tried

Still to your accents I listen with pride

Blest as I was when I sat by your side

Long, long ago, long ago.

(By Thomas Haynes Bayly, 1833.)

The Titanic

Oh, they built the ship Titanic to sail the ocean blue
And the people said the water would never get through
But the Lord with mighty hand said that ship will never land
It was sad when the great ship went down.

Chorus: It was sad (it was sad), it was sad (it was sad)
It was sad when that great ship went down (to the bottom of the)
Husbands and wives, little children lost their lives
It was sad when the great ship went down.

Oh, they started out from England and headed for the shore
But the rich refused to 'sociate with the poor
So they put 'em down below where they'd be the first to go
It was sad when the great ship went down.

Chorus

Oh, they put the lifeboats out on the cruel and raging sea
And the band kept playing "Nearer My God to Thee"
And the little children cried as the water swept inside
It was sad when the great ship went down.

Chorus

Well, the moral of this story as you can plainly see
Is to wear a life preserver when you go out to sea
The Titanic didn't make it though mighty as could be
It was sad when the great ship went down.

Chorus

Key of D

Oh, they built the ship Ti - tan - ic to sail the o - cean blue, And the

peo - ple said the wa - ter would nev - er get through, But the

Lord with might - y hand said that ship will nev - er land, It was

sad — when the great — ship went down. It was sad (it was sad), it was

sad (it was sad), It was sad when that great — ship went

down (to the bot - tom of the), Hus - bands and wives, lit - tle

chil - dren lost their lives, It was sad — when the great — ship went down.

When the Work's All Done This Fall

A group of jolly cowboys discussing plans at ease
Says one, "I'll tell you something, if you will listen, please,
I am an old cowpuncher and here I'm dressed in rags
And I used to be a tough one and take on great big jags.

"But I've got a home, boys, a good one, you all know
Although I have not seen it since long, long ago
I'm going back home, boys, once more to see them all
Yes, I'm going to see my mother when the work is done this fall.

"After the round-up is over and after the shipping is done
I'm going right straight home, boys, ere all my money is gone
I have changed my ways, boys, and no more will I fall
And I am going home, boys, when the work is done this fall.

"When I left home, boys, my mother for me cried
Begged me not to go, boys, for me she would have died
My mother's heart is breaking, breaking for me, that's all
And with God's help I'll see her when the work is done this fall."

That very night this cowboy went out to stand his guard
The night was dark and cloudy and storming very hard
The cattle they got frightened and rushed in wild stampede
The cowboy tried to head them, riding at full speed.

While riding in the darkness, so loudly did he shout
Trying his best to head them and turn the herd about
His saddlehorse did stumble and on him did fall
The poor boy won't see his mother when the work is done this fall.

They picked him up so gently and laid him on a bed
His body was so mangled the boys all thought him dead
He opened wide his blue eyes and, looking all around,
He motioned to his comrades to sit near him on the ground.

"Boys, send Mother my wages, the wages I have earned
For I am afraid, boys, my last steer I have turned
I'm going to a new range, I hear my master call
And I'll not see my mother when the work is done this fall.

"Fred, you take my saddle; George, you take my bed;
Bill, you take my pistol after I am dead,
And think upon me kindly when you look on them all
For I'll not see my mother when the work is done this fall."

Poor Charlie was buried at sunrise, no tombstone at his head
Nothing but a little board and this is what it said:
"Charlie died at daybreak, he died from a fall,
And he'll not see his mother when the work is done this fall."

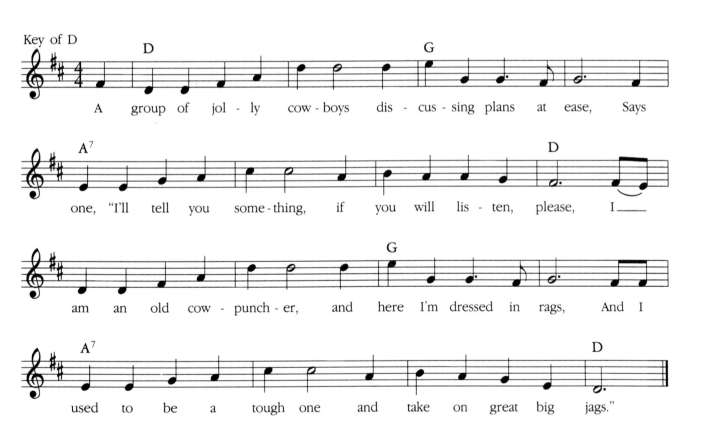

Key of D

D   G
A group of jol - ly cow - boys dis - cus - sing plans at ease, Says

A⁷   D
one, "I'll tell you some - thing, if you will lis - ten, please, I____

                                         G
am an old cow - punch - er, and here I'm dressed in rags, And I

A⁷   D
used to be a tough one and take on great big jags."

The Soldier's Poor Little Boy

The snow was fastly falling
And the night was coming on
When a poor little boy half-frozen
Crept up to the rich lady's door.
He happened to spy at her window so high
What filled his heart with joy
"Oh, for mercy's sake, some pity on me take,
I'm a soldier's poor little boy.

"My mother died when I was young
And my father went to the war
He fought in many a battle brave
And was covered with wounds and scars.
For many a mile in his knapsack
He carried me with joy
But now I'm left quite parentless
I'm a soldier's poor little boy.

"The snow is fastly falling
And the night is coming on
And if you don't protect me
I'll perish before the storm.
And that would grieve your innocent heart
Your piece of mind destroy
To find in the morn, dead at your door,
A soldier's poor little boy."

The rich lady rose from her window so high
And opened to him the door,
"Come in, my poor unfortunate child,
You never shall roam anymore.
My son, my son, my son was slain
My pride and all my joy
And so long as I live a shelter I shall give
To a soldier's poor little boy."

(A listener who sent this song writes, "My mother was one of a large family and several of her great-uncles had served in the Civil War. At family gatherings my Uncle Dwight would often be asked to sing this song and he would do so with great feeling. I can remember tears rolling down my cheeks as I listened.")

Key of F

The snow was fast - ly fall - ing, And the night was com - ing — on, When a poor lit - tle boy half - fro - zen, Crept up to the rich la - dy's door. He hap - pened to spy at her

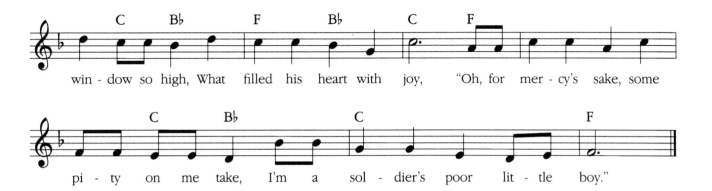

win - dow so high, What filled his heart with joy, "Oh, for mer - cy's sake, some

pi - ty on me take, I'm a sol - dier's poor lit - tle boy."

Babes in the Woods

Oh, don't you remember a long time ago
When two little babes, their names I don't know
Went strolling away one bright summer's day
Got lost in the woods, I heard people say
Poor babes in the woods.

And when it was night, so sad was their plight
The moon had gone down and the stars gave no light
They sobbed and they sighed and they bitterly cried
Poor babes, they lay down and died
Poor little babes in the woods.

And when they were dead, the robins so red
Took mulberry leaves and over them spread
All the night long the branches among
They mournfully whistled and this was their song
Poor babes in the woods.

(A version of this song was registered as a street ballad in London in 1595.)

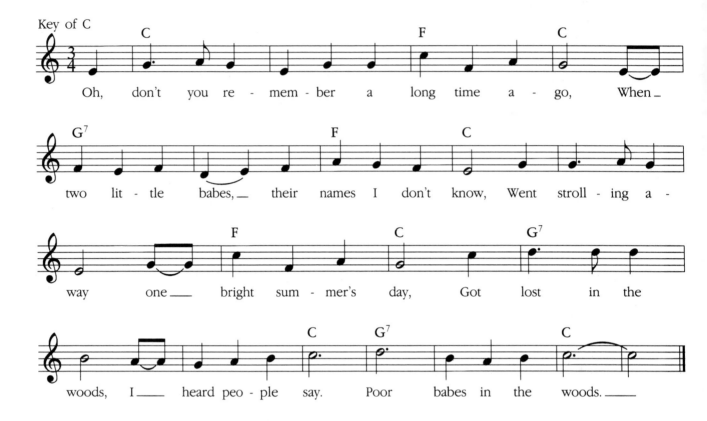

Key of C

C   F   C

Oh, don't you re - mem - ber a long time a - go, When

G⁷   F   C

two lit - tle babes, — their names I don't know, Went stroll - ing a -

F   C   G⁷

way one — bright sum - mer's day, Got lost in the

C   G⁷   C

woods, I — heard peo - ple say. Poor babes in the woods. —

Sweet and Low

Sweet and low, sweet and low
Wind of the western sea
Low, low, breathe and blow
Wind of the western sea
Over the rolling waters go
Come from the dying moon and blow
Blow him again to me
While my little one
While my pretty one sleeps.

Sleep and rest, sleep and rest

Father will come to thee soon

Rest, rest on Mother's breast

Father will come to thee soon

Father will come to his babe in the nest

Silver sails all out of the west

Under the silver moon

Sleep, my little one

Sleep, my pretty one, sleep.

(Words by Alfred, Lord Tennyson, music by Joseph Barnby, 1863. From Tennyson's "Medley" in *The Princess*.)

287

Skip to My Lou

Skip, skip, skip to my Lou
Skip, skip, skip to my Lou
Skip, skip, skip to my Lou
Skip to my Lou, my darling.

Flies in the buttermilk, shoo shoo shoo
Flies in the buttermilk, shoo shoo shoo
Flies in the buttermilk, shoo shoo shoo
Skip to my Lou, my darling.

Lost my partner, what'll I do?
Lost my partner, what'll I do?
Lost my partner, what'll I do?
Skip to my Lou, my darling.

I'll get another one prettier than you
I'll get another one prettier than you
I'll get another one prettier than you
Skip to my Lou, my darling.

Can't get a redbird, a bluebird'll do
Can't get a redbird, a bluebird'll do
Can't get a redbird, a bluebird'll do
Skip to my Lou, my darling.

Vive la Compagnie

Let every good fellow now join in this song
Vive la compagnie!
Success to each other and pass it along
Vive la compagnie!

Chorus: Vive la, vive la, vive l'amour
Vive la, vive la, vive l'amour
Vive l'amour, vive l'amour
Vive la compagnie!

A friend on your left and a friend on your right
Vive la compagnie!
In love and good fellowship let us unite
Vive la compagnie!

Chorus

Now wider and wider our circle expands
Vive la compagnie!
We sing to our comrades in faraway lands
Vive la compagnie!

Chorus

Farther Along

Tempted and tried, we're oft made to wonder
Why it should be thus all day long
While there are others living about us
Never molested though in the wrong.

Chorus: Farther along we'll know all about it
Farther along we'll understand why
Cheer up my brother, live in the sunshine
We'll understand it all by and by.

When we see Jesus coming in glory
When he comes home from his home in the sky
Then we shall meet him in that bright mansion
We'll understand it all by and by.

Chorus

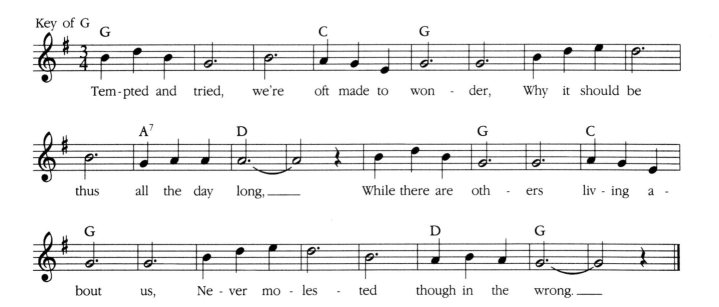

Tem-pted and tried, we're oft made to won - der, Why it should be

thus all the day long, _____ While there are oth - ers liv - ing a -

bout us, Ne - ver mo - les - ted though in the wrong. _____

Down in the Valley

Down in the valley, the valley so low
Hang your head over, hear the wind blow
Hear the wind blow, love, hear the wind blow
Hang your head over, hear the wind blow.

Write me a letter, send it by mail
Send it in care of Birmingham Jail
Birmingham Jail, love, Birmingham Jail
Sent it in care of Birmingham Jail.

Roses love sunshine, violets love dew
Angels in heaven know I love you
Know I love you, dear, know I love you
Angels in heaven know I love you.

Tell Me Why

Tell me why the stars do shine
Tell me why the ivy twines
Tell me why the sky's so blue
And I will tell you just why I love you.

Because God made the stars to shine
Because God made the ivy twine
Because God made the sky so blue
Because God made you, that's why I love you.

Index of Song Titles

Index of First Lines

The Top Tunes

Contributors to the Department of Folk Song

Dorothy Day Aarness, St. Louis Park, MN
Jean Skoglund Abbe, Alameda, CA
Kathy Abbott, Atlantic Mine, MI
Maria Abdin, Tucson, AZ
Bill Abler, Chicago, IL
Dona Dowling Abt, Albany, CA
Bob Adams, Longmont, CO
Jane Adams, Carbondale, IL
Kevin Adams, New York, NY
Barry Adamson, Cincinnati, OH
Stan Adelman, Auburndale, MA
Sylvia Adelman, Wilmington, DE
Lee Agnew, Norman, OK
Peter Agoos, Boston, MA
Lynn Aiken, Tempe, AZ
Chuck Albertson, Pullman, WA
Gail Albro, Elkton, OR
Allison Aldrich-Cobb, Mansfield, MA
Mabelle Alexander, Littleton, NH
Melinda Alexander, Ames, IA
Shellie Alexander, Portland, TX
Jane Alexander-Manifold, Lafayette, IN
Joan Alkula, Orangeburg, SC
Mrs. Andrew Allan, Elyria, OH
Rufus Alldredge, New Orleans, LA
Deborah Allen, Hanover, NH
Frances Allen, Springfield, IL
Tony Allred, Severna Park, MD
Earl Almquist, Herman, MN
Nicholas Altenbernd, Boston, MA
Joel Alter, Minneapolis, MN
Bob Altman, Hawaiian Gardens, CA
Bonnie Aman, Kent, WA
Jennifer Ambler, Homer, IL
Maxine Amundsen, Lamberton, MN
John D. Amundson, Battle Creek, MI
Adrienne Anderson, HI
Gay Anderson, East Lansing, MI
John Anderson, Granville, NY
John T. Anderson, Waterloo, IA
R. J. Anderson, Huntington Beach, CA
R. E. D. Anderson, Brevard, NC
Rox Anderson, Somerville, MA
Ruth Anderson, Huntington Beach, CA
Sandy Anderson, East Point, GA

Willie Anderson, Nashville, TN
Betty B. Andrews, Alexandria, VA
Cheryl Angelos, Laramie, WY
Steve and Pat Ankeny, New Castle, IN
Libby Antarsh, New York, NY
Christopher Arata, Salsberry, IN
Jan Archer, Tucson, AZ
Barbara C. Armenta
Ruth Armon, Elvine Park, PA
L. Armstrong, Westchester, NY
Linda Armstrong, New Rochelle, NY
Robert Armstrong, Memphis, TN
William S. Armstrong, Vancouver, WA
Jill Arnel, Oregon City, OR
Choela Leslie Arnold, San Antonio, TX
Rick Aronow, Fresh Meadows, NY
Suzy Arter, Kennewick, WA
Nancy Ashley, Columbus, OH
Carrie Ashton, Sewanee, TN
Maritt Aska, Websterville, OH
Charles Austin, Teaneck, NJ
J. Scott Avery, Indianapolis, IN
Katrine Avery, Providence, RI
Sharon AvRutick, New York, NY
Molly Ayer, Torrington, CT
Virginia Babcock, Post Mills, VT
Mary Bacon, Honolulu, HI
Astrid Bailey, Menominee, WI
Helen M. Bailey, Portland, ME
Irwin Bailey, Willoughby, OH
Lucille Bailey, Muncie, IN
Maurice J. Bailey, Menominee, MI
Bobbi Bailin, North Falmouth, MA
Ken Baines, Sault Ste. Marie, Ontario
Vivian Bakal, Paterson, NJ
Holden Baker, Greenfield, MA
Rebecca Baker, Republic, WA
Mrs. Robert Baker, Lorell, ME
Stephen Baker, Greenville, SC
Jean Balderson, New York, NY
Jay Baldwin, Sausalito, CA
Virginia Baldwin, Pavilion, NY
Mrs. Bob Bales, Homer, IL
Carol Ball, Culver City, CA
Dick Ballard, Moses Lake, WA

Dianne Ballon, Monroe, ME
Guy Bankes, Levittown, PA
Carter Bannerman, Bainbridge Island, WA
Thomas Barany, Oak Park, IL
Philip Baratta, La Jolla, CA
Nancy L. Barber, Atlanta, GA
Jorn Barger, Bartlett, IL
Donna L. S. Barkow, Denham Springs, LA
Linda Barnes, San Francisco, CA
Jerry Barney, Fergus Falls, MN
Donna Barr, Seattle, WA
Anna Barry, Sugar Grove, NC
Carol Barrymore, Firth, NE
Heidi Barthelemy, Berkeley, CA
Ricardo Barthelemy, San Juan Nuevo, Mexico
Julia Bartlett, Point Reyes Station, CA
Herb Barton, Wrentham, MA
Bob Bartsch, Louisville, KY
Diane Bartz, Providence, RI
Norma Bates, Nashville, TN
Richard Bay, Novato, CA
Ray Bayley, Prairie du Sac, WI
Kelcey Beardsley, Portland, OR
Everett W. Beath, Decatur, IL
Sara Beck
Paul Becker, Bedford, IN
Richard Becker, Broomfield, CO
Barbara J. Beeching, Newington, CT
Ingrid Beery, Wedgefield, SC
Barbara Bell, Troy, VA
John Bell, E. Providence, RI
Katherine Bell, Seattle, WA
Mike Bell, Boulder, CO
Charles Belov, San Francisco, CA
Ruth Benjamin, Eaton Rapids, MI
Carolyn Bennett, Evansville, IN
Ralph Bennett, Nanticoke, PA
Bob Benson, Burlington, VT
Sarah Bent, Fair Haven, NJ
Cherie Bentley, Colt, AK
Eddie Bentley
Jeela Bentley, Christiansburg, VA
Ann Berg, Cambridge, MN
Barbara Bergin, Concord, MA
Sharon Bergstrom, Hopkins, MN
Alberta Bertelsen, Rock Island, IL
Darla Beverage, Knoxville, TN
Jessica Beyer, Seattle, WA
Leslie Beyer, Cedarburg, WI
Jon R. Biemer, Portland, OR
Doris M. Bill, Mount Vernon, OH
Darya Bilyk, Somerville, MA
Francis V. Binderback, Newport, MN
Kirk Bingham, N. Grosvenordale, CT
Bruce L. Birchard, Los Angeles, CA
Elaine Bishop, Austin, TX
Lois and Bob Bisig, Lane, KS
Jenny and Steven Bixby, Kalamazoo, MI
Robert Bixby, Kalamazoo, MI
Carol Bixler, Moline, IL
Jim Blackman, Annapolis, MD

Pat Blackman, Huntsville, AL
Evelyn Blackmer, New York, NY
Linda Blair, New Haven, CT
Meredith O. Blair, Clinton, TN
Evelyn and Dick Blaisdell, Kapaa, HI
Elaine Blakeman, Eau Claire, WI
Suzanne Blanchard, Hamilton, NY
Liz Blaylock, Ankoka, MN
Joan Blessing, Norwich, CT
Val Blom, Boston, MA
Edi Blomberg, Lopez, WA
Jimi Blum, Camdenton, MO
Jimi Blum, Ladson, SC
Jan Blundell, Oakland, CA
Randy Blythe, Franklin, VA
Wayne T. Blythe, Franklin, VA
Jules Bobroff, Tallahassee, FL
Ginna Boccetti, Morehead City, NC
Mrs. Alfred Boerner, Sarasota, FL
Robert Bogan, Janesville, WI
Carol Bohmbach, Sacramento, CA
Al and Hedy Boissevain, Georgetown, CA
Kit Bolle, Washington, DC
Erika Bookman, Dallas, TX
Joyce M. Boose, Lancaster, PA
Judy and Jerry Booth, Morrill, ME
Essie Borden, New York, NY
Verna Bormann, Cook, MN
Dana Bosley, Seattle, WA
Lisa Botts, Decatur, IL
Judy Bouder, Liverpool, PA
Timothy Bowen, Pensacola, FL
Elaine Bowers, Omaha, NB
Frank and Thelma Bowman, Whitesburg, TN
Mike Boyd, Greenbelt, MD
Travis Boyd, Lawrence, KS
Barbara Boyk, Ann Arbor, MI
Norris Braaten, Hankinson, ND
Inez Brabham, Sumter, SC
David Braden, St. Paul, MN
Carol Bradsher, Greenville, SC
Ann Braeman, Lincoln, NE
David Branch, Milwaukee, WI
Joyce Branch, Frederic, WI
Alex Brander, Bedminster, NJ
Todd Brandon, Louisville, KY
Bruce Brandt, Brookline, MA
Susan Brandt, Stayton, OR
Cindi Brath, Ketchikan, AK
Jan Braun, Hastings, MN
Cathy Brechtelsbauer, Moneta, VA
Karen Brei, Davenport, IA
Virginia Brennan, Pleasant Ridge, MI
George Bridgman, Minneapolis, MN
Jessica Briefer, Ann Arbor, MI
Deborah Brien, Concord, MA
Jean Briggs, Hendersonville, NC
Catherine Brigham, Campbell, CA
Robert Brigham, Mountain View, CA
Elizabeth Bright, Chisholm, MN
Shelly Britton, St. Paul, MN

Eunice Brock, Chapel Hill, NC
Chris Broune, Brooklyn, NY
Cecelia Brown, Madison, WI
Gianine Brown, Piermont, NY
Juliana Brown, Raleigh, NC
Nick Brown, Los Osos, CA
Russell Brown, Effingham, SC
Thomas Brown, Morgantown, WV
William Brown, Philadelphia, PA
Judith Bruff, Cazadoo, CA
Kervin Brungardt, Peoria, IL
Barbara Brunk-Harnish, Chicago, IL
Pamela Budd, Burnsville, NC
Barbara Buehner, Milwaukee, WI
Betty Bullion, Minneapolis, MN
Hank Bullwinkel, Baltimore, MD
Lucy Burk, Mount Holly, NJ
Robert Burke, Miami, FL
Mary D. Burkett, Paw Paw, MI
Patty Burkholder, Harrisburg, PA
Helen Burnsteed, Bowling Spring, TN
Ellis Burruss, Brunswick, MD
Susan Meredith Burt, Bloomington, IN
Karen A. Busch, Smithton, IL
James Buschman, East Lansing, MI
Janet Bush, Arlington Hts, IL
Merrily Butler, New York, NY
Elizabeth Cadorette, Northboro, MA
Mike Cady, Red Wing, MN
George F. Cahoe, Cuahoga Falls, OH
Marian Calabro, N. Bergen, NJ
Michele Caldwell, Spencertown, NY
Muffy Caldwell, Grassycreek, NC
Steve Callahan, Creve Coeur, MO
Betsy Calvert, Urbana, IL
Mary Calvo, Waupaca, WI
Cindy Cameron, Champaign, IL
Alice Campbell, St. Paul, MN
Caren Canfield, Ripley, OK
Rodney B. Canfield, Bristol, CT
Phil Cantor, Brooklyn, NY
Richard Caplan, Chicago, IL
Charles Carignan, Windham, NH
Ann Carlson, Lyndeborough, NH
Gorden Carlson, Torrance, CA
Mark and Dorothy Carlson, Blacksburg, VA
Sue Carlson, Santa Rosa, CA
Susan Carpenter, Amherst, MA
Susan Carpenter, Yellow Springs, OH
Carin Carper, Conifer, CO
Tony Carrabes, Alexandria, VA
Rockwell Carrier, Avon Park, FL
Jerry Carris, Atlanta, GA
Sarah Carson, New York, NY
Pat Carstensen, Eatontown, NJ
Cheely Carter, Millington, TN
Jackie Carter, Iowa City, IA
Ann Catelli, Northampton, VA
A. Caterson, Palos Verdes, CA
David Celsi, New York, NY
Donald M. Chaffee, Wellesley, MA

Peg Chagnon, Glens Falls, NY
Sandrea Chait, Nelsonville, OH
Debbie Chakour, Oregon, IL
Mary Chalk, Topeka, KS
James D. Chalupnik, Seattle, WA
Lorna Chambreau, Monroe, WA
Steve Chandler, Moscow, ID
Kim Chapman, Lansing, MI
Sue Chapman, Milltown, IN
Dean Charlton, Knoxville, TN
Tricia Chatary, Barryton, MA
Jeannine Chatterton-Papineau, Peoria, IL
John Cheeseman, Urbana, IL
Kay Cheever, Brookings, SD
Mokurai Cherlin, Palo Alto, CA
Marsha Childers, Boonville, MO
Martha S. Chiles, Herndon, VA
Dorothy Chilkott, Pontiac, MI
Donald Choate, Deerfield, IL
Mike Cholet, Bakersfield, CA
Larry Chott, Muncie, IN
David Chrestenson, Oswego, IL
Jeffrey Christensen, Weston, CT
Crystal Christenson, Omaha, NE
Barbara Christy, Carson City, NV
Tom Ciborowski, San Manuel, AZ
L. Waldemar Claeson, Bloomington, MN
Milt and Rose Clark, Whitefish Bay, WI
David B. Clarke, Concord, MA
Mary Class, Eliot, ME
Mary Margaret Clements, Nashville, TN
Joel Cler, Peoria, IL
Donna K. Cleverdon, Arlington, VA
Ed Clopton, West Branch, IA
Dave Coate, Pittsburgh, PA
Ralph Cobb, Williamsburg, VA
Frank Coco, Middlebury, VT
Peg Coffey, Indianapolis, IN
Chris Coffin, Portland, OR
Kevin Cole, Lansing, MI
Norma Cole, Farmington, MI
Steve Cole, Wareham, MA
Diane Coleman, Independence, VA
Martin Collier, Chicago, IL
Clint Collins, Wilmington, DE
Grace and Arthur Collins, Las Vegas, NV
Lynn Collins, Jackson, MI
Philip Collins, Plymouth, MN
Diane Colvin, Fairborn, OH
Sherna M. Comerford, Hyattsville, MD
Peg Conan, DeWitt, NY
Laura Conkey, Hanover, NH
Marilyn Connelly, Kailua, HI
Lynn Connette, Richmond, VA
Peter and Marie Connors, Kakabeka Falls, Ontario
Charles Conrad, Racine, WI
Tom Constanten, Oakland, CA
Frances Conway, Greenville, SC
Caren C. Cook
Esther Cook, Minneapolis, MN
Steve Cook, Portland, OR

Priscilla Cooley, Byron, NY
Judy Cooper
Robert Cooper, Savannah, GA
Blanche Corbett, Salisbury, CT
Kelly Corcoran
Mary and Tom Corcoran, Spokane, WA
Peggy Core, Traverse City, MI
Lynn Corrie, Urbana, IL
Kathryn Costello, Lakefield, MN
Barbara Cotts, Ithaca, NY
Joe and Carol Coulter
Eleanor M. Covington, Fresno, CA
Hallie Cowan, Agawam, MA
Anne Cox, Ann Arbor, MI
Birk Cox, Richmond, VA
C. Edwin Cox, Charlotte, NC
Harold M. Cragg, St. Paul, MN
Hugh Craig, Arlington, VA
Asho Craine, Ann Arbor, MI
Sukie Crandall, N. Plainfield, NJ
Jennifer Crane, Oshkosh, WI
Bill Crawford, Manchester, IA
Dan Crawford, Manchester, IA
Elaine Creaden, Lawrence, KS
Jon Cremins, Charlemont, MA
Jay Critchley, Provincetown, MA
Ruth Crockett, Honolulu, HI
Ann G. Crosby, Raleigh, NC
Mrs. Cecil Cross, Jefferson City, MO
Tim Crouse, KS
Cheryl Crow, Bakersfield, CA
Jonna Crow, Seattle, WA
Carol Crowe, Minneapolis, MN
Bill Crownover, Knoxville, TN
Gene Crutcher, Birmingham, AL
Allisande Cultler, Ann Arbor, MI
James R. Cunningham, Olympia, WA
Mrs. John Cunningham, Roanoke, VA
Nancy Current, Seattle, WA
Kay Curry, Berkeley, CA
Mrs. Aina Cutler, Wellesley Hills, MA
Cora Dahl, Kingsport, TN
Dianne Daley, Missoula, MT
Jody Dalton
Dianne Daly, Missoula, MT
Sam Daniels, Gaithersburg, MD
Bob Darcy, Stillwater, OK
Dean and Edith Darling, Bellevue, NE
Richard Darling, Bloomington, IN
Steve Darling, Long Beach, CA
Kip Darner, Seattle, WA
Karen Dash, Los Angeles, CA
Judy Dautel, So. Dartmouth, MA
Tom and Rachel David, Erie, PA
Paul Davinroy, Boulder, CO
Dorothy W. Davis, Durham, NC
E. Mott Davis, Austin, TX
Julius Davis, Greenfield, CA
Martha and Rick Davison, Schoolcraft, MI
Edie de Chadenedes, Friday Harbor, WA
Jennifer de Chadenedes, Seattle, WA

LeRoy De Gregory, New York, NY
April de Young, Brooklyn, NY
E. R. Deal, Fort Collins, CO
Nancy A. Deal, Fort Collins, CO
Gordon Dean, Richfield, MN
Ellen H. Deaton, St. Augustine, FL
Barbara DeCoster, Evanston, IL
Madge Defee, El Paso, TX
Matthew DeFord, Mooresville, IN
Marcia Deihl, Cambridge, MA
Jean Marie Deken, Clayton, MO
Jodi and Jim DeLapp, Cottage Grove, OR
Steven DeMarte, Long Beach, CA
Jim Deming, St. Paul, MN
Jackie Dempsey, Webster, NY
Anne C. Denlinger, Merion, PA
Connie DePond, Altoona, IA
Charles DeShong, Tulsa, OK
Sarah Desjardins, Westport, MA
D. DeVoe, Bridgewater, CT
Barbara Devonshire, Littleton, CO
Laurel Dewey, Glendale, CA
Emil Dickstein, Youngstown, OH
Charles Dimmick, Cheshire, CT
Margaret Dimock, Rough & Ready, CA
A. Nelson Dingle, Dexter, MI
Christine Dingman, Farmers Branch, TX
Barbara Dixon, Salem, OR
Michele Doerflein, Memphis, TN
Bill Doescher, Portland, OR
Trevor B. Dolby, Butte, MT
Ellen and Don Dollar, Gatlinburg, TN
Michael Dolnick, Silver Spring, MD
Amy and Jim Domanico, Oswego, NY
Eileen F. Doughty, Reston, VA
Victor Doumar, Huntsville, AL
Russell Dowda, Albany, NY
Donna Dowling, Albany, CA
Bill Downall, West Roxbury, MA
Greg Downing, Staten Island, NY
Walter Downing, Sandy Hook, CT
Julie Downs, North Bend, OR
Robert Downs, New Castle, PA
Cheri Noel Doyle, Eagle Rock, CA
Anne Draper, Hermann, MO
David Draves, Durham, NH
Leonard Drey, St. Louis, MO
Robin Dreyer, Burnsville, NC
Frank Driscole, University City, MO
Sibley Driscoll, Corinth, VT
Diane Dropsho, Madison, WI
Bill and Cindy Drumm, River Edge, NJ
Jim Dubuar, Seattle, WA
Mrs. Chester Duck, Allison Park, PA
Edwin Dudley, North Haven, CT
Diana Dulhend, Willow Springs, MO
Joyce Ury Dumtschin, Portsmouth, OH
Dennis Dunham, Marysville, KS
David Dunklee, Brattleboro, VT
Emma Dunn, Bourbon, MO
Larry Dunnewold, St. Louis Park, MN

Penny Durham, Menlo Park, CA
Scott Durkee, Bar Harbor, ME
M. A. Durren
Harold Dutch
Ann Dutton, Modesto, CA
Nancy Dwyer, Pittsburgh, PA
Patricia Ann Dziewit, Westminster, MD
Mary Kay Eakin, Waterloo, IA
Ann S. Earley, W. Brookfield, MA
Jack Gavin Early, Jr., Birmingham, AL
Suzie Earp, Santa Fe, NM
Elizabeth Easterling, Placerville, CA
Jeff Eaton, Fort Worth, TX
David Eckman, Coatesville, PA
William Edelstein, Santa Barbara, CA
Craig Eder, Washington, DC
Don Edrington, Fallbrook, CA
Teon Edwards, W. Lafayette, IN
Keith Egnor, Penn Yan, NY
Sheldon Einhorn, Philadelphia, PA
Deb Eisenhauer, LaPorte, CO
Allan Eitzen, Barto, PA
Kathy Eldred, Binghamton, NY
Brooke Elgie, Olympia, WA
Richard D. Ellers, Warren, OH
Margaret Elliot, San Jose, CA
Marion S. Ellis, Easton, PA
Hugh A. Ely, East Hampton, NY
Polly and John Ely, Cedar Rapids, IA
Jeffrey M. Engholm, Galesburg, IL
Solveig Englund, Tampa, FL
Mary Lou Enlow, Pasco, WA
Mona Enquist-Johnston
Carol Entin, Seekonk, MA
Jerry Enzenauer
Laurel Eppstein, Starksboro, VT
Linda Erdberg, Arlington, VA
Avis and Jon Erickson, Normandy, MO
Becky Erickson, Brookside, NJ
Cathy Henley Erickson, Claremont, CA
Richard Erickson, Staten Island, NY
Tim Erickson, Berkeley, CA
Sue Ethridge, Detroit, MI
Susan Euler, Edina, MN
Loren Evarts, East Haven, CT
Ronald Evett, Holliston, MA
Jim Evinger, Rochester, NY
Richard Ewald, Westminster, VT
Marjorie Ewell, Rochester, NY
Martha Fairbank, Durham, NC
Joel Faitsch, Pittsfield, MA
Bob Fakundiny, Rensselaer, NY
Sue Fallon
R. H. Fanders, Council Bluffs, IA
Ashleen Fariss, Tucson, AZ
Irene Farlee, Los Angeles, CA
Sandy Farley, Redwood City, CA
Warren Fay, Portland, OR
Pam Feehan, DeSoto, TX
Sue Fenimore, Lynnwood, WA
Don and Sally Ferriby, Frankenmuth, MI

Muriel Ferris, Sacramento, CA
Ruellen R. Fessenbecker, Nashville, IN
Matt Fichtenbaum, Chelmsford, MA
Diane Fiedler, Boston, MA
Marlen Field, Hillsdale, MI
Larry Fields, San Diego, CA
Dave Fihn, Detroit Lakes, MN
Angela Fina, Amherst, MA
Anne Finch, Rensselaer, NY
Paula Fink, Ann Arbor, MI
Donald Finley, Missoula, MT
Louisa Finn, Fairfax, CA
Joseph J. Firebaugh, Ann Arbor, MI
Roger M. Firestone, Norristown, PA
Bill and Ann Fisher, Oak Park, IL
Bill Fishman, Los Angeles, CA
Stephanie Fittschen, Opelika, AL
Kathy Fitzgerald, Salt Lake City, UT
Leslie A. Fitzpatrick, Pittsburgh, PA
Sue Fleming, Ann Arbor, MI
Suzanne Fleming, Pitman, NJ
Mickey Fletcher, Rock Springs, WY
Martha Floener, Chicago, IL
Anita Fobes, Pleasant Lake, MI
Hannah Folsom, Carmichael, CA
Rick Ford, Chicago, IL
Steven Forsell, Tuscaloosa, AL
Suzanne Fosberg, New Orleans, LA
George Fosmire, Dallas, TX
Lloyd Foster, Temple Hills, MD
Mark S. Foster, Minneapolis, MN
Martha Foster, Gallipolis, OH
Dale and Dotty Fox, Hopkinton, MA
Jean Fox, Columbus, OH
Sally Goers Fox, Tanunda, Australia
John Frank, New Haven, CT
Lucy Frantzman, Brownville, ME
Merian Brown Frederick, Ann Arbor, MI
Kathleen Fredlund, Camarillo, CA
Ann Frederick
Ron and Pat Frederickson, Amherst, MA
Janet Freeman, Wingate, NC
Paul Freeman, Milwaukee, WI
Rebecca French, Grinnell, IA
Sparrow B. Frenkel, Dallas, TX
Rosemary Frenza, Ann Arbor, MI
Bill Freund, Hatchville, MA
Herman Freund, Sharon, CT
Bill Frey, Wilton, CT
Nancy Corbit Frick, St. Paul, MN
Anne Friend
Ariel Friesner, Eugene, OR
J. Frisby, Maxwell AFB, AL
Anna Fritz, Gillett, WI
James Fritz, Auburndale, WI
Gabriel Frommer
Sara Frommer, Bloomington, IN
Dave Fryant, Elmira, NY
Velma Frye, Wakulla County, FL
Betty Fuller, Long Beach, CA
Charles Fuller, New Auburn, WI

Fred Fuller, Williamston, MI
John Fuller, Harvard, MA
Doug Fulton, Tucson, AZ
Carolyn Furman, Girard, IL
Ralph Gabby, New York, NY
John W. Gable, Damascus, VA
Spence Gainey, Kingsport, TN
Don Gallagher, Washington Grove, MD
Ken Gallant, Philadelphia, PA
Greg Gappa, Platteville, WI
Theresa Gardner, Richmond, VA
Cathy Garra, Evanston, IL
G. Garrison, Dade City, FL
Harriet Gates, Stanton, CA
Howard P. Gates, Jr., Locust Grove, VA
Mary Kate Gaynor, Ocean View, NJ
Greg Geise, Minneapolis, MN
Karen Geisler, Grass Valley, CA
Davey Gerhard, Bernardsville, NJ
John Gerson, Spartanburg, SC
Louisa Gerstenberger, Fredericksburg, VA
Alex Gibson, Manchester, MA
Walker Gibson, Amherst, MA
Anna Gieschen, Fargo, ND
Dick Gilbert, Lincoln, NE
Tom and Deborah Gilboy, Louisville, CO
Bob Gile, Merrillan, WI
Dodi Giles, Madison, WI
Robert D. Gillette, Cincinnati, OH
Richard Gilpin, St. Louis, MO
Kelly Glazner, Las Cruces, MN
Paul Goddard, North Fork, CA
Elisabeth Godolphin, Harrisville, NH
Emily Gohn, Chimacum, WA
Laurence Gold, Madison, WI
Sandy R. Goldapp
David Golden, Eugene, OR
Eve Golden, Secaucus, NJ
Tony Goldenberg, Seattle, WA
Bernice Goldman, Riverdale, NY
Stanley Goldsmith, Aberdeen, NC
Linda Goldstein, Littleton, NH
Susan Goldstein, Philomath, OR
John Goman, Minneapolis, MN
Carol Good, Lima, OH
Barbara Goodell, Loda, IL
Jay and Marilyn Goos, Moorhead, MN
Suzanne Noble Gordon, Cambridge, MA
Carol Goris, Knoxville, TN
Elizabeth Gorney, San Francisco, CA
Muffet Gracey, Sunderland, MA
Jill and Colin Graham, Vancouver, B.C.
Mrs. Boo Graham, Athens, OH
Pat Graham, Chapel Hill, NC
Franklin Grapel, Cottekill, NY
Nancy Graumlich, Sylvania, OH
Rebecca Graves, Vashon, WA
Dan Gray, Oakland, CA
Lyn Gray, Sonora, CA
Mrs. Douglas Gray, Oneonta, NY
Pattie Gray, Oneonta, NY

Carroll Green, La Habra Heights, CA
Elizabeth Green, Temperance, MI
Hal and Kathy Green, Des Moines, IA
Ed Greenawald, Greensboro, NC
Bob and Barbara Greenaway
Karen Greenbaum, Claremont, CA
Anne Greene, Marina Del Rey, CA
Scotty Greene, Franklin, PA
Jean Greensfelder, Nevada City, CA
Leslie Greer, Eugene, OR
Mary Greer, Hudson, OH
Anne Gregory, Winchester, MA
Eloise Gregory, Grass Valley, CA
John Gregory, Springfield, KY
Nancy Greive, Stanton, CA
Karol Gresser, Burnsville, MN
Nancy Grewe, Stanton, CA
Elaine Gridley, Colchester, IL
Nancy Griffin, Knoxville, TN
Leigh Griffith
Kathy Grimm, Winfield, MO
Violetta Grobe, Ann Arbor, MI
Vaughn E. Groom, Guthrie, OK
Ray Grosser, Eubank, KY
L. C. Grove, Tucson, AZ
Carlton Groves, Rice, MN
John Grubic, Sacramento, CA
Cindy Gugich, Lopez Island, WA
Mary Guild, Cambridgeport, VT
Kelly E. J. Guilfoil, Spokane, WA
Thelma Gunia, Los Angeles, CA
Erik Gunn, Rochester, NY
Pam Gunstrum, Old Saybrook, CT
Mike Guslick, Grafton, WI
Sue Guss, Corvallis OR
Bob Haagland, Charlotte, NC
Peg Haakenson, Wyncote, PA
S. Haas
Betsy Habich, North Reading, MA
Mrs. D. L. Hadley, Pierson, FL
Trisha Haley-Miller, Calais, ME
Donald S. Hall, Rochester, NY
Pam and Joe Hallberg, Medford, MA
Helen Haller, Ithaca, NY
Judy Halverson, Alexandria, MN
Ron Halvorson, Colfax, WI
Morton Hamermesh, Minneapolis, MN
Judy Hampton, Stevens Point, WI
Eleanor Hancock, Silver City, NM
Corky Handley, Albany, CA
Ernest Hanes, Akron, OH
Jill Hanna, Lexington, KY
Laurie Hansen, Lutsen, MN
Lois Hansen, Springfield, VA
Craig Hanson
Jane Hanson-Tafel
Louis Happe, Evansville, IN
Judy Harada, Pacifica, CA
Ron Harding, Downer's Grove, IL
Charity Hardison, Ann Arbor, MI
Mark Harlik, Hamilton, TX

Lois Harney, Endwell, NY
Peggy Harrell, Clarksville, TN
Mary Ann Harris, Oxnard, CA
Rose Harrison, Vernon, CT
George Hart, New Wilmington, PA
Becky Hartman, La Crosse, WI
Kathy Hartman
Grandma Harwood, Cape Canaveral, FL
Micky Hastings, Fresno, CA
Alice Hauck, Providence, RI
Derek Hauck, Missoula, MT
Ellen Hauer, Johnstown, PA
Jerald Thomas Haughay, Corydon, IA
K. S. Haugland, St. Paul, MN
Amy W. Hauslohner, Troutdale, VA
George F. Hawk, Los Angeles, CA
Karen Hawkins, Maple Grove, MN
Dick Hawks, Hinsdale, IL
Sharon Haworth, Macomb, IL
Rose Mary Hayden, Arlington, VA
Dennis Hayes, Spencer, IA
Francis Hayes, Gainesville, FL
Jack Hayes, Lawrence, KS
Mona Johnson Hearn, Olympia Fields, IL
Sally Hearon, Charlotte, NC
Jane Heart, Machias, ME
Allene Heath, Eugene, OR
Ellen Heath, Middletown, CT
Mrs. A. M. Heath, Eugene, OR
Jan and Howard Hebel, Hamden, CT
John Hedtke, Seattle, WA
Kate Heideman, Hancock, MI
Chuck Heidorn, Boston, MA
Dennis Hein, Rochester, NY
Yvonne Hein, Rochester, NY
Jack Heinzmann, Berlin, CT
Jean Heinzmann, Berlin, CT
Jean Heise, Urbandale, IA
Paul and Sharon Helbert, Timberville, VA
Shyana Helin, Nevada City, CA
Virginia Helin, Nevada City, CA
Gabe Heller
Elizabeth Hellman, New York, NY
Marilyn Helmers, LeMars, IA
Marilyn Heltzer, St. Paul, MN
Virginia Hench
Gladys Henderson, Salem, OR
Jim and Marie Henderson, Knoxville, TN
Sally Henderson, Mechanicsburg, PA
Susan Hendrickson, Catonsville, MD
Erna Hennick, San Diego, CA
Kay Henriksen, Lexington, KY
Georgianna Henry, Eunice, LA
Jim and Helen Henry, Longford, KS
Sharon Henry, Clementon, NJ
Rebecca Herb, Berkeley, CA
Nancy Hersey, Akron, PA
Karen Hescock, Benson, VT
Mary Hespen, Bozeman, MT
Jane Heyer, Winfield, IL
Herman Heyn, Baltimore, MD

Catherine Hibbitt, RI
Jeannette Hickman Kingsley, Wayzata, MN
Michael Hieber, Hamilton, OH
Julie Higginbotham, Jackson, TN
Mary B. Higgins, Versailles, IN
Carolyn Hill, High Point, NC
Jennifer Hill, Dillingham, AK
Jo Hill, Las Vegas, NM
Pat Hill, Blodgett, OR
Stephen Hill, Excelsior, MN
George and Rita Himes, Ridgefield, CT
Sam Hinton
Anne and Stephen Hintz, Oshkosh, WI
Joyce Donen Hirschhorn, Killingworth, CT
Robert Hirstein, Norfolk, VA
John Hitchner, Camarillo, CA
David Hoadley, Clifton Park, NY
Isabelle Hoag, Davenport, IA
Ina Hobson, El Cajon, CA
Scott Hochman, Brooklyn, NY
H. C. Hodson, Bloomington, IN
Rani Hoff, Erie, PA
Lucy Hoffhines, Elizabeth, CO
Barbara Hofmaier, New Haven, CT
John Hohanson, Decatur, GA
Marilyn Hoijer
Frank Holan, Westminster, VT
David Holden, Knoxville, TN
Agnes Hole, Madison, WI
Francis D. Hole, Madison, WI
Elizabeth Hollenhorst, Duluth, MN
Katherine Holliday, Auburn, WA
Martie Holmer, Boston, MA
Elizabeth Holmes, Mineral Point, WI
Ted Holmes, Winterport, ME
Meredith S. Holte, Golden Valley, MN
Adeline Hooper, New York, NY
Noreen Horneck, Elkhart Lake, WI
Ellen Horsburgh, Fremont, NH
Mary Hortin, Fair Oaks, CA
Will Hoskins, Heiskell, TN
Charles Hoskinson, St. Louis, MO
Richard Hough-Ross, Peacham, VT
Bonnie House, Bedminster, PA
Nancy Hovland, Murrysville, PA
Alison Howard, Strafford, MO
Barbara Howard, Albany, CA
John Howard, Lockport, IL
Julie Howard, St. Cloud, MN
Dana Hoyle, Portland, OR
Alison Hubbard, Chicago, IL
Don and Reba Huber, Deerfield, IL
John Hudson, Bethesda, MD
Ruth Huebner, Swanton, MD
Theresa Huey-Stone, Tallahassee, FL
Dave Hug, Fort Collins, CO
Jane Hughes, St. Catherine's, Ontario
Dan Hulbert, Floyd, VA
Corinne Hull, Richmond, IN
Nancy O. Hull, Lancaster, SC
Mary Beth Hunn, Sitka, AK

Joan Hunt, Eugene, OR
Katie Hunter, Tallahassee, FL
Sandy Huntley, Greenville, SC
Dan Huntsperger, Blaine, MN
Lori Hurd, Mason City, IA
Ruth Huston, Longmeadow, MA
Margaret A. Hutcheson, Sandwich, MA
Ed Hutchinson, Creston, NC
Sara Hutchinson, New Castle, DE
L. Hyatt, Ridgewood, NJ
Alice Hyde Minneapolis, MN
Ruth Hyde-Hanus, Clarksville, IN
Darrell Hyder, N. Brookfield, MA
Bert Hyman, St. Paul, MN
Rosemary Hyman, Hawkeye, IA
Jo Ickler, Ashland, MA
Kathryn H. Iliff, West Chester, PA
W. P. Ingalls, Richland, WI
Richard Ingram, Seattle, WA
Betty Inman, Charlevoix, MI
Lisa Irons, Noble, OK
John Irvine, Park Ridge, NJ
Carl Isaacson, Georgetown, SC
Gordon Iseminger, Grand Forks, ND
Marilyn Jackson, San Francisco, CA
Pat Jackson, San Francisco, CA
Rebecca Jackson, Indian Hills, CO
Mrs. F. A. Jacobi, New York, NY
Sally Jacobs, Orono, ME
Tollef Jacobson, Arlington, VA
Doug Jaeger, Wilmington, DE
Nina Jaffe, Burlington, VT
Robert F. Jambor, New Brunswick, NJ
Jane and Ben James, Birchrunville, PA
Louise James, Iowa City, IA
Dibb Jamison, Walla Walla, WA
George Jamison, Sandstone, MN
Robert Janett, Arlington, MA
William Janning, Dayton, OH
Janet Janzen, Wichita, KS
Linda Jeffries, Ann Arbor, MI
T. and B. Jeffries, Fresno, CA
Barbara Jeffus, Fresno, CA
Don and A. J. Jenkins, Indianapolis, IN
Boyd Jensen, Covington, VA
Elizabeth Jensen, Jamaica Hills, NY
David Jenson, Freeport, ME
Peter and Kitty Jerjisian, Oberlin, OH
Alvin Jeske, Sumner, IA
Mera R. Jetton, Findlay, OH
Grace Jillson, Boston, MA
Anne Johnson, Charleston, WV
Audrey Johnson, St. Paul, MN
Barbara Johnson, Lecoma, MO
Bonnie Nestor Johnson, Oak Ridge, TN
Cranford Johnson, Winston-Salem, NC
Dan Johnson, Rhinelander, WI
David Johnson, Ann Arbor, MI
Delores Johnson, Atlanta, GA
Doug Johnson, St. Paul, MN
Leslie Johnson, Eldred, NY

Marj Johnson, Portland, OR
Marjorie Johnson, San Luis Obispo, CA
Michael Johnson, Denver, CO
Monty Johnson, Natural Bridge, VA
Patricia Johnson, Pulaski, NY
Ron Johnson, Long Beach, CA
Bob Johnston, Kane, PA
Cheri Jolivette, Holland, MI
Brenda and Chuck Jones, Durham, NC
Carol Jones, Philadelphia, PA
Charles A. Jones, Houston, TX
Charlie Jones, Columbia, MO
David Jones, St. Louis, MO
Beverly Joranko, Waterloo, IA
H. Jordan, Elberta, AL
Dana Josslin, Los Angeles, CA
James Juhnke, North Newton, KS
Alfred Julian, Blairstown, NJ
Will C. Jumper, Ames, IA
Daryl and Cheri Junk, Durham, NC
Paul Kaarre, Gurnn, MI
Jean Kahler, Chapel Hill, NC
Susan Kahn, Leverett, MA
Randy Kallansrud, Baltimore, MD
Jan Kalnbach, Nashville, TN
Bertha Kapner, Pittsburgh, PA
Janet Karow, Sumptor, OR
Donald Kaspersen, Concord, NC
Jim Kauer, Kennett Square, PA
Denny Kayser, Hudson, NH
Katherine Keena, Savannah, GA
Rick Keena-Levin, Chapel Hill, NC
Gail Keeney, Bethesda, MD
Nancy Keeton, Cottage Grove, OR
Judy Kegley, Ames, IA
Lyle Kehm, Urbandale, IA
Wilma Kellogg, Sycamore, IL
Anne Kelly, St. Paul, MN
Ron Kelsey, Lamberton, MN
Marian Kemper, Pittsburgh, PA
S. Bryan Kendrick, Winston-Salem, NC
Eliot Kenin, Oakland, CA
Sam Kennedy, Brookline, MA
Mrs. John Kennefick, Davenport, IA
Tom Kenney-Montgomery, Rockville, MD
Kate and Ada Kerman, Prospect Park, PA
Judie Kern, Chowchilla, CA
Mary Kessler, Minneapolis, MN
Sylvia Khan, No. Hollywood, CA
Bill Kilgour, Madison, WI
J. P. Killough-Miller, Eugene, OR
Brenda Kimble, Champaign, IL
Amy Jo King, Oxnard, CA
Carolyn King, Grand Forks, ND
Jane King, Doylestown, PA
Richard B. King, Syracuse, NY
Joan King-Angell, Oakland, CA
Peter Kingsley Hickman, Wayzata, MN
Susan Kinsey, Geneseo, NY
J. Scott Kiphart, Vestal, NY
Don Kipper, Seattle, WA

Mary Dascher Kirchner
Janna Kisner, Roseville, MN
Sandra Kisner, Ithaca, NY
Mary Klein, Los Angeles, CA
Nancy Klingman, Billings, MT
Stuart D. Klipper, Ann Arbor, MI
Ruth Klippstein, Scottsville, VA
Gene Knepprath, Sacramento, CA
Edward Knittel, Youngstown, OH
Eunice E. Knox, Presque Isle, ME
Arlene Knutson, Bloomington, MN
David Kobos, Oregon City, OR
Lynn Kohl
Karla Kohlmann, Rosebush, MI
Harold Kohn, Columbus, OH
Mary Kolasinski, Minneapolis, MN
Penny Kommalan, Pasadena, MD
Tom Konda
Nancy Nixon Koppin, Ann Arbor, MI
Kathy Kotila, Saegertown, PA
Margaret Kraght, Glendora, CA
Cathy Krause, Long Beach, CA
Anna Mae Krebs, Provo, UT
Maynard Krebs, Tofte, MN
Sylvia Krell, Austin, TX
Roger Krenkler, Thousand Oaks, CA
Peter Krinke, Anoka, MN
Pam Kristan, Dorchester, MA
Vic and Roxane Krivitski, North Wildwood, NJ
Shirley Kruger, Minneapolis, MN
John and Martha Kuch, Charlotte, MI
Henry Kuehn, Minneapolis, MN
Vincent Kueter, DeSoto, IL
Edith Lyman Kuether, Chevy Chase, MD
Dylan Kuhn, Fort Collins, CO
Joyce Kukuk, Naperville, IL
Betty Kunz, Boulder, CO
Sharon Bryant Kupit, Durham, NC
Gene and Verla Kurtz, St. Petersburg, FL
Dorothy Kussmaul, Philadelphia, PA
Marcia Kuszmaul, Anchor Point, AK
Mark Kutnink, San Francisco, CA
Peg Kuula, Santa Fe, NM
Renee Lajcak, Oshkosh, WI
David Lamb, Seattle, WA
Jim Land, Boulder, CO
Marcia Lane, New York, NY
Jessie Lang, Kearny, NJ
Alison Langley, Baltimore, MD
Margaret Langshore, Hamilton, MI
Avi Lank, Milwaukee, WI
Dov Lank, Columbus, OH
Glenny Lanning, Springfield, MO
Manny and Franny Lanseros, Centreville, AL
Jason LaRosa, Naugatuck, CT
Eleanor Larson, Columbia, SC
G. Paul Larson, Grand Forks, ND
Jean Larson, San Francisco, CA
Susan Larsson, Madison, WI
Ed Lashman, Dedham, MA
Ron and Linda Lasiter, Chicago, IL

Nancy Louise Lathrop, Los Angeles, CA
Lyn Lauffer, West Berkshire, VT
Martha Lavell, Philadelphia, PA
Nick Lavigne
Brian P. Lawler, San Luis Obispo, CA
Nan Lawless, Owls Head, NY
Carol Lawrence, Oshkosh, WI
Patricia Lawrence, Baton Rouge, LA
Jim Lawson, Enid, OK
John Layne, Camp Hill, PA
Cherie Lazaroff, Tucson, AZ
Barbara Lea, New York, NY
Norma Lea, McPherson, KS
Wendy Leavens, Las Vegas, NM
Mrs. Harold Leavy, Marion, MI
Carlton R. Lee, Cokato, MN
Laurie Lee, Council Bluffs, IA
Lucy Lee, Newport News, VA
Nadia Lee, Baltimore, MD
Peter V. Lee, Pasadena, CA
Thomas C. Lee, Delavan, WI
Myron Leet, Wilkes-Barre, PA
Kathy Lefferts, Seattle, WA
Gerald Lehmann, Marshall, MI
Virginia Lelander, Bowling Green, OH
Winton Lemoine, Tucson, AZ
Joanne M. Lenigan, Chambersburg, PA
Chris Leuba, Seattle, WA
Mrs. Louis Levi, Florence, AL
Allen Levin, Chicago, IL
Wanda and Rob Levin, Burnsville, NC
Ellen Levine, New York, NY
Jane Lewis, Champaign, IL
Lorelyn Lewis, Santa Monica, CA
Maggie Lewis, Seattle, WA
Muriel Lewis, Silver Spring, MD
Janice Leslie Ley, Petoskey, MI
Marjorie Lietz, New Bremen, OH
Hannah Lincoln, Pleasantville, NY
Martha Lind, Alameda, CA
Henry Clay Lindgren, San Francisco, CA
Abby Lindstrom, Gaithersburg, MD
Mary Jean Link, Belmont, MA
Mark Linville, Cincinnati, OH
Justine Lipovsek, Wauwatosa, WI
Peggy Lipson, Mill Valley, CA
Eileen Lischer, St. Louis, MO
Arlene Listing, Racine, WI
Virginia Lisveners, Virginia Beach, VA
Judy Lium, N. Concord, VT
Suzanne Locke, Ione, CA
Peter Lockrem, Carbondale, IL
Rick Lockwood, Baltimore, MD
Brian Loe, Providence, RI
John C. Lohr, Baltimore, MD
Bill Long, St. Charles, MO
Carol Long, Dallas, TX
Mary M. Longelfeld, Madison, WI
Kathryn J. Lord, Storrs, CT
Eric Loring, Amherst, MA
Willie Losinger, Harbor Springs, MI

Mrs. Hunter Lott, Bryn Mawr, PA
Dana Loud, Rochester, NY
Thomas J. Lough, Grosse Point, MI
Margaret T. Lovejoy, Janesville, WI
Gladys Lowrey, Silver Spring, MD
Dave Loy, Pasadena, CA
Carol Ludwig, Wichita, KS
Christine Luedeking, Moscow, ID
Dorothy Lund, Eagle River, WI
Janet Lund, Minneapolis, MN
Helen Lundeen, Fergus Falls, MN
Judith Luoma, Chattanooga, TN
Bill Lutholtz, Indianapolis, IN
Isaac Lutz, Fort Branch, IN
Marilyn Lutz, Ellicott City, MD
Enid Lynch, Bruce, SD
Franz Lynn, Aberdeen, MD
Wendy Lyons, Suffield, CT
Erik Maakestad, Champaign, IL
Eleanor Maan, New Milford, PA
Guenther Machol, Saratoga, CA
Pam Mack, Blacksburg, VA
Anne MacKinnon, Casper, NY
Evelyn MacKinnon, Madison, NH
David M. MacMillan, San Diego, CA
Wendy Macpherson, Austin, TX
Catherine, MacWilliam, Spencerport, NY
Kathleen Madden, Amherst, MA
Susan Madden, Salt Lake City, UT
Helen Malkerson, Oakland, CA
Pam and Jack Mallek, Cleveland Heights, OH
Mark Mandel, Framingham, MA
Glenn Paul Manion, New Hyde Park, NY
Larry Manire, Providence, RI
Marilyn Mann, Orange, MA
Gen Manning, Wendell, MA
Mildred A. Manny, Yellow Springs, OH
Anne Maret, Cleveland, OH
Martha Mark, Brea, CA
J. M. Marken, Superior, WI
Cindy and Sage, Marquette, Fairbanks, AK
Patricia Marrin, New York, NY
Joe Marshall, Falls Church, VA
Gloria Martin, Mt. Lk. Terr., WA
Joseph P. Martino, Sidney, OH
Elsa Martz, Manchester, MA
Marcia Marvin, Portland, OR
Jan and Tom Masaros, Waupaca, WI
Barbara Mason, Sanger, TX
Dorothy Mateka, Winona, MN
Kristina Mattson, Rockford, IL
Marion Maurer, Greenfield, MA
Alena Maurice, Urbana, IL
Edith Maxwell, Boston, MA
M. E. Maxwell, Westmoreland, NH
Pat Maxwell, Andrews AFB, MD
Edward May, Howardsville, VA
Margaret May, Vienna, VA
Jeanne Mayer
Steve Maynard, St. Louis, MO
Carl Mazel, Chatsworth, CA

Mary McAdoo, Temple, NH
Ann McAlister, Nashville, TN
Bob and Mary Kay McCann, West Chester, PA
Joyce McConeghey, Alameda, CA
Frances McCormick, Andover, MA
Mac McCormick, Norman, OK
Sheila McCormick, Clayton, MO
Justine McCoy, Manassas, VA
Jane McEvoy, Harrisonburg, VA
John and Helen McFarland, Charleston, IL
Ellen McGrew, Raleigh, NC
Mark McIntyre, Port Lions, AK
Gerry McKeen, Dallas, TX
Carolyn McKenna, Northampton, MA
Janet McKenna, Northampton, MA
Kathie McLaren, Cedar Rapids, IA
Eileen McLaughlin, Littleton, CO
Rita McLaughlin, Philadelphia, PA
Janet McLean, Canton, OH
Alice McMahon, Philadelphia, PA
Gwen McVickar McMahon, Greenville, IN
Mona McMahon, Winona, MN
Erma and Hughie McMenemy
Gregory McNamee, Tucson, AZ
M. N. McPherson, Charlotte, NC
C. J. McPike, Clovis, CA
Merle Meacham, Chimacum, WA
Diane Mech, Ladysmith, WI
Roberta Medford, Los Angeles, CA
G. W. Meek, Silsbee, TX
Elizabeth Mehlberg, Madison, WI
Richard Meinke, Downers Grove, IL
Matt A. Meis, Oakland, CA
Richard Mengler, Corvallis, OR
Freda Meredith, Dixmont, ME
Mary Mergenthal, St. Paul, MN
Lisa Merrin, Boulder, CO
Barb Merterr, Shoreview, MN
Tim Messick, Davis, CA
Patty Meyer, Victor, MT
A. Coletto Mezza, St. Paul, MN
Jim and Diane Mica, Pittsburgh, PA
Rosalie Mikalac, Arlington, VA
Anne Marie Miller, Atlanta, GA
Dave Miller, Los Angeles, CA
Dave Miller, Seattle, WA
Eleanor Miller, Rochester, NY
Jan Miller, South Gate, CA
Jane Miller, Delaware, OH
Kaye Miller, Philadelphia, PA
Kelly J. Miller, Kutztown, PA
Larry Miller, New Orleans, LA
Muriel Miller, Deerwood, MN
Reid Miller, Madison, WI
Rick Miller, Louisville, KY
Barbara Millikan, Sheridan, OR
Barry Mills, Seattle, WA
Kay Mills, Halstead, KS
Molly Miron, Brookings, SD
Frederick Mitchell, Berkeley, CA
Stella Mitchell, Los Angeles, CA

Tom Mitchell, Vernon, CT
Doug Modica, Sioux Falls, SD
Ethel Modroch, West Redding, CT
Sandra Moffat, Orford, NH
Elaine Mohr, Sandpoint, ID
B. Moody, Hyattsville, MD
Jackson Moody, Youngstown, OH
Carrie Mook, Memphis, TN
Alice Moore, Southampton, PA
Cathy Moore, Ames, IA
Danny Moore, Bakersville, NC
Janice Moore, Hiawatha, KS
Jim Moore, Birmingham, AL
John R. Moore, Laurel, MD
Marjorie Moore, Winchester, MA
John Moorman, Chisago Lakes, MN
Sherwood Moran, Springfield, OH
Vivian Moran, Madison, WI
Don Morgan, Elmer, NJ
Leonard Morgenstern, Moraga, CA
Marilyn Morin, Orange, MA
Diana Morley, Manchester, VT
Marilyn Morn, Orange, MA
Jo Louise Morrice, Lake Odessa, MI
Lee and John Morris, Hyattsville, MD
Marilyn Morris, Urbana, IL
Penny Morrison, Anaheim, CA
Erika Morrissey, Cambridge, MA
Beth and Ed Morsman
Sandi Morton, Metaline Falls, WA
Al Moseley, Melbourne, FL
Michael Moskow, Cleveland Hts., OH
Rebecca Moskow, Cleveland Hts., OH
Deb Mount, Toledo, OH
Julie Muehlberg, Minneapolis, MN
Carol Mulligan, Concord, NH
Marc and Bob Mullinax, Wake Forest, NC
Patty Mullins, Silver Spring, MD
Bill Munger, Tulsa, OK
Al Murray, Winchester, MA
Lysbet Murray, Plano, TX
Ruth Murray, Papillon, NE
Eric Myers, Coram, NY
Hillbilly Hal Myers, West Logan, WV
Myles M. Myers, Knoxville, TN
Barbara Myhr, Philadelphia, PA
Carolyn Myrick, Temple, NH
Paul Nahay, Hyattsville, MD
Tom Nakamura, Hampton, VA
Nan Narboe, Portland, OR
Ken Nattinger, Port Angeles, WA
Deborah Neale, Atlanta, GA
David Nebenzahl, Flagstaff, AZ
Mark Nedzbala, San Francisco, CA
Cassie Neely, Spring Lake, MI
Therry Neilsen-Steinhardt, Manchester, NH
George Neitzert, Columbia, MO
Edith Nekut, Lancaster, PA
Ken Nellis, Perry, ME
Betty Nelson, Cottontown, TN
Brenda Nelson, West Bath, ME

Dave Nelson, Eden Prairie, MN
Diane Nelson
Laurie Nelson, Nevada City, CA
Margaret C. Nelson, Claremont, CA
Mark Nelson, Knoxville, TN
Stephen Nelson
Beth Neundorfer, Brighton, IL
Kandace Neville, Rancho La Costa, CA
Bob Newby, Milwaukee, WI
David M. Newman, Brockport, NY
Judy Nichols, Batavia, OH
Richard Niebunck, New York, NY
Donald S. Nisbett, Tecumseh, KS
Emily Nitchie, Vineyard Haven, MA
Dorothy Sue Noland, Sacramento, CA
Greg Norbert, Jenkintown, PA
Dan Nordquist, Everett, WA
Elizabeth Northern, Morgantown, IN
Jim Norton, White Bear Lake, MN
Joey Norton, Monroe, WI
Alma Nyguen, Sinking Spring, PA
Audrey O'Neill, Plymouth, NH
David O'Neill
Betty Oakberg, Oak Ridge, TN
Hal Ober, Vancouver B.C., Canada
Holly Oberle, Miami, FL
Thomas Odell
Dave Oestreich, Okemos, MI
Mavis Oeth, Dubuque, IA
Glenna Ohlms, Nokesville, VA
Karl Oldberg, Santa Monica, CA
Ray Oliver, N. Highlands, CA
S. Olsen, Wooster, OH
Anne Olson, Clarendon Hills, IL
Jeane Olson, Dallas, TX
Linda Olson, Brookings, SD
Pat Oparowski, Medford, MA
Doris Oppenheimer, Somerville, MA
Liz Oppenheimer, New York, NY
Bill Orme-Johnson, Cambridge, MA
Kitty Ortman, Missoula, MT
Robert Osband, New York, NY
Oliver Osmond, Chicago, IL
Marjorie Ottenberg, Saratoga, CA
Steve Owens, West Hartford, CT
Ellynn Packard, Cohasset, MA
Dorothy Page, Springfield, MO
Lara and Elaine Palincsar, Alexandria, VA
Helen Palmer, Pittsburgh, PA
John Palmer, St. Paul, MN
Mary Palmer-Jenkins, Sumter, SC
Ruth Palumbo, Beaverton, OR
Fran Parker, Stevens Point, WI
Marion Parker, Seattle, WA
Leslie Parrish, Sebastopol, CA
Bob and Joyce Parsons, Twinsburg, OH
Miriam Pattison, Tucson, AZ
Bob Payton, Minneapolis, MN
Jerrilyn Pease, Simsbury, CT
Robert Pease, San Francisco, CA
Rosamond Peck, Waverly, PA

Roland M. Peek, St. Paul Park, MN
Bob Peffley, Lynchburg, VA
Bruce Pencek, Ithaca, NY
Tim Peoples, Charlotte, NC
Chere Pereira, Corvallis, OR
Rosalie Perfler, Orangevale, CA
Dorothy J. Perkins, Media, PA
Jane Perkinson, White Plains, NY
Greta Schmidt Perleberg, Wichita, KS
Josephine Perleberg, New Berlin, WI
Don Peters, Indianapolis, IN
Sally Niemand Petersburg, Minneapolis, MN
Cal Peterson, Moorhead, MN
Edith Peterson, Wausau, WI
Janet Peterson, Dodge Center, MN
Joyce Peterson, No. Easton, MA
Kevin Peterson, Pinkham Notch, NH
Faith Petric
Jean Pfeiffer, Wallingford, PA
Scott Pflug, Fresno, CA
Patty Phares, Miami, FL
Beverly R. Phillips, Madison, WI
Jenny Phillips, Savannah, GA
Nancy Phillips, Arvada, CO
Nancy Phillips, Connersville, IN
Suzanne Phleger, Minneapolis, MN
Charlotte Pickering, Bloomington, MN
John Picone, Pittsburgh, PA
Mary Lou Piech, Springfield, MO
Kathi Piedzwelis, Cedar Rapids, IA
Candace Pierce, Walla Walla, WA
Deb Pierce, Newton Center, MA
Marion Pierson, Granite City, IL
Randy Pike, Portland, ME
William G. Piston, New Orleans, LA
Walter Pitkin, Weston, CT
Margaret Plaganis, Hartford, CT
Carrie Plaman, Brooten, MN
Harriet Ploeger, Kirkland, WA
Phil Pockras, New Castle, PA
Walter Pocock, Severna, PA
Meegan Podlech, Salem, OR
Arthur C. Polansky, Fort Washington, MD
Bill Pond
Alison Pontynen, Iowa City, IA
Dave Poreth
Dave Poretti
Denis Portier, Lansing, MI
Amanda Pough
Eric Powell, New Richmond, WI
Andrea Powers, Mt. Horeb, WI
Flo Pratt, Newark, DE
Mary Pratt, New Haven, VT
Lori Prentice, Cedar, MI
Karen Prescott, Boulder, CO
Doug Price, Ann Arbor, MI
John Priebe, Waukesha, WI
Roslynn L. Pryor, Downey, CA
Helen Purcell, Wellfleet, MA
Ken Purcell, Reading, PA
Jane Pyle, Pittsboro, NC

Barbara Quick, Lawrence, KS
James Quigley, Philadelphia, PA
Doris Quinn, Latham, NY
Tania Quinn, Lincoln, NE
Robin Rader, Suffern, NY
Judith Rae, Indianapolis, IN
Sue Raher, Missoula, MT
Bill Ralph, Rome, PA
Charles E. Randall, Wenatchee, WA
Karen Randall, New York, NY
Rick Randall, Homer, AK
Jean Randles, Louisville, KY
Margaret Ranger, Spokane, WA
Jorgen Rasmussen, Ames, IA
Janet Rastall, Lexington, MA
Louise Rathburn
Mrs. R. C. Rathburn, St. Paul, MN
H. F. Raup, Kent, OH
Kirsten Reberg, Grand Rapids, MI
Jim Rebhan, Richmond, CA
Nina Reck, Amherst, MA
Elaine Reed, Fargo, ND
J. Reed, Palmyra, NJ
Joan Reed, Sullivan, MO
Judy Reed, Palmyra, NY
Fred R. Reenstjerna, Roanoke, VA
Tony Reeves, Spencer, IA
Jessie Regner, Citrus Heights, CA
Barbara Reiber, Woodstown, NJ
David Reichgott, Richboro, PA
Edward Reid, Greensboro, FL
Faith Reigle, Elizabethtown, PA
Barbara Reimer, Leisterstown, MD
Kathy Remington, Missoula, MT
Edgar Renfrew, Lock Haven, PA
Fred Renfroe, New Haven, CT
Karen Rhodes, Orange Park, FL
Robert Rice, Fly Creek, NY
Elaine Rich, Bluffton, OH
Mike Rich, Fallston, NC
Joe Richards, Smyrna, DE
Lynda Richards, Rolla, MO
Peter and Bev Richardson, McMinnville, OR
Susan Riegel, Greensboro, NC
Bill Riley, Boston, MA
Hazel Ristow, Hazelhurst, WI
Gerald R. Rittenberg, Williamston, MI
Larry Rittenberg, Madison, WI
Richard Roark, Loveland, CO
Nancy Ann Robbins, Roseville, MN
Ann Roberts, Richmond, CA
Kay Roberts, Sherman Oaks, CA
Rebecca Roberts, Ithaca, NY
Dillon Robertson, Winston-Salem, NC
Ellen Robertson, Cambridge, MA
Tom G. Robinson, Barnegat Light, NJ
Hope Robson, Amherst, MA
Christine Roccaro, New York, NY
Barbara Rogers, Ontario, CA
Margaret Rohdy, Canton, NY
Katy Rollins, Milwaukee, WI

John S. Rolston, Anchorage, AK
Evan F. Romer, Cranbury, NJ
James Romer, Rockport, ME
Ervin Roorda, Spokane, WA
Harrison Roper, Houlton, ME
Hank Rosen, South River, NJ
Ken Rosenbaum, Alexandria, VA
Eric Roskos, Nashville, TN
John Ross, New York, NY
Truman Ross, Comins, MI
Audrey Roth, Solon, OH
Don Roth, Oak Park, MI
Ruth Roth, Morgantown, PA
Lorraine Rovig, Des Moines, IA
Pat Clark Royalty, Atlanta, GA
D. Rubenstein, Brooklyn, NY
Doris Rubenstein, Minneapolis, MN
Hardin and Karen Rubin, St. Paul, MN
Charles Rufin, Pickerel Lake, WI
Jean Rumsey, Custer, WI
John Rund, Tucson, AZ
Frances Russell, Burbank, CA
Gary Russell, Eugene, OR
Stephen Russell, Wellfleet, MA
Kevin and Ellen Rustad, Anoka, MN
Susan Rustad, Minneapolis, MN
Megha Ryzen, Carbondale, IL
Linda Saarinen, Cambridge, MA
Shirley and Bert Boyd, Sacramento, CA
Dona Saforek, Iowa City, IA
Wally Saleanik, Randalltown, MD
Phillips Salman, Cleveland Hts., OH
E. Sampson, Bemidji, MN
Faith Sandberg, San Jose, CA
Constance Sanders, Cincinnati, OH
Ken Sanford, Charlotte, NC
Don Sauer, Ft. Atkinson, WI
Allen Saugstad, Kintyre, ND
Stephen Saupe, St. Cloud, MN
Joyce Sauter, Denton, TX
Kit Sawin, Newark, DE
Winifred D. Sayer, Amherst, MA
Sue Scaduto, San Francisco, CA
Hillary Scarborough, So. Orange, NJ
J. Sceats, Gainsville, FL
Al Scheer, Littleton, CO
Elvera Scheidler, Alpena, MI
Teri Scherber, New Hope, MN
Reed Scherer, Columbia, SC
Mona Schleper, Center, CO
Sue Schluender, Lakeland, FL
Agnes Schmidt, St. Louis, MO
J. R. Schmidt, Oak Park, IL
Judy Schmidt, Eagle River, AK
Gordon Schnaper, Tewksburg, MA
Mary Ann Schneider, Champaign, IL
Miriam Schneider, So. Freeport, ME
Ernst Schoen-Rene, Chico, CA
Ed Schor, Albuquerque, NM
John Schrank, Madison, WI
Joan Schrouder, Eugene, OR

Leo Schubert, Moline, IL
Patricia R. Schuessler, Summerville, PA
Helen Schulberg, San Francisco, CA
Kate Schultz, San Francisco, CA
Richard Schultz, Fort Atkinson, WI
James Schulz, Tigerton, WI
Mary P. Schumacher, Southaven, MI
Cliff Schutjer, Mansfield, OH
Peggy Schwab, Carmichael, CA
Mary Schwaiger, Phelps, WI
Anne Schwartz, Hopkinsville, KY
Jeffrey Schwartz, Lawrence, NY
Peter and Nancy Schwinn, Hampstead, MD
Meredith Schwirtz, Santa Rosa, CA
Helen Scott, El Cajon, CA
Joe Scott, Southeastern, PA
John C. Scott, Cincinnati, OH
Charles Scull, Magalia, CA
Helen Scull, Magalia, CA
Michele Scullane, North Dartmouth, MA
Rex Secrist, River Falls, WI
Anne Seeley, Sacramento, CA
Franklin Seiberling, Coralville, IA
Ruthy Seid
Donnie Seidenfaden, Alexandria, VA
Walter Seipp, Ravenna, OH
Jim Selcraig, Carrolltown, TX
Kathleen Serrell, Portland, OR
Barbara Sferra, Cincinnati, OH
Denny and Sue Shaffner, Rockton, PA
Bill Shane, Minneapolis, MN
Celia Shanks, Knoxville, TN
Bob Shannahan, Weare, NH
Toby Sharp, Oklahoma City, OK
John Shaver, Sierra Vista, AZ
Joe Shaw, Northfield, MN
Bob Sheffield, Binghamton, NY
Peg Sheldrick, Lincoln, NE
Nancy Hamilton Shepherd, Stow, MA
Talia Sher, Boxborough, MA
Jackie Sheridan, Port Wing, WI
Janette D. Sherman, Southfield, MI
Mirra Shernock, Thibodaux, LA
Richard Shipley, Salem, OR
Patricia Shrewsbury, Faribault, MN
Heidi Shuler, Pensacola, FL
Frances Sieler, Gardena, CA
Bob Siller, Tappan, NY
David Simington, Brewster, NY
Shirley Simmons, Tucson, AZ
Aletta Simon, St. Paul, MN
Carol Simon, Beloit, WI
Cheryl Simons, Oakland, CA
Katie Simpson, Springfield, MO
Lyn Sims, Columbus, OH
Sally Sims, Columbus, OH
Marjorie Sinclair, Westbrook, ME
Maggie Siner, Leesburg, VA
J. W. Singer, Stamping Ground, KY
Bob Skocpol
P. W. Slagle, North Vernon, IN

John Slater, Massillon, OH
Sarah Sloan, Urbana, IL
Lois M. Slusser, Oak Ridge, TN
Jane E. Small, Beulah, MI
Jeffrey Smart
Joe Smilgius, Brisbane, CA
Bob Smith, Columbus, OH
Carl Smith, Milford, MI
Claudia Smith, Lawrence, KS
Cyndi Smith, Tigard, OR
David Smith, Laurel, MD
Dory Smith, Sequim, WA
Eileen K. Smith, Los Angeles, CA
Elizabeth A. Smith, Reform, AL
Jean Smith, Nashville, TN
Jeff and Katy Smith, Sanford, ME
Jim Smith, Mesquite, TX
Judy Holcombe Smith, Somerville, NJ
Laurel Smith, Lanexa, VA
Marcel Smith, Tuscaloosa, AL
Marylou Smith, Beckwourth, CA
Matt Smith, Snyder, NY
Mike Smith
Roger M. Smith, Milwaukee, WI
Verna Smith, Seattle, WA
Virginia Hall Smith, Pownal, VT
Claudia Smith-Orton, Lawrence, KS
Bob Smithson, Ames, IA
Jennifer Snodgrass, Berkeley, CA
Esther Snow, Minneapolis, MN
Howie Snyder, Solon, OH
Ray Sobel, Lebanon, NH
Arthur W. Soderlund, Springville, UT
Suzanne Sokoloski, Richmond, VA
Mary Kay Solecki, Vichy, MO
Mrs. Donald Sommer, St. Petersburg, FL
Julie Sorenson, DeKalb, IL
David Soss, Salt Lake City, UT
Sally Southwick, Minneapolis, MN
Halbert Speer, Sea Cliff, NY
Ann Speth, Orange, CA
David Spilman, Curlew, WA
Paul Spivey, Walpole, NH
Karen Spjut, Somerville, MA
LaMar Spohr, Lombard, IL
Mrs. Arthur Sprague, Columbia, SC
Roberta Stammer, Erie, PA
Arthur Stamps, San Francisco, CA
Barbara Stanton, Jackson, MI
Mildred Stapleton, Corvallis, OR
Nancy Staub, Berkeley, CA
Sandy Stave, Yorba Linda, CA
Barry Stearns, Waltham, MA
Cathy Stecker, Malden, MA
Wilbur Steevart, Greenwood, OH
Patsy Steimer, Charlotte, NC
Sonja Ann Stepperud, New York, NY
Paul Steucke, Anchorage, AK
Lucinda Stevens, Ann Arbor, MI
Renee Stiglich, Troutville, VA
Holly Stinson, Wasilla, AK

Judith Stix, St. Louis, MO
Cheryl Stock, Diamond Bar, CA
Cindy Stocker, Lockport, IL
Linda Stoikowitz, El Cerrito, CA
Len Stokes, Westchester, NY
John Stolberg, Big Rapids, MI
Lois Stoller, Orrville, OH
Darnall Stone, Danbury, CT
Yoni Stone, Hermosa Beach, CA
Berta Storey, Atlanta, GA
Eric Stott, Norwich, NY
Kristin Stout, Seattle, WA
Thomas Stout, Wakefield, RI
Marian Stow, S. Bloomington, OH
Gloria Strait, Longview, WA
John Stranack, Ft. Lauderdale, FL
Teddi Stransky, Wichita, KS
David H. Stuart, Columbus, OH
Beatrice Stubbs, Dillard, GA
Lorraine Stube, Duluth, MN
Sharon Stuessy, Madison, WI
Charlie Stumpf, Hazleton, PA
James E. Sturm, Hellertown, PA
Pat Stweart, Taylors, SC
Margaret Sudekum, Grand Rapids, MI
Brad and Joanne Suhm, Sheboygan Falls, WI
Barbara Sullivan, Windsor, Ontario
Doris Sullivan, Kennewick, WA
Shari Sullivan, San Jose, CA
Ruth Ann Sundberg, Alliance, OH
April Sutor, Marshall, MN
Rolf Svanoe, Whitewater, WI
Sue Swanson, Morgantown, WV
Randy Swart, Arlington, VA
Patricia Sweazey, Seattle, WA
Frances Sweeney, NJ
Ben Swihart
Cheri Sykes, St. Paul, MN
Lesli Sykes, Providence, RI
Kay Synrud, Hawley, MN
Terri Tacheny, St. Paul, MN
Ruth Taferner, N. Fryeburg, ME
Lois Tamowski, Zimmerman, MN
Kendra Tanner, Davis, CA
Gerry Tatham, Clarksville, TN
Carl and Jo Tatlock, Rochester, NY
Livingston Taylor, Frankfort, KY
Lowell Taylor, Alden, NY
Virginia Taylor, Southern Pines, NC
Sonja Teas, Sitka, AK
Jaxon Teck, Rockaway, NJ
Jean Teichroew, Takoma Park, MD
Curt Tenall, Juneau, AK
Freda Tepfen, Arlington, WA
Ginger Terault, Knoxville, TN
Ken Tessier, Milford, CT
Ginger Tevault, Knoxville, TN
Jennifer Thistle, Painted Post, NY
Margaret Thomas, Lutherville, MD
Bill Thompson, San Francisco, CA
Harriet and C. W. Thompson, New Orleans, LA

John E. Thompson, Nekoosa, WI
Linda M. Thompson, San Francisco, CA
Steve Thompson, Grand Forks, ND
Sue Thompson, Eau Gallie, FL
William Thompson, San Francisco, CA
Cynthia Thomson, Amherst, MA
John R. Tiffany, Iowa City, IA
Neila Tillman, Lansing, MI
Jamey Tippens, Elfand, NC
Wedgeley Todd, Duane, IA
S. T. Toleno, Golden Valley, MN
Katie Tolin, Happy Camp, CA
Pandora Tonart, Seattle, WA
Margaret Tonkinson, Rochester, NY
Deborah Toomey, Willow Grove, PA
Dorothy Topping, Okeechobee, FL
Mrs. E. A. Torrance, Tallahassee, FL
Clifford Towle, Hutchinson, KS
Myles Tracy, Chico, CA
Greg Traxler, Minneapolis, MN
Mickey Trent, Dallas, TX
Joseph Trimble, Silver Spring, MD
Yvonne Truhon, Schofield, WI
Joe M. Truman, Londonderry, OH
Carolyn Trundle, Boynton Beach, FL
Ginny Tschanz, Lakewood, CO
David Tulis, Knoxville, TN
B. Turby, West Topsham, VT
Nina Turitz, Brentwood, MD
Alta Turner, Verona, NJ
Francesca Tyrnauer, Surfside, CA
William Tyrrell, Albany, NY
Luann and Jon Udell, Baltimore, MD
Meta Ukena, Pelham, NY
Sandy Umhaver, Lexington, KY
Virginia Lee Underwood, Chickasha, OK
Suzanne Unger, Rock Springs, WI
Bill Unsworth, Green Springs, OH
Polly Valentine, Alexandria, VA
Jean Vallee, Atlanta, GA
William Van Ark, Oceanside, NY
John Van Gilder, Seattle, WA
Patricia Van Hartesveldt, Reseda, CA
Josh and June Van Houten, Williston, VT
John C. Van Pelt, Bangor, ME
Johanna Van Wert, Philadelphia, PA
Sharon A. Van Yperen, North Creek, NY
Joan Vance, Minneapolis, MN
Elizabeth VanderSchaaf, Cedar Rapids, IA
Ellen Vanderslice, Ann Arbor, MI
John A. Varela, McLean, VA
Bob Vargas, Lewisburg, PA
Don and Chris Veeder, Boone, IA
Kay Ver Schure, Holland, MI
Diane and Jim Veresh, Lansing, MI
John Vick, Perronville, MI
Ann Vilner, Minneapolis, MN
Stephen Vincent, Arlington, MA
Wilton Vincent, Auburn, CA
George Vivimo-Hintze, Rome, PA
Andy Voda, Putney, VT

Susan Volk, Britton, SD
Volkert Volkersz, Snohomish, WA
Regina Voorhies, Sacramento, CA
Helen and Morris Wade, New Rochelle, NY
Carol Wagner, Roseville, MN
Howard D. Wagner, Stephen, MN
Kathy Wagner, Lexington, KY
Mark and Jocelyn Wagner, Scio, OR
Lucy Walborn, Columbus, OH
Barbara Walden, Minneapolis, MN
Jan Walker, Portland, OR
M. O. Walker, Tulsa, OK
Marcus Walker, Newton Centre, MA
Jean Wall, Albuquerque, NM
Bruce Wallace, Blacksburg, VA
Harlan Wallum, Detroit Lakes, MN
Robert Wallum, Missoula, MT
Bob Walser, Mystic, CT
David Walsh, Wendell, MA
Dennis Walsh, Elmira, NY
Barb Walter
Charles Walter, Johnson City, TN
Rosemary Walton, Hampton, VA
Dana Ward, San Luis Obispo, CA
William L. Ward, Shawnee, KS
Linda Wardell, Wilmington, DE
Pamela Warfield, Bethesda, MD
Fran Warner, Wilmington, DE
Ruth Wathen-Dunn, Lexington, MA
Glen Way, So. Charleston, WV
Claire Wayne, Sunnyvale, CA
Tom Weakley, Arlington, VT
Rita Weatherholt, Seattle, WA
Jean Weaver, Coon Rapids, MN
Joy Weaver, Islip, NY
Voni Weaver, Newton, MA
Alice Webber, Berkeley, CA
Loir Lee Weber, River Falls, WI
Max H. Webster, Bennington, VT
Etta Weigl, Webster, NY
Blair Weille, New York, NY
Virginia Weinland, Chappaqua, NY
Karel Weissberg, Arlington, VA
Stephanie Weissman, Som, MA
Chris Weitz, Mondovi, WI
Dianne Weitzenkamp, Oak Park, IL
Doug Wellman
Herb Wells, Wolfeboro, NH
Paula Wendland, Arlington, MA
Christina Werling, Macomb, IL
Nina Werner, Brooklyn, NY
Steve and Sarah Wersan, Cupertino, CA
Kathy Wesley, Newark, OH
Matthew West, Hope, RI
Jennifer Weston, Daisytown, PA
Evelyn Whalen, Atlanta, GA
Herbert Wheeler, Novato, CA
Linda White, Tri-Cities, WA
Mary Whiting, Hastings on Hudson, NY
Lynn Whitten, Geneseo, NY
Mia and Lia Whittle, Dundalk, MD

Joani Whyman, Batavia, NY
Marilynn Wickens, Haslett, MI
Christian Wig, Hartville, OH
Gazella Wike, Irvine, CA
Lara Wild, Portland, OR
Susan Wilde, Bishop, GA
Deetje Wildes, Clinton, WI
Mrs. Clarence Wildes, Clinton, WI
Nancy Wilkinson, Bryn Mawr, PA
Twila M. Will, Wausau, WI
Lois Willand, Minneapolis, MN
Antoinette Willard, Oak Ridge, TN
Thelma Willett, Grand Forks, ND
Audrey Hillman Williams
David Williams, Seattle, WA
Dyke Williams, Deephaven, MN
Elizabeth Williams, Mill Valley, CA
Evelyn Williams, Huntsville, AL
Oliver P. Williams, Philadelphia, PA
Pam Williams, Richfield, UT
Roger B. Williams, Lawrence, KS
Shayne Willis, Gate City, VA
Tim Willson, Richford, VT
Margaret Wilner, Auburn, CA
Anne H. Wilson, Craftsbury, VT
Barbara Wilson, Sand Springs, OK
Carol Wilson, Mason, WI
Charlene Wilson, Santa Barbara, CA
Curtis Wilson, Urbana, IL
Genevieve Wilson
Jenny Wilson, Kent, OH
Jerriann Wilson, Severna Pk., MD
Michael Wilson, Madison, WI
Wylie Wilson, Washington, DC
Nancy Wilterdink, Menomonie, WI
Richard Windels, Cheshire, CT
Marilyn Winter, Carmichael, CA
Shirl and Becky Wirkler, Farmersberg, IA
Mary Wiseman, Fort Worth, TX

Glen Wittrock, Sioux Falls, SD
Harry Woehn, Philadelphia, PA
Steve Wolicki, Camp Hill, PA
Eric Wollman, Brooklyn, NY
Anna Wood, Springfield, IL
Lacey Wood, Centreville, MD
Bruce Woodcock, New York, NY
Frieda Woodruff, Durham, NC
Gordon Woods, Salt Lake City, UT
Jennifer Woods, East Lansing, MI
Virginia Woodward, Chagrin Falls, OH
Ralph R. Woodworth, Bloomington, IN
Cathy Wright, Huntingdon, PA
Jenny Wright, Charlestown, NH
M. B. Wulf, Manchester, NH
(The) Wymans, Portland, ME
Karla Wyse, Brattleboro, VT
Carol Yaffe, Columbia, SC
Joseph Yager, East Liverpool, OH
Esther Yanai, Moorestown, NJ
Bill Yates, Oxnard, CA
Fred Yoos, Geneseo, NY
Dean Young, Yuba, WI
Mark Young, Springfield, PA
Philip Young, Portland, OR
Sara Young, West Hartford, VT
Suzanne Zander, St. Paul, MN
Laurie Zant, Palo Alto, CA
Aileen Zanteson, Tujunga, CA
Harold and Lois Zapolsky, Highland Park, NJ
Jeannie Zarucchi, Arlington, VA
Joan Zawaski, Oakland, CA
Bill Zeiger, Los Angeles, CA
Bill Zeigo
Susan R. Zelitch, Philadelphia, PA
Rebecca Zettler, Armonk, NY
James D. Ziegler, Billings, MT
Tom Zike, Anderson, TX
Dawn Zimmer, Contoocook, NH

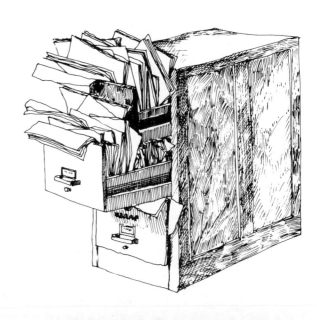